# JAPANESE TAKEOVERS

# JAPANESE TAKEOVERS

## The Global Contest
## for Corporate Control

W. CARL KESTER
HARVARD BUSINESS SCHOOL

**Harvard Business School Press**
**Boston, Massachusetts**

© 1991 by the President and Fellows of Harvard College
All rights reserved.
Printed in the United States of America.
95  94  93  92  91          5  4  3  2  1

The paper used in this publication meets the requirements of the American National
Standard for Permanence of Paper for Printed Library Materials Z39.49–1984.

Library of Congress Cataloging-in Publication Data
Kester, W. Carl.
    Japanese takeovers : the global contest for corporate control / W.
Carl Kester.
        p. cm.
    Includes bibliographical references and index.
    ISBN 0-87584-235-6 (hardcover : acid free paper)
    1. Consolidation and merger of corporations—Japan. 2. Corporate
governance—Japan. 3. Corporations, Japanese. I. Title.
HD2907.K45 1990
338.8'3'0952—dc20                                    90-40430
                                                     CIP

TP

*To my wife,*
*Jane,*
*and our children,*
*Kelsey, Eric, and Kirsten*

# CONTENTS

# PREFACE

The 1987 O'Melveny & Myers Centennial Grant provided the impetus as well as financial support for this book. Established in 1985 to commemorate the hundredth anniversary of the founding of the O'Melveny & Myers law firm in Los Angeles, the grant's purpose is to promote research on the internationalization of American business. The particular subtopic underwritten by the grant in 1987 was "The Impact of International Capital Markets."

Both the general field and the particular subtopic are of immense importance to today's business and legal communities. Between 1945 and about 1979, international commerce was characterized by American economic dominance. This dominance has since receded on a number of fronts, including the world's capital markets. For years now, a powerful constellation of forces has brought about an unprecedented degree of global capital market integration. Market deregulation, financial product innovation, and so-called securitization—the bundling of bank credit instruments into marketable forms of paper—have contributed to the shaping of a financial world that knows no national borders. The annual volume of new corporate bonds issued in the Euromarkets now approaches that occurring in the U.S. domestic market. American money-center banks have been superseded in size by their Japanese counterparts, and both groups are competing fiercely around the world with each other and their European rivals.

How might these trends in global capital markets affect American business interests? While their collective impact on the world economy will undoubtedly be significant, it also appears to be fairly clear. Forces of integration have launched international capital markets on a trajectory leading toward heightened competition within the financial services sector accompanied by greater financial flexibility and lower financing costs for the manufacturing sector.

The United States has, however, long benefited from relatively open and efficient capital markets. It is arguable, therefore, that the most important effects of international capital markets on American firms will not be those transmitted directly through reductions in financing costs or the expansion of financial flexibility. Rather, they are likely to be those transmitted indirectly through changes induced in the behavior of foreign competitors newly exposed to open capital markets. Of all foreign rivals likely to be affected by world capital market trends, and likely in turn to influence American companies heavily, none are more prominent than Japanese manufacturers—large, powerful competitors governed by a unique system of unwritten rules largely unfamiliar to their Western competitors.

Thanks to their tremendous competitive successes in global product markets, and to their unfettered access to global capital markets since 1984, large Japanese corporations stand at the threshold of the 1990s with unparalleled amounts of cash and other forms of financial slack. This war chest has been made all the more formidable by the substantial rise of the yen's global purchasing power since 1985.

The way in which this vast stockpile of wealth is deployed will have a tremendous impact on the world's economic landscape. For this reason, its deployment is fraught with considerable political significance as well. Japan's economic success has gone beyond the miracle that the world admires to a relentless expansion that much of the globe now views with concern if not alarm. Political pressure on Japan to contain itself, or at least become less one-sided about its economic expansion, has had scant effect. Even now, as we grapple with the problems of persistent Japanese trade surpluses and difficult access to Japan's markets, a new front of potential conflict has arisen—the outright ownership and control of entire corporations.

Many Westerners, particularly Americans, feel threatened by the prospects of a sustained increase in Japanese M&A activity. They fear a loss of control over their country's economic destiny as the locus of corporate strategic decision making shifts to Tokyo. On the brighter side, if the Japanese market for corporate control were to open to Westerners, heightened Japanese M&A activity would create viable new opportunities to secure a Japanese work force, gain access to local Japanese distribution, or forge a vital strategic alliance with a major Japanese company. In the long run, it might even beneficially alter the norms by which Western companies are owned and governed, regardless of Japanese presence abroad.

Historically, Japanese corporations have been remarkable for their relative lack of participation in the market for corporate control. The late 1980s saw a change in this regard, at least with respect to the purchase of foreign companies. Japanese corporations became successful bidders for a number of prominent American companies.

In Japan, however, there are still very few large-scale acquisitions and only limited opportunities for foreign corporations to do much more than buy out the Japanese partner in a joint venture, or perhaps purchase the Japanese subsidiary of another foreign company. This has given rise to further charges of one-sided access to markets and mounting Western concern over the effects of Japanese financial hegemony in this era of integrated global capital markets.

It was against this backdrop of concern over the changing ownership and control of corporations that I undertook an examination of Japanese M&A activity. I did so well aware of the fact the most pressing issues for many observers were essentially questions of policy. Should nations feel threatened by Japanese takeovers, and if so, what should they do about them? Should Japan take steps to encourage a more active and open market for corporate control at home?

Sound judgments regarding these normative economic issues cannot be reached without first achieving an objective understanding of the economic phenomena at hand. Thus the questions I held uppermost in mind as I approached the topic were less normative and more exploratory in nature. What explains the historic reluctance of Japanese companies to acquire or merge with others? What stimulated change in the 1980s? Do the soaring values of the yen and Japanese stock prices in the 1980s adequately account for the recent increase in Japanese takeovers of foreign companies? What direction is Japanese M&A activity likely to take in the future? Will it become more Western in its pace and style? Will foreign bidders ever enjoy the same degree of access to Japanese targets as Japanese bidders have to foreign markets?

The key, I found, to unlocking answers to these questions is a comprehensive understanding of the Japanese corporate governance system—the incentives, safeguards, and dispute-resolution processes that control and coordinate the activities of the Japanese corporation's many stakeholders. Consequently, this book is as much an exposition of the economic logic that underlies that system as it is an explanation of Japanese M&A activity itself. The two are inextricably intertwined.

This book presents a decidedly institutional view of Japanese M&A activity. It is concerned more with tying together the struggles among major groups of corporate stakeholders (shareholders, lenders, employees, suppliers, customers, and so forth) with merger and acquisition activity than it is concerned, for example, with the documentation of market trends, an explication of various methods for buying a Japanese company or selling a foreign one to a potential Japanese purchaser, or the measurement of shareholder gains and losses associated with takeovers in Japan. These topics are either treated adequately elsewhere or must await further passage of time so that more data and perspective can be brought to bear on them.

My data have been gathered from a variety of sources, but mostly from my own international field research of the past several years. I have had the opportunity of interviewing over 40 executives in 15 different Japanese industrial corporations (for a list of the industrial and financial corporations at which I interviewed, see the Appendix). Interviews were also held at a similar number of Japanese financial institutions (five commercial banks, two trust banks, two long-term credit banks, four securities houses, and two life insurance companies). While a book could easily be devoted to the global acquisition activities of these financial institutions, my focus from the start has been on the M&A activities of Japan's largest industrial corporations.[1] I included financial institutions in my sample primarily to provide insight into the attitudes and expectations of large providers of capital regarding their corporate clients, and to benefit from their direct experience as advisers in the M&A business.

The composition of companies studied was determined primarily by the willingness of executives to cooperate with my research and the public availability of data about the companies in question. Nevertheless, I deliberately attempted to balance the sample roughly between "sunrise" and "sunset" industries in Japan, industrial and consumer product firms, and group and nongroup members. Thus the field sample is comparatively large. All companies researched either were active in some way in mergers and acquisitions, were attempting to manage the growing tension among stakeholder groups, or were themselves (e.g., banks and insurance companies) key stakeholders in some of the manufacturing companies being studied.

Some companies' decisions and actions receive special attention in this book as subjects of case studies or detailed examples. It must be noted that the situations selected for closer examination are not uniformly typical of Japanese corporate behavior. Indeed, some are highlighted precisely because they are "outliers" that may suggest important future trends. Clearly this line of argument is not without its risks. But my purpose is not simply to rediscover the stylized facts and conventional wisdom about Japan that, for all their past helpfulness, sometimes obscure our vision of future possibilities. Rather, it is to go beyond received doctrine to provide decision makers with a new, more powerful, and more reliable framework for interpreting and predicting the behavior of Japanese companies in a modern world characterized by Japanese financial hegemony. To achieve this, the light of inquiry must be focused on spots where innovation is occurring, for it is there that we are most likely to obtain our clearest glimpses of tomorrow.

---

1. Because of this industrial focus, I do not treat Japanese overseas real estate transactions. These too have been extensive and might well merit a separate study.

My interpretation of the field data takes place within the context of two major strains of economic literature: the literature of "transaction-cost economics" (most commonly associated today with Oliver Williamson and, before him, Ronald Coase) and that of "agency theory" (most commonly associated today with Michael Jensen and William Mecklin and, before them, Adolph Berle and Gardiner Means).[2] The former literature is concerned primarily with the governance of contractual relations among economic organizations. The central question of this literature most germane to an analysis of Japanese mergers and acquisitions is: When should companies integrate (vertically or horizontally) so as to be self-sufficient in some capacity, and when should they simply procure their needs on the open market? In short, what is the optimal boundary between the administrative hierarchy of firm and the market? Reliance on arm's-length transactions in the market allows for greater specialization in production activities and the realization of scale economies, but also poses risks associated with self-interested opportunism.[3] Absorbing key suppliers, customers, or subcontractors may afford greater control and relieve some of the hazards of self-interested opportunism, but often at the expense of efficiency. The high-powered incentives the market provides can be difficult to replicate and manage inside an organization; moreover, other conditions that Williamson calls "bureaucratic disabilities" may exist. The problem is to devise a system of governing business relations that optimally balances the economies and hazards of transacting in the market with those of administratively controlling the same activities within a hierarchical organization.

2. For representative examples of this literature, see Oliver Williamson, *The Economic Institutions of Capitalism* (New York: Free Press, 1985); Ronald H. Coase, "The Nature of the Firm," *Economica N.S.* 4 (1937), pp. 386–405; Michael Jensen and William Meckling, "Theory of the Firm: Managerial Behavior, Agency Costs, and Capital Structure," *Journal of Financial Economics* 3 (October 1976), pp. 305–360; and Adolph A. Berle and Gardiner C. Means, *The Modern Corporation and Private Property* (New York: Macmillan, 1932).
3. After a company invests in some expensive and highly specialized assets, for example, an important customer or supplier could threaten to abandon its relationship with the company if terms of trade are not shifted in its favor. Legal adjudication of such disputes may be too slow, costly, and cumbersome to rely on constantly as a means of handling such problems.

The agency literature, in contrast, focuses more on the problems associated with the separation of ownership and control in the modern corporation. Again, for reasons of self-interested opportunism, agents (e.g., managers) hired to do a job cannot always be counted on to act in the best interests of the principals (e.g., shareholders) that engaged them. Within the context of modern stock corporations, considerable value may be dissipated by managers whose interests are not perfectly aligned with those of investors. Rational investors will recognize this possibility in advance and reflect expectations of self-interested actions by managers in the prices paid for the corporation's securities. The more interesting problem, however, is to create cost-effective monitoring, bonding, and incentive systems that will reduce the losses associated with the separation of ownership from control. When prevailing systems prove inadequate, the existence of a market for corporate control may be used to concentrate ownership. This in turn enables new owners to change the company's patterns of investment, cease other deleterious policies, alter maladjusted contracts, and perhaps change management itself.

Despite differences in these theories, both may be viewed as subbranches of a broader stream of literature concerned with the economics of contracting. Both take up the universal problem of coping efficiently with the hazards of dependence on self-interested second and/or third parties to accomplish some economic aims. And both are essential to a complete understanding of the Japanese corporate governance system.

When viewed comparatively from the distant perspective of typical Western (more specifically, Anglo-American) corporate governance systems, the Japanese system can seem strange and even irrational. Primarily cultural differences would seem to explain its constitution. But when examined closely through the analytic lenses of both transaction-cost economics and agency theory, Japanese corporate governance is revealed to be an economically rational and, in fact, extremely effective means of coping with these hazards. Further, this effectiveness is a crucial determinant of Japanese M&A activity.

# ACKNOWLEDGMENTS

I owe a considerable debt of thanks to many people and organizations that contributed to the development of this book. I am especially grateful to the O'Melveny & Myers law firm and its chairman, Warren Christopher. I was honored and privileged to be named recipient of the 1987 O'Melveny & Myers Centennial Grant, which substantially funded my research for this book. Several people at O'Melveny & Myers also generously supported me with their interest, advice, and experienced points of view, in particular John Stamper and Ko-Yung Tung. Additional financial support from the Harvard Business School's Division of Research is also gratefully acknowledged.

Foremost among individuals to whom I am indebted is Noriko Kameda who assisted me as a research associate throughout the project. Her remarkable blend of managerial, diplomatic, and research skills were of unequalled importance to my work. Her efforts ranged from the organization of field research trips to insightful analyses of the data to the writing of exhaustive reports on various aspects of the topic. She quietly and, it seemed, almost effortlessly cleared my path of one roadblock after another. Indeed, this book would not have reached fruition without Nori's diligence.

Special help in the field research was provided by Professor Sadahiko Suzuki of the Graduate School of Business Administration at Keio University. He generously agreed to collaborate with me during my first field research trip to Japan and has since accompanied me on numerous other interviews. Besides his warm friendship, he has consistently made available to me his considerable expertise concerning Japanese corporate finance.

He helped me sort fact from fiction in Japan, enabled me to penetrate below the surface of some vital but obtuse comments made during interviews, and generally kept me oriented in the complex world of Japanese business practices.

My gratitude is also due to the many executives and companies that cooperated in my research. Besides those organizations identified in the Appendix as members of my field sample, I benefited from interviews with managers at The First Boston Corporation; the Keidanren; Merck Sharp & Dohme International; Merrill Lynch Capital Markets and Merrill Lynch Japan, Inc.; Ministry of Finance; Ministry of International Trade and Industry; Morgan Guaranty Ltd.; Morgan Stanley & Co. Incorporated; Nomura Research Institute; Salomon Brothers, Inc.; and Skadden, Arps, Slate, Meagher & Flom. Other individuals who shared their expertise and hospitality include my former Harvard Business School classmate, Kazuo Hayakawa; Kanji Ishizumi; J. Brian Waterhouse of James Capel Pacific Limited; Masayuki Yasuoka of Bankers Trust Company; and Michael Young, director of the Center for Japanese Legal Studies at Columbia University. Richard Hill was instrumental in helping me gain access to a number of financial institutions by graciously writing letters of introduction. I hope these people and the many others I interviewed both realize the full extent of my gratitude and derive some satisfaction from their contributions to the research.

A number of my colleagues at the Harvard Business School were invaluable in shaping my research plans and the final product. Timothy Luehrman was a particularly valuable resource on whom I relied constantly for advice. His own research into Merck & Co.'s acquisition of Banyu Pharmaceutical and the greenmailing of Fujiya Co., Ltd. provided essential underpinnings for my discussion of both these situations, and he also made numerous other substantive suggestions. Likewise, Michael Yoshino consistently provided me with invaluable support and constructive criticism. Thoughtful comments on early drafts of the manuscript were provided by Alfred D. Chandler, Jr., Dwight Crane, Gordon Donaldson, William E. Fruhan, Jr., Samuel L. Hayes III, Michael Jensen, Jay Lorsch, and Richard

Ruback. At other stages of inception and development, sound advice was given me by Joseph Bower, Colyer Crum, Robert Eccles, Robert Kaplan, Jay Light, Scott Mason, Thomas McCraw, and Jeremy Stein. By his constant expressions of interest in my work, Dean John McArthur was a steady source of encouragement throughout.

Others have made valuable contributions to this book in various ways. I am indebted to Michelle Chen for organizing interviews at a number of Japanese financial institutions. It was through her efforts that I was introduced to Yukari Yamaguchi, who provided considerable assistance in the research about Japanese greenmailing. Richard Melnick took responsibility for compiling and analyzing much of the numerical data from Japan, as well as for responding to a wide array of other research requests. Philip Hamilton and Barry Feldman expertly managed the Nikkei NEEDS data base that was my principal source of historical financial statement data for Japanese corporations. For the most complete, up-to-date data on Japanese acquisitions in the United States, I relied upon *Japan M&A Reporter* published by Ulmer Brothers, Incorporated of New York. I am grateful to Ulmer Brothers, particularly Daniel Schwartz and Barbara Pfeiffer, for their reliable and timely cooperation. Invaluable assistance in the physical production of the manuscript was provided by Brenda Fucillo, Erin McCormack, and virtually the entire staff of the Word Processing Center of the Harvard Business School, all of whom made useful suggestions and patiently coped with my many revisions.

I benefited enormously from editorial advice at several crucial junctures in the development of the manuscript. Barbara Feinberg made numerous recommendations that improved the manuscript both structurally and stylistically. She also sustained me with unflagging enthusiasm for the project. Carol Franco and Natalie Greenberg of the Harvard Business School Press refined the manuscript still further and strengthened it at a number of pivotal points. I am also grateful for the considerable time, effort, and editorial expertise contributed by my wife, Jane Manilych, who examined the manuscript in detail. I relied heavily on her counsel when weighing editorial recommendations.

Finally, special recognition must be given to Jane and our children for their devoted interest, encouragement, and sacrifices on my behalf during the past several years. The strength of their love made the gulf between aspiration and attainment seem that much less imposing and that much more rewarding to cross. Thus, it is to them that this book is dedicated.

# 1
# INTRODUCTION

TOKYO, 1987

The conference room in which I was seated had understated elegance. The low-seated, cushioned furniture was modern and Western, but far from trendy. In the corner, a fine example of *ikebana* blended color and texture into harmonious balance. A single antique ceramic vase was the focal point of the wall opposite me. These simple elements imparted a sense of timeless Japanese harmony and tradition to the environment, the precise effect, no doubt, sought by the decorator. The room reflected the prestige of the company, one of Japan's foremost financial institutions, and bespoke the dignity of its directors, one of whom I had come from Boston to interview.

I had been sent to him to learn about Japanese mergers and acquisitions, a subject on which he was a recognized expert. I came with a long list of questions that I hoped to squeeze into our short time together. But it soon became evident that the agenda was his, not mine. Sitting stiffly before me, speaking a steady stream of Japanese in low, evenly modulated tones, and surrounded by silent, somber aides, he evoked the image of a latter-day *daimyo* with his samurai retainers. With barely a chance to get a word in edgewise, I sipped the green tea that had been set before me and sat back to listen to what amounted to a lecture on the intricacies of traditional Japanese business protocol and its influence on dealmaking in Japan.

Much of it was already familiar to me—discouragingly so, for it basically added up to the conclusion that Japan was for the

1

Japanese, that its commercial culture was beyond the compre-
hension of most non-Japanese, Westerners and Asians alike,
and that nothing less than a cataclysmic event would change
these basic truths. Neither the motives nor the techniques for
combining companies in the West were portable to Japan was
his basic message.

"But hasn't Japanese business undergone rapid and profound
change before?" I finally asked. "Is it not possible that we might
see at least *some* change in Japanese merger and acquisition activity by the end of this century—perhaps a few hostile takeover
bids, for example?" In the back of my mind were the fierce
struggles for power and ascendancy among rival Japanese clans
that I had read about in history books. Japan was no stranger to
internal conflict. Why shouldn't we expect to see such struggles
again—this time in boardrooms and on trading floors rather
than on battlefields?

He countered matter-of-factly. "Unless we stop being Japanese, I see no prospect for significant change," the interpreter
said on his behalf. "It will take more than a few decades to reverse five hundred years of tradition." The end of the meeting
was signaled with a prim smile that seemed to communicate
something between patience and boredom with my Western na-
ivete about Japanese ways.


NEW YORK, 1989


The attendance at the Japan Society of America conference on Japanese mergers and acquisitions exceeded all my expectations. I anticipated being one of a few hundred people rat-
tling around an oversized hotel function room. Instead I found
myself in a New York Hilton ballroom that was filled nearly to
capacity with people from all over North America, Asia, and Europe. The talkative, noisy crowd seemed to contain nearly as
many Japanese as Americans.

It was a typical conference scene. When the audience was not
listening to John Nevin talking about the sale of Firestone Tire
& Rubber to Japan's Bridgestone Corporation, or to James

McDonald's description of life at Gould under Japanese ownership, it was busy gulping coffee, shaking hands, talking deals,
and exchanging cards. Other than a few reporters and academ-
ics such as I, most in attendance were dealmakers of various
stripes—bankers, lawyers, financiers, consultants, and so forth.

The speakers were generally well received. They told the audience what it came to hear: there will be lots more deals done
with the Japanese; life under Japanese ownership is not so bad
after all; Exon-Florio is bad for America; cutting a deal with the
Japanese is far less mysterious than some people would have you
believe, but sufficiently complicated to ensure a steady demand
for professional advice.

The most forceful statement of the day came from Joseph Perella, cofounder and chairman of the board of the American
merchant bank, Wasserstein, Perella & Co., Inc., which special-
izes in mergers, acquisitions, and corporate restructurings. Contrary to conventional wisdom, he asserted the whole world, including Japan, is gravitating to a "single standard of M&A
dealmaking"; he called it "the Anglo-Saxon standard."

Perella did not define that approach in detail. But what he
meant was evident from the context. He was forecasting a world
that in the long run would feature essentially a single, globally
integrated market for corporate control. It would be a relatively
free market, regulated locally to be sure, but driven primarily by
price and open to anyone with enough capital to be a serious
player. Value-maximizing investors would use takeovers to replace underperforming managers, change corporate policies,
and dramatically restructure companies with the aim of increasing equity values. Thanks to modern financing capabilities, size
in and of itself would not be an adequate deterrent to attack.
Inevitably, some deals would be large, bitterly contested, and depend crucially on the judgments of a cadre of globally active risk
arbitrageurs. These raptors of the capital markets would take
and dispose of large stakes in the equity of target companies,
seeking quick gains in the process. They would confer victory on
whoever paid the most cash soonest. It would, in short, be a
global market that looks a lot like what is seen today in the
United States, the United Kingdom, Canada, and Australia,

with Japan joining the Western world in hard-nosed contests for corporate control.

Judging from the thoughtful expressions and knowing nods around me, it was a forecast that the Americans and at least some of the Japanese both believed and liked.

## A NEW VIEW OF JAPANESE M&A ACTIVITY

These two views—continuance of business as usual in Japan versus Japanese imitation of the West—epitomize the two most extreme but nevertheless dominant hypotheses about the future course of Japanese M&A activity. Nearly anyone with a viewpoint in this field can be found in one camp or the other. I too have alternately held and ultimately rejected both. Each has a degree of plausibility, to be sure. Indeed, three years of research taking me into executive offices from London and New York to Hong Kong and Tokyo, and prompting me to sift through decades of data about Japan's largest companies, have taught me that support for either view can be selectively culled from the world of experience and statistics.

But I have also learned that both positions are ultimately half truths. Each is born of one-sided experience with the subject. Neither, I found, squared satisfactorily with the empirical plane defined jointly by history, culture, and economics.

This book has been written to advance a new hypothesis. I make the case that the Japanese market for corporate control will change significantly in terms of style, conduct, and volume, but will *not* converge completely with the Anglo-American model prevalent today. The reason to expect change without total convergence has to do with both Japanese culture and fundamental economics, though more the latter than the former. Specifically, it has primarily to with the economics of contractual exchange that explains how and why Japanese corporate stakeholders relate to one another in the current business environment. Should complete convergence of the Japanese and Anglo-American markets for corporate control ever occur, it will be due as much to a degree of Western conformity with Japanese corporate governance techniques as to simple Japanese imitation of the West.

## JAPANESE CORPORATE GOVERNANCE AND THE MARKET FOR CORPORATE CONTROL

Whatever parallels one may draw between Japanese corporations in the 1980s and those of the United States two decades ago (e.g., slowing real growth, rising excess cash, declining debt, increasing unrelated diversification), there is no inevitability about the convergence of Japanese and Anglo-American activity in the market for corporate control. The reason convergence cannot be preordained boils down to a fundamental premise: companies headquartered in these two economic superpowers have historically developed vastly different systems of corporate governance.

As I use it, the term "corporate governance" means something more than merely the process by which the board of directors and top management control the actions of managers at lower levels in the organization. Such controls are part of a broader system of corporate governance, but only part. Here, "corporate governance system" means the entire set of incentives, safeguards, and dispute-resolution processes that orders the activities of various corporate stakeholders, each seeking to improve its welfare through coordinated economic activity with others.

What primarily sets the Japanese corporation apart from economic institutions elsewhere is its unique system of corporate governance. This system, more than anything else, has decisively influenced Japanese merger and acquisition activity throughout the country's modern economic history. It has largely obviated the necessity for a deep and active market for corporate control at home, limited the activity of Japanese companies in the market abroad, and yielded a paucity of attractive targets for foreign bidders. It has also produced a distinctly Japanese standard for those M&A transactions that do take place. Trust is the key ingredient to success, with emphasis placed on the preservation of existing claims held by various corporate stakeholders (e.g., employees, shareholders, creditors, customers, suppliers, subcontractors, and so forth). So far, price, deal structure, and the potential for immediate financial gain by the acquirer tend to be of secondary importance, even in many cross-border acquisitions.

It is, however, a system under great pressure. Changing patterns of corporate finance are altering crucial relationships with traditional suppliers of capital. At the same time, strategic restructuring is diversifying many large manufacturers. Both trends are providing relief from market tests: the former from capital markets, the latter from product markets. This freedom has allowed Japanese companies to stockpile enormous amounts of cash, take risks in financial markets, sit on highly valuable but nonessential real estate, and devote considerable corporate resources to the benefit of current employees.

Accompanying these developments have been several small but important changes in the Japanese market for corporate control. Some traditionally stable shareholders are showing signs of disloyalty to incumbent management and a willingness to sell out for a profit. Successful large-scale greenmailing in the hands of legitimate, albeit maverick, investors is on the rise. Even unfriendly foreign bidders are finding opportunities to acquire equity stakes in Japanese targets, and their threats are being taken seriously. In short, there is a gradual movement toward a more open, Anglo-American style market for corporate control.

It is unlikely, however, that a complete transition to the Anglo-American standard will ever be made. There will be more large-scale combinations among listed companies in Japan. The Japanese market will feature hostile attacks by corporate raiders more frequently. Forcing an errant management to refocus its attention on shareholder priorities may also be a more common motive for takeovers. But these trends will give Japanese takeover activity only the trappings of an open and active market for corporate control. In fact, transitions in the control of Japanese corporations will remain a largely administered affair dominated by a few large banks and other major shareowning stakeholders. Raiders will be the hounds that flush errant companies into the open, only to chase them back into the part of that herd from whence they came. Seldom will the target companies be fought over in a genuine contest for control.

Limited openness in the Japanese market for corporate control will continue because of the economic efficiencies intrinsic to the traditional Japanese corporate governance system. Embattled though the system may be, the economies it fosters in the creation and preservation of long-term business relationships are too great to suppose that it will be abandoned entirely. It is more apt simply to take another turn in the evolutionary path as Japanese corporate stakeholders learn to cope with the current relaxation of capital and product market discipline.

## TESTING THE M&A WATERS

Significant changes are occurring in the capital and ownership structure of Japanese industrial corporations. On one hand, enormous trade surpluses coupled with slower economic growth are contributing to a buildup of financial slack on Japanese corporate balance sheets. Bank debt is being steadily reduced and excess cash is accumulating. On the other hand, global capital market integration and Japanese financial liberalization are predictably weakening ties with traditional stable shareholders. Today, when large Japanese corporations have to turn to external financing to meet their funds needs, they are far more likely to issue securities than to borrow from financial intermediaries. As a direct result of these two trends, Japanese business has been experiencing a widening of both the scope and the wherewithal for the exercise of managerial discretion in the allocation of corporate resources.

Against this backdrop came the effects of a sudden, sharp rise in the real purchasing power of the yen beginning in 1985. Through its impact on global and even local competitiveness, the strengthened yen has functioned as a kind of economic "black ship," forcing Japanese manufacturers to address the need for change if they wish to ensure prosperity—and for a few, perhaps even survival—in the next century. More expenditure on basic research and development, the funding of new enterprises, and joint ventures with foreign companies have been among the major responses to the pressure for change. Yet another emerging response is the acquisition of other companies at home and abroad.

The trend toward merger and acquisition as a means of corporate restructuring in Japan has been developing for some time. A 1985 survey of Japanese manufacturers by Yamaichi Securities revealed that 83% of the respondents thought that mergers and acquisitions were becoming popular in Japan; 56% believed that mergers or acquisitions could help them achieve corporate objectives; and 42% had at least attempted a combination of some sort.

Thoughts have begun to turn into action. In 1987, 2,299 mergers and amalgamations of other types occurred among domestic Japanese corporations, a record level for Japan.[1] A widening of activity to include foreign targets and, rarely, foreign bidders is evident as well. The number of acquisitions of U.S. companies by Japanese buyers reached 79 in 1989, up from 40 in 1986 and only 17 in 1984. Although majority ownership of only 30 preexisting Japanese companies has been acquired by foreign buyers during the 1981–1987 period, this number represents twice that of all prior years. Judging from the M&A advisory capacity that major banks and securities firms in Tokyo put in place by 1987 (see Exhibit 1–1), more than a few seasoned professionals are betting heavily that these trends will continue.


THE JAPANESE RELUCTANCE TO COMBINE

While suggesting a significant future trend, the figures also reveal the relative paucity of the Japanese M&A deal flow

---

1. Data on mergers and various forms of business amalgamations (other than stock acquisitions) are compiled and reported by the Japanese Fair Trade Commission. Such combinations have risen steadily from a level of about 500 a year in the mid-1950s to present levels in excess of 2,000 a year.

Exhibit 1-1 *Numbers of Professionals Assigned to M&A Advisory Work in Japanese Financial Institutions, 1987–1988*

| | Size of M&A Staff[a] | | |
| --- | --- | --- | --- |
| | *Domestic* | *Overseas* | *Total* |
| *City Banks* | | | |
| Sumitomo Bank | 25 | 12 | 37 |
| Sanwa Bank | 13 | 12 | 25 |
| Dai-Ichi Kangyo Bank | 12 | 10 | 22 |
| Bank of Tokyo | 7 | 10 | 17 |
| Mitsui Bank | 11 | 6 | 17 |
| Mitsubishi Bank | 12 | 10 | 22 |
| Tokai Bank | 5 | 6 | 11 |
| Fuji Bank | 10 | n.a. | 10 |
| Daiwa Bank | 8 | — | 8 |
| Kyowa Bank | 1 | 6 | 7 |
| Taiyo Kobe Bank | 6 | — | 6 |
| Saitama Bank | 4 | — | 4 |
| Hokkaido Takushoku Bank | 1 | — | 1 |
| Subtotal | 115 | 72 | 187 |
| *Long-Term Credit Banks* | | | |
| Industrial Bank of Japan | 9 | 13 | 22 |
| Long-Term Credit Bank | 5 | 1 | 6 |
| Nippon Credit Bank | 8 | 4 | 12 |
| Subtotal | 22 | 18 | 40 |
| *Security Houses* | | | |
| Yamaichi Securities[b] | 33 | 9 | 42 |
| Nomura Securities[c] | 23 | 8 | 31 |
| Daiwa Securities | 11 | 9 | 20 |
| Nikko Securities[d] | 18 | — | 18 |
| Subtotal | 85 | 26 | 111 |
| Total | 222 | 116 | 338 |

n.a. = not available

[a]Figures are for professional staff assigned to mergers and acquisitions advisory work in the business information, corporate development, financial development, information development, or international business departments of these institutions. Figures do not include professional staff at affiliated foreign merchant banks in which the institution holds a minority bank interest.

[b]Affiliated with Lodestar Partners in the United States through a 25% investment in a buyout fund managed by Lodestar.

[c]Affiliated with Wasserstein, Perella & Co., Inc. in the United States through a 20% interest acquired in 1988.

[d]Affiliated with the Blackstone Group in the United States through a 20% interest acquired in 1989.

compared to that of other industrialized nations. The United States, for example, has experienced at least four distinct M&A waves, beginning as early as the late 1880s and recurring as recently as the late 1960s. In the most recent wave, the annual number of announced combinations reached an all-time high of 6,107 in 1969. Although the numbers of combinations announced in the 1980s are substantially below that record level (peaking at 3,336 combinations in 1986), the dollar magnitude of the deal flow since 1980 (averaging more than $120 billion per year in the aggregate value paid for acquired companies between 1981 and 1987) perhaps qualifies the 1980s as yet another distinct wave in the history of U.S. mergers and acquisitions.

Japan, in contrast, has never had a M&A wave as such. Several government-sanctioned combinations—for example, between Prince Motors and the Nissan Motor Corp. in 1966, and between Fuji Iron & Steel and Yawata Iron & Steel to form Nippon Steel in 1970—have played a vital role in the creation of Japan's industrial might. However, these have been fairly unusual and isolated. Most of the 2,000 or more mergers occurring annually in Japan today are small, privately negotiated deals. Fully 80% of those taking place between 1981 and 1985 were transactions resulting in companies with *total* book equity capital of ¥5 billion (about $20 million at past exchange rates) or less. Sixty percent produced companies with book capital of less than ¥1 billion ($8 million). Based on a sample of 186 combinations publicly announced between 1982 and 1987 for which actual purchase prices were disclosed, the average price paid for a Japanese company was a mere ¥520 million (less than $4 million at prevailing exchange rates).

International combinations involving Japanese corporations have been similarly small in number and size. The pace of Japanese takeovers in the United States clearly quickened in the late 1980s, as it did for nearly all major foreign buyers of U.S. companies. But until the very end of the decade, Japan remained firmly entrenched in fifth place among foreign buyers (see Exhibit 1–2). Often during the decade, its average annual number of acquisitions barely exceeded (1982–1984 and 1986),

Exhibit 1-2 *Number of U.S. Acquisitions by Country of Buyer, 1979–1988*

| Country | Total |
| --- | --- |
| United Kingdom | 692 |
| Canada | 423 |
| West Germany | 152 |
| France | 132 |
| Japan | 120 |
| Switzerland | 90 |
| Netherlands | 86 |
| Australia | 76 |
| Sweden | 67 |
| Italy | 35 |
| Total Foreign Acquisitions | 2,075 |

*Source:* W.T. Grimm & Co., *Mergerstat Review, 1988*, p. 65.

or was even superseded (1985) by, Switzerland's and the Netherlands'.[2] Despite some stunningly high premiums paid for a few major U.S. companies in the late 1980s, the median price paid in this period reached a peak of only $37 million in 1988 and was typically under $10 million in all other years.

These figures are remarkably low for an economic superpower that can boast a $1.6 trillion annual GNP, 2.4 million incorporated businesses, and a public equity market nominally capitalized at $3.4 trillion, the largest in the world. What explains the historic reluctance of Japanese companies to combine with others at home or abroad? The few explicit legal or regulatory barriers to M&A in Japan are no more potent deterrents than those found in other industrialized nations. For a complete explanation, one must look beyond legal restrictions to some powerful extralegal impediments.

Culture

The most commonly cited impediment is cultural norms. The Japanese concept of family, or *ie* (an *ie* might best be thought of as a perpetual descent group defined as much, if not

---

2. See W.T. Grimm & Co., *Mergerstat Review,* 1989, p. 55.

more, by intertemporal continuity of property as by consanguineous kinship), has functioned powerfully in Japan's postfeudal
era to shape Japanese attitudes about modern industrial enterprises. The Meiji reformers, for example, seized the concept of
*ie* to promulgate the simile of nation-as-family with the divine
emperor as its living head as a way to lend social legitimacy to
the far-reaching changes they were seeking. It was but a natural
extension for early, visionary professional Japanese managers to
use a parallel simile for companies to help justify their organizational innovations. The company-as-family simile persists in
the minds of many Japanese managers even today, lending an
unsavory connotation of "fleshpeddling" to the idea of selling a
company. Even the conventional Japanese words for takeover,
*nottori* (also used for hijacking) and *baishu* (also meaning bribery), reflect and reinforce this negative image of M&A activities.

Corporate Governance
        Yet another powerful deterrent to M&A activity in Japan
is the classic Japanese system of corporate governance. The cornerstones of this system have been (1) implicit contracting
founded on trust; (2) extensive reciprocal shareholdings and implicit reciprocal trade agreements with a few key stakeholders;
(3) managerial incentives aligned toward overall corporate
growth and away from transfers of value among stakeholders;
and (4) early selective intervention by key stakeholders, especially main banks.

    Because of these and other elements of the governance sys-
tem, the net economic benefits of mergers and acquisitions may
have been smaller for Japanese companies than for others. The
advantage of outright control over, say, an upstream supplier or
downstream user may generally be less when there is extensive
information sharing among transacting companies bound by reciprocal shareholdings or close monitoring by a few financial
intermediaries.

    To the extent that transacting parties are confident that each
will act in good faith, heavy reliance on implicit contracting may
also reduce the need for complete integration of ownership.

Smoothly functioning implicit contracts better enable managers dealing personally and directly at the trading interface to effect quick, subtle adjustments in the terms of those contracts in response to sudden environmental changes. This ability mitigates the need to exert direct administrative control over, say, an important supplier, subcontractor, or customer.

In principle, by tying themselves to one another in industrial groups bound by an intricate network of reciprocal ownership and reciprocal trading agreements, yet eschewing outright ownership and control, Japanese companies have been able to enjoy the best of both worlds. They have been able to harness the high-powered incentives of the market that derive from independent ownership of assets while relying on selective intervention by large banks, trading companies, or other key equity owners to adapt contracts to new circumstances as needed. When given a choice between owning another company outright or embracing it with implicit, bilaterally self-enforcing contracts, most major Japanese companies have opted for the latter whenever possible.

## A SYSTEM UNDER STRESS

Hence, Japanese companies have resorted to mergers and acquisitions less frequently than others for good reasons, economic as well as cultural, and arguably economic *more* than cultural. What, if anything, might tempt these companies to depart from past practices that apparently have served them so well? Indeed, what is tempting companies such as Sony, Bridgestone, and Nippon Mining to reach beyond Japan for corporate ownership?

Two important developments of the 1980s stand out. The first, giving rise to the emerging interest in mergers and acquisitions by many Japanese companies, is the sense of urgency with which managers in large, mature companies regard the need to undertake strategic restructuring of their businesses. The second, which will shape the nature of Japanese M&A activity over the long run, is the gradual degeneration of some essential elements of the Japanese corporate governance system, company-bank relationships in particular.

The Pressure to Restructure

Since the first oil shock of the 1970s, many Japanese industrial corporations have been attempting to sustain competitive advantage in their mature core businesses while searching for new avenues of growth and profitability to replace that core eventually. At the same time, they have tried to avoid placing the burden of adjustment on any one corporate stakeholder. This process gained momentum in the 1980s with the sudden, dramatic rise in the purchasing power of the yen, which has further threatened the profitability of industries such as steel, textiles, shipbuilding, and household consumer products that were the principal engines of Japanese economic growth in earlier decades.

Two factors distinguish the adjustment problems faced by Japanese businesses in the 1980s: (1) the depth of the modern excess personnel problem, and (2) the intensity of the pressure being placed on Japan by its trading partners to take initiatives to correct trade imbalances. For all the progress that has been made in shrinking capacity in some of Japan's mature or declining industries, dealing with redundant workers and managers remains a thorny problem at many large companies. Previously successful tactics such as worker "loans" to suppliers, subcontractors, and even industrial customers, early outplacement of aging employees at all ranks, and simple reliance on natural attrition to bring the work force in line with true needs have succeeded primarily in deferring final adjustment of personnel requirements to the 1990s. Thus the need to reduce the work force at Nippon Steel by 3,500 people in the late 1970s burgeoned into a 19,000 reduction need by the end of the 1980s.

At the same time, with its emergence in the last decade as an economic superpower, Japan has lost the advantage of being small. Few if any large Japanese companies can rely on export growth today as heavily as in the past to maintain full employment while implementing (or even deferring) a plan for restructuring over a long time horizon. Indeed, just the opposite is true. The rest of the world is demanding that Japan help other economies by shifting its consumption patterns to include more imported items, and the charge is to do so fairly quickly.

Nevertheless, the basic impulse of Japanese managers today remains very much as before: to continue growth of the enterprise as a means of fulfilling the expectations of some key stakeholders (labor, in particular) and avoiding, or at least forestalling, potentially divisive and costly recontracting among the broad coalition of stakeholders making up the corporation. But what are the alternatives? For manufacturers in mature industries such as Nippon Steel, growth opportunities in existing core businesses are few if any.

For many Japanese companies, substantial new growth can be achieved only through diversification into new markets. However, internal development of new businesses from the ground up—the approach historically favored by Japanese managers and the one most consistent with the traditional incentive alignments of large Japanese corporations—is believed to require more time than managers deem acceptable in present circumstances. Moreover, attractive investment opportunities in the growth businesses most frequently targeted for entry by restructuring Japanese corporations—telecommunications, computer electronics, advanced materials, and biotechnology—tend to be shared with other competitors around the world. If new Japanese entrants to these businesses are to avoid being pre-empted by competitors, they must acquire market share at home and abroad at a faster pace than is generally afforded by internal development of products, manufacturing, and marketing know-how. Confronted with this reality, Japanese managers are gradually overcoming their unfamiliarity with, and even distaste for, mergers and acquisitions in order to implement restructuring plans considered crucial to the life and profitability of their companies.

The Cost of Corporate Financial Emancipation

Yet another characteristic separating the current period of adjustment for the modern Japanese corporation from earlier periods is the abundance of liquidity found on most of their balance sheets. Even though profitability came under pressure during the 1980s, the availability of financial resources to effect a restructuring did not. For perhaps the first time, modern Japanese corporations find themselves awash in cash, the result of having executed highly successful past strategies in product markets while maintaining low dividend payout policies.

It is no mere coincidence that this period of abundance has also been accompanied by atrophying company-bank relationships. The increased availability of internally generated cash to fund projects has reduced the need to raise funds externally, thus diminishing the financial dependence of industrial enterprises on banks. In addition, the growth and gradual deregulation of capital markets at home and the opening of capital markets abroad have distanced Japanese industrial companies still further from banks.

There is a hidden cost to the financial emancipation of past success, however. In the absence of the discipline previously exerted by both product and capital markets, Japanese management now finds itself with far greater discretion in the allocation of corporate resources than ever before. Unwilling to breach long-standing implicit contracts with key stakeholders, especially lifetime employment commitments, and unable to execute past strategies of simply growing themselves out of their current plight, some companies use this discretion to sustain marginal businesses and/or pursue unrelated diversification strategies. Thus the economic rents (returns to factors of production such as capital and labor in excess of the opportunity cost of their use in that activity) of these enterprises may be being reallocated from suppliers of capital to other stakeholders, primarily employees.

Despite the low priority traditionally accorded to shareholders in Japan, it is unlikely this trend can continue for long. One by-product of the increasingly global market in which Japanese financial institutions must compete, and of their weakening relationships with industrial clients, has been a growing concern for obtaining higher direct returns on their equity investments. For banks in particular, this has been reinforced by the 8% capital requirements recently promulgated by the Bank for International Settlements, a level substantially above the 2–4% normally maintained by the large Japanese city banks. Today, in contrast with the volume-oriented banking practices of the past, nearly all major Japanese banks monitor closely the precise cash return on investment they receive on their open positions with client companies. This information is not compiled for convenience only. Many banks now rank clients according to the aggregate return on investment they provide. In some cases, relationships have been severed if an adequate return has not been forthcoming.

## TOWARD A NEW JAPANESE MARKET FOR CORPORATE CONTROL

Given the increasing performance orientation of large financial institutions in Japan, and the widening latitude enjoyed by Japanese managers in the allocation of corporate resources, a tension is emerging within the delicate coalition of stakeholders that makes up the Japanese industrial enterprise. Already, this tension is erupting into overt conflict among corporate stakeholders, resulting in some genuine contests for corporate control *within* Japan.

A rash of at least 22 successful "greenmailing" attacks on cash- and real estate-rich companies occurred between 1984 and 1988. Some (e.g., Fujiya in 1986) reportedly had quiet behind-the-scenes support of supposedly stable Japanese shareholders. As of June 1988, an estimated 120 *shite* groups—private Japanese investors and companies with experience in greenmailing and/or risk arbitrage—were holding positions in 150 different companies listed on the Tokyo Stock Exchange. In a dramatic break with Japanese business norms, one of the greenmailers, the Koshin group, successfully acquired control of Kokusai Kogyo (an aerial surveying contractor owning a substantial real estate portfolio in central Tokyo) in late 1988, the first overtly hostile takeover in modern Japanese history.[3]

Although one may be tempted to adopt the view that Japan is

3. This takeover is being investigated by the Tokyo District Prosecutor's office for suspected misuse of inside information. Under pressure from the banks that funded Koshin's investment, Mitsuhiro Kotani resigned his chairmanship of Kokusai's board in June 1990.

gradually converging with the West as far as the conduct of its market for corporate control is concerned, such a conclusion is too much of an extrapolation from recent events. Though weakened by current trends, the Japanese corporate governance system will continue to function prophylactically with respect to hostile takeovers.

Maverick Japanese shareholders will play a greater and a profitable role as agents of change in the future market for corporate control. No doubt there will be a few surprising and notable successful hostile takeovers at their hands. But in the end, they will neither dominate nor determine contests for control in an essentially free and open market such as that seen in the West. That privilege will remain with the banks and other major shareowning stakeholders. Unsolicited transfers of ownership are likely to occur only if these key shareholders acquiesce to it. In a curious, perhaps surprising symbiosis, traditional stable Japanese shareholders will come to depend on maverick corporate raiders to exert the discipline previously provided by the rigors of survival in product markets and the heavy dependence of the manufacturing sector on financial intermediaries for its capital. Instead of being an open, free-wheeling market in which corporate ownership winds up in the hands of the highest bidder, the future Japanese market for corporate control is more likely to be a rather controlled market, implicitly "administered" by main banks and other core shareholding companies.

It should be emphasized that this outcome will be determined more by *economic* than cultural considerations. It is not because of a Japanese social taboo against takeovers that complete convergence with today's Anglo-American market for corporate control will not occur. Rather, it is the intrinsic efficiencies of the Japanese corporate governance system that will allow major elements of that system to remain in place as the Japanese economy opens, thereby deflecting the evolutionary path of the Japanese market away from its Anglo-American counterpart. Indeed, these same efficiencies may one day lure some Western companies away from their traditional corporate governance practices and perhaps usher in a new era in the evolution of the global market for corporate control.

# PART I
# Relationship
# Management Versus
# Asset Ownership

Japanese M&A activity is presently in a state of flux. While increasing in scope and volume and exhibiting some tactical maneuvers that are more typically Anglo-American than Japanese, it nevertheless remains distinctly different from takeover activity in much of the Western world.

To develop an understanding of why the Japanese market for corporate control is fundamentally different, Part I provides a largely retrospective view of Japanese corporate governance and takeover activity. It begins with a case study of the Kikkoman Corporation, which traces the roots of the classic Japanese corporate governance system to a process of conflict and resolution among Japanese corporate stakeholders that began in Japan's earliest industrial organizations. From this historical perspective, contemporary changes in Japanese M&A activity may be seen as but the latest stage in a continuous process of "creative destruction" identified by Joseph Schumpeter as so characteristic of capitalism.

Following the establishment of this historical baseline, there is a detailed description of the classic Japanese corporate governance system and an analysis of how and why it successfully blunted corporate stakeholders' potentially destructive self-interested opportunism. It is this success that allowed Japanese companies to build and sustain efficient, long-term business relationships with one another, largely obviating the need for an active market for corporate control. Within the context of this system, large Japanese companies have preferred to bind themselves to one another in contractual relationships and manage those relationships over time, rather than exercise outright ownership and control over another company. This has made them comparatively reluctant bidders and infrequent targets, both at home and abroad. Moreover, when they do combine domestically, a distinctly Japanese standard of dealmaking applies, as shown in the case of the merger that produced Nippon Steel in 1970.

When Japanese companies have seized outright control of a foreign firm, it has usually been to preserve a valuable long-term business relationship being threatened in some significant way. We see this in Dainippon Ink and Chemicals' takeover of Reichhold Chemicals, Sony's purchase of CBS Records, Bridgestone's successful tender offer for Firestone Tire & Rubber, and Nippon Mining's acquisition of Gould, Inc. In the comparatively few instances of foreign takeovers of Japanese companies, similar long-term business relationships preceded the acquisitions, and Japanese standards of dealmaking were followed. Merck's acquisition of Banyu Pharmaceutical presents a virtual blueprint for success that other foreign companies eyeing Japanese targets will find valuable in their planning.

# 2
# STAKEHOLDER CONFLICT AND THE EVOLUTION OF THE JAPANESE CORPORATION

Imagine organizing a company and electing at the outset to establish the following policies and procedures: The company will be leveraged to the hilt. It will have perhaps two or three times as much debt in its capital structure than is typical for other companies in its industry. It will be dependent on a single bank or a small group of banks for virtually all of that debt, most of which will be short term and secured against just about every asset the company owns.

The company will rely on a relatively small handful of suppliers and subcontractors in its trading relationships. Its dealings with them will be fairly informal. It will negotiate hard but will minimize reliance on painstakingly detailed written contracts. Once an understanding is reached, the trading partners will be trusted to uphold the spirit of the agreement, informally modifying the terms of trade as needed to adjust to changed circumstances.

The managers who will run this firm are to be hired right out of college (just a few good ones, however), trained at the company's expense, and effectively promised jobs for life. There will be little or no performance-based compensation, and promotion will be based primarily on seniority. Similarly, factory workers will be hired for life, with pay tied primarily to seniority. Decision making will be a highly decentralized, bottom-up process.

The goals of the company will be growth and longevity, with profitability a distant third priority. In fact, independent shareholders will rank fairly low on the list of constituencies whose interests management is to represent. There would be no outside directors. The board of directors will be composed entirely of

21

senior managers who will probably hold no equity in the company. Dividends will be small. Cash not needed for reinvestment will be saved for a "rainy day" in bank deposits, government securities, or equities of other companies.

Today few people would feel sanguine about such a company's prospects for lasting success. In fact, unless you were wealthy enough to provide most if not all of the equity capital yourself, it would seem challenging enough to get such an enterprise off the ground, let alone sustain its viability. Yet many of these policies are stylized versions of characteristics that have been common among many of Japan's largest modern corporations.

At first glance from a Western perspective, the enterprises would appear to be economic anomalies, successful *despite* rather than *because of* the agreements and expectations that bind various corporate stakeholders (managers, workers, creditors, shareholders, suppliers, customers, government regulators, and so forth) together. The fact that they *are* so successful causes many Westerners to view them with awe and even suspicion. Their peculiar contracting arrangements are often dismissed as blunt attempts to restrict trade, symptoms of an entrenched managerial elite, or merely idiosyncrasies of the Japanese culture.

In fact, however, these and other characteristics typical of modern Japanese companies are important elements of the classic Japanese system of corporate governance, which has been a major determinant of Japanese merger and acquisition activity in the postwar era. As a prelude to a more detailed exposition of the system, the following case study traces the evolution of the Noda Shoyu Company from a rudimentary kinship network in feudal Japan to a cartel in the Meiji Restoration to a modern corporation known today as the Kikkoman Corporation. As a rural, agri-based group of companies, the Noda Shoyu Company and its affiliates differed in some respects from its larger urban cousins, the Mitsui, Mitsubishi, and Sumitomo groups, which tended to focus investment in transportation and financial assets required to support trade. Nevertheless, the passage of the Noda Shoyu Company through its various organizational stages is fundamentally similar. Thanks to Mark Fruin's rich and exhaustive history of Kikkoman, it is a company whose evolution can be analyzed carefully with an eye toward understanding how and why Japanese companies are governed as they are today.[1]

Two points are evident: (1) change and successful organizational adaptation, not "five hundred years of tradition," have been the cornerstones of the Japanese corporation since the Meiji era; and (2) in Japan, as elsewhere, economic self-interest more than culture has been the primary driver behind that change and adaptation. In view of the mythology that too often obscures reality concerning Japanese business, it is important that these points be appreciated early and borne in mind throughout as we appraise the modern Japanese corporation and assess its role as a major player in the global market for corporate control.

## THE EARLY GOVERNANCE OF BUSINESS RELATIONSHIPS

*Shoyu,* or soy sauce, a naturally fermented brew of steamed soybeans and roasted wheat, was long a traditional product of the Japanese countryside. For centuries it has been an important seasoning in Japanese cooking. Produced originally in small batches, *shoyu* manufacture was largely a cottage industry during most of Japan's feudal period (pre-1868). Rapid growth in the demand and output of *shoyu*, particularly around Edo (modern Tokyo) began to occur with the urbanization of the Japanese population in the Tokugawa period (1603–1867).

In 1661, Hyozaemon Takanashi XIX began producing *shoyu* in Noda, an agricultural community 40 kilometers northwest of Tokyo. The next year, he was joined there by Shichizaemon

---

1. Facts concerning the Noda Shoyu Company are derived from a history of the Kikkoman Corporation by W. Mark Fruin, *Kikkoman: Company, Clan, and Community* (Cambridge, MA: Harvard University Press, 1983). I have benefited substantially from the many scholarly insights contained in that important history. The particular interpretation of the facts given here, as well as any errors in the presentation of those facts, is my responsibility.

Mogi I, who began production of *miso*, another soybean by-product used as a seasoning or soup base. A century later, in 1764, the eldest son in the Takanashi family married a daughter in the Mogi family and became the adopted son of Shichizaemon Mogi V. Soon he established a *shoyu* factory with the financial backing of his natural father and eventually became recognized as head of a separate branch household in the Mogi line. Thus a business alliance accompanied the marriage, and the two Noda families became united in the production of *shoyu*. Further family expansion into *shoyu* production occurred when Shichizaemon Mogi added the product to his manufacture of *miso* in 1766.

The Family as Enterprise

In Japan as elsewhere in the pre-industrial world, a close association existed between family and business enterprise. Indeed, there was virtually no concept of the latter independent of the former.

The Japanese models of family most relevant to an appreciation of early Japanese business organizations and stakeholder interests are those of the *ie* and the *dozoku*. Unlike the Western concept of family, which is delineated by kinship and segmented by nuclear units, the Japanese *ie*, or "stem family," is a perpetual descent group defined by continuity of property and genealogy. A *dozoku* is similar to a clan in that it is made up of several *ie* related to a main household and connected by descent through males. Often, members of the *ie* are not genetically related to the male head of the household.

It is within the context of this *ie/dozoku* concept of family that the Mogi-Takanashi business alliance and, indeed, many of the principal features of enterprise control and management in nineteenth-century Japan must be appreciated. Kinship and entrepreneurship were inextricably intertwined, and economic considerations dominated kinship considerations as often as not. Eldest sons who were not deemed suitable for managing the household and business would be passed over for property inheritance in favor of younger male siblings. In fact, it was not uncommon for main households to *adopt* an able young man to become the family heir if no consanguineous male heir existed or if those who did exist were inadequate.[2]

New enterprise development was also executed through family branching—a device by which a main household established a related but separate household with its own genealogical and corporate identity.[3] Family branching provided an invaluable network of cooperative kinsmen in early industrial Japan, which was characterized by highly uneven distributions of labor, capital, raw materials, and, above all, information about market conditions. A *dozoku* focused on one industry; in effect, it mimicked a large single-product cooperative in which production was locally decentralized, but information about local market conditions, output, and production technology was transferred internally via communication with the main household.

The kinship network represented by a *dozoku* also functioned as a kind of private capital market for family members: kin would finance important new projects within the *dozoku* and would trade production assets among themselves. Reliance on the family for financial support and liquidity necessarily limited growth to the rate at which the wealth of the *dozoku* accumulated. But in return for this constraint, the internal market for funds and assets supported the family's goal of maintaining the continuity of property.

***Ownership versus control.*** The flexibility of household membership and resulting enterprise control afforded by adoption was another important feature of the Japanese family that served a vital economic function: the resolution of conflicts between principals (owners) and agents (hired administrators) in the management of the family business. Early family organizations typically displayed rudimentary degrees of specialization that sharply divided the management of the "factory" (e.g., the production of *shoyu*) from the management of the "front office" (e.g., the determination of output volume, the purchase of soybeans, the scheduling of production, the marketing of finished

---

2. Fruin, *Kikkoman*, p. 294
3. Ibid.

products, and any other function not directly part of the physical production process).[4] Largely separated from both functions were the individual family owners themselves. Although they were the principals of the business, having provided the capital to found the factories, their managerial role was limited to essentially ritualistic top-management tasks. In the production of *shoyu*, effective control over the front office was delegated to *banto* (trusted retainers), and factory responsibilities were delegated to *toji* (factory brewmasters) and *oyakata* (labor recruiters).[5]

The wide separation between ownership and control, coupled with ineffectual monitoring systems, presented a situation ripe for abuse. Managers could easily act in their own self-interests at the expense of the principals. Potential replacement constituted an important check on untrustworthy managers, though awareness of abuse was a prerequisite to such redress. This was difficult to develop in the absence of reliable accounting systems.

But where the stick does not work, the carrot might: rewarding managers for loyalty to family interests offered another means of ensuring that hired agents acted in the best interests of principals. For the reward to work properly, however, the wealth and status of the agents must be closely linked over time to the wealth and status of the principals. In modern Western corporations, this tends to be accomplished by vesting key managers with equity interests of one form or another. In early Japanese family enterprises, it often took the form of adoption into the family.

Exploiting the feudal ideal of a vassal being loyal to his lord even unto death, *banto* were expected to tie the destinies of their families to that of the owning households. Their motive for doing so was the real possibility that they would eventually be rewarded with a family tie of some type. This tie took the form of outright adoption or marriage of the *banto* to a family daughter, in effect vesting the *banto* with a "general partnership"

4. Ibid., p. 42.
5. Ibid., p. 2.

equity interest in the enterprise. Alternatively, the *banto* family and the owning family might establish a tie in the next generation through the marriage of sons and daughters. The latter ties were more common in the case of the Mogi family, which was blessed with many competent heirs.

***Trust and stakeholder harmony.*** From an economic point of view, the early Japanese family was cunningly ambiguous in its design. As in the concentric circles of waves from a stone dropped into water, it was comparatively easy to identify its epicenter but difficult to distinguish its boundaries. This ambiguity lent flexibility to the Japanese *ie* and *dozoku*, and rendered them organizational forms uniquely well adapted to the economic rigors of the day. In particular, they were forms conducive to relatively low-cost resolution of potential conflicts among various stakeholders in the enterprise.

For the Mogi family, attitudes about economy, family cooperation, and trust among stakeholders in matters of business were sufficiently well developed to have been codified into a family constitution during the late eighteenth or early nineteenth century. Fruin reports the following written precepts of the Mogi family:

Sincerity first and profits will follow. Neglect neither.

Take care to preserve the harmony and unity of the household.

Avoid luxury and cultivate simplicity and earnestness.

Avoid matters not connected with family business.

Learn to make money and not to lose it.

Competition makes for progress, but avoid reckless competition.

Attend to your health. Eat simple food no different from that taken by your employees.

Economize on personal expenses and give what remains to charity, taking care to preserve a sufficient estate for your successors.

Cultivate a positive attitude toward making money and be cautious in times of uncertainty.

Twice a year call a family assembly; praise family members
according to their character, not according to their profits.[6]

In effect, beginning with the first article, the Mogi family constitution reminds Mogi managers from household heads to factory *toji* that the best route to long-term wealth creation is a
demonstrated capacity to recognize the claims of other corporate
stakeholders, to resist the temptation of myopic self-enrichment
at their expense, and to honor (as much as practically possible)
implicit contracts established with them. Through such fair
dealing, harmony and the attendant economic benefits of family
branching will be preserved, as will the ability to contract implicitly with important nonfamily stakeholders such as employees, customers, suppliers, Noda townspeople, and others.

Then as now, in Japan as in the rest of the world, it was simply
good business to develop a reputation for trustworthiness. As I
will explain in Chapter 3, the ability to enter into implicit contracts, which are generally more flexible and less costly to adjust
than formal written contracts, can be an important source of efficiency in the management of business relationships. As long
as there is an expectation of entering into favorable *future* agreements with one's stakeholders or partners in commerce, it will
pay to honor existing implicit contracts despite the possibility of
immediate personal gain through breaking them.[7] With its in-
tergenerational view of the future and focus on the continuity of
property ownership, the Mogi family's early emphasis on trustworthiness as a basis for conducting profitable business was not
only ethical, but entirely logical from a purely economic point of
view.[8]

---

6. Ibid., p. 20.
7. See Andrei Shleifer and Lawrence H. Summers, "Breach of Trust in Hostile Takeovers," in A.J. Auerbach, ed., *Corporate Takeovers: Causes and Consequences* (Chicago:
University of Chicago Press, 1988), pp. 33–56.
8. Writing down "house rules" was not unique to the Mogi family. Other great entrepreneurial houses such as Mitsui and Sumitomo had written rules as well (see, for example,
the Mitsui family constitution in Johannes Hirschmeier and Tsunehiko Yui, *The Development of Japanese Business: 1600–1980*, 2d ed. [London: Allen & Unwin, 1981], pp. 63–
64).

INDUSTRIAL CROSSROAD

Economic and political turbulence followed the opening of Japanese ports by Admiral Perry in 1854. A debasing of the currency resulted in drastic price inflation that saw the price of soybeans rise eightfold between 1859 and 1867, wheat and salt ninefold, and sake tenfold. At the same time, Japanese entrepreneurs were exposed to fierce competition from foreigners who were often better equipped to compete in Japanese markets.

Ultimately, the upheavals of the period gave birth to the Meiji Restoration of 1868 and the overthrow of the Tokugawa Shogunate. The emperor Meiji was restored as the true head of government, and a powerful drive toward industrial modernization began. Dissenting samurai spawned a number of sporadic revolts, culminating in the Satsuma Rebellion of 1877. Financing the fight against the rebels led to a renewal of inflation followed by an increase in taxes and a sharp cut in government spending. The result was severe deflation and recession from 1881 to 1885.

Market Hazards: Cartelization and the Displacement of Kinship Networks

Adding to the economic woes of the *shoyu* brewers of Noda was the amalgamation in 1871 of the *tonya* merchants (distributors who bought on consignment and sometimes branded goods themselves) into the "River-Road" Shoyu Tonya (rivers and roads were the two principal modes of transport to Tokyo). In 1879, the group was reorganized into the Tokyo Shoyu Tonya Association to meet government requirements. *Shoyu* manufacturers wishing to distribute product in Tokyo through member *tonya* were required to give the association exclusive distribution rights and consign goods to it at terms set by the association. The manufacturers' only alternative was to allow the association to sell *shoyu* under its own brand names.[9] In short, the association gave the *tonya* near monopoly control over *shoyu* distribution in Tokyo and thus posed a significant threat

---

9. Fruin, *Kikkoman*, p. 60.

to the livelihood of the Noda brewers, who made over half their sales in Tokyo, the largest and fastest-growing single market for *shoyu* in Meiji Japan.

Reaction by the Mogi family was varied. Ultimately, however, fragmented individual responses were inadequate to counter the threat posed by a large and well-organized monopoly. Coordinated action finally took shape in a competing group established by *shoyu* producers in 1881, the Tokyo Shoyu Company. Interestingly, it was organized as a *company* in which members owned shares, not as an association. Important differences accompanied this alternative organizational form. They reflected attempts to achieve superiority over the *tonya* association through better monitoring and control systems designed to reduce the scope for stakeholder conflict arising from hidden action by some at the expense of others. For example, the rules governing the company required a monthly balancing of books and an annual report to members, who were permitted to inspect financial records at any time. Company profits could be calculated by anyone, and members could determine their share of the profits based on their fractional participation in the company.

The *tonya* association, in contrast, maintained closed and secret accounts. Prior to the distribution of sale proceeds, members could draw cash from the Tokyo Shoyu Company by borrowing up to 70% of the value of their inventory on deposit with the company at no interest, whereas association members had to wait for semiannual cash payouts from the sale of products sold on consignment.[10]

The organizational benefits the company provided were clear enough and resulted in the secession of a number of families from the *tonya* association. The *tonya*, in return, redrafted their agreement to include severe penalties for manufacturers and distributors that elected association with the Tokyo Shoyu Company. In effect, the organizational form itself, at least as it related to the rights and privileges of members and their ability to share

---

10. Ibid., p. 63

fairly in the economic rents produced by the groups, became a basis of rivalry between the two. So strong were the different economic incentives and costs that strong family alliances were greatly strained as families began to choose between the groups.

Ultimately, the size and first-mover advantage of the *tonya* association proved insurmountable to the newer company. Despite unprecedentedly large marketing expenditures to promote the producers' own brand names, the grip of the *tonya* could not be shaken. A disastrous flood during the 1889 spring monsoon finally forced the weakened Tokyo Shoyu Company into bankruptcy.

Perhaps sensing the futility of combating the powerful *tonya*, the Noda brewers initiated an independent course of action even before the demise of the Tokyo Shoyu Company. Rather than bear the enormous costs of surmounting artificial barriers to entry into *shoyu* distribution in the Tokyo market, the Noda brewers sought to preserve their economic rents by erecting their own barriers to inhibit entry into the *production* of *shoyu*. The Noda Shoyu Brewers Association, a cartel, was established in 1887. The cartel would last for 30 years and at its peak would include 22 families in 12 different communities. At the outset, its ostensible purpose was to share information among unrelated producing families, though this function eventually became but the first step toward the coordination of decision making on the basis of the shared information.[11] Eventually, the cartel would determine *shoyu* prices, wage rates, the volume of raw material purchases (thereby indirectly controlling output), and shipping schedules.

In the dynamic industrial environment of Restoration Japan, the *shoyu* producers' cartel displaced kinship networks as a basis for coordinated commercial activity. The cartel was a seemingly ubiquitous organizational solution to the problem of realizing the economic advantages of large-scale production without incurring the "costs" (from the producers' point of view) of fragmented action. The *ie* and *dozoku*, in contrast, were unique Jap-

---

11. Ibid., p. 65.

anese sociological institutions that for centuries had been well adapted to the rigors of commercial activity in a feudal economy, but were deficient as a commercial organizational form in a modern industrial state. In effect, the rise of the *shoyu* cartel in 1887 marked the ascendancy, at least temporarily, of basic economic interests (among them, the profit motive) over traditional forms of commercial activity rooted in centuries of Japanese culture and Confucian ethics.[12] Kinship considerations were far from being discarded, to be sure. But with the emergence of the cartel, kinship no longer constituted the exclusive basis for joint action.

Controlling Stakeholder Interests

In displacing the kinship network, the Tokyo Shoyu Company faced the problem of how to exert control and resolve potential conflicts among stakeholders. Its solution was half political and half managerial. It partially defused potential conflict among members by judiciously restricting the extent of its reach over members' business activities, thus narrowing the range of conflict. In general, pooling information and coordinating decision making were confined to areas where there were clear benefits to joint action, but limited scope for the appropriation of unique, family-specific sources of competitive advantage that would result only in the transfer of value from the "donating" family to the membership at large. For example, the cartel controlled the volume of and prices paid for raw materials, but left private the techniques used by different families to combine these materials into their brews. Likewise, wage rates were set by the cartel, but there was no pooling of workers, some of whom possessed unique knowledge and skills related to family brewing techniques.[13]

To control hidden action by members in those areas to which cartel authority extended, the cartel simply implemented more

---

12. Although cartelization as a solution to industrial restructuring was not unique to Japan, neither was it without precedent or culturally foreign. Guilds were an enduring feature of Tokugawa Japan until their abolition in 1872. A long tradition of information sharing and cooperation within kinship networks also offered a sociological basis for the establishment of cartels.
13. Fruin, *Kikkoman*, p. 55.

professional management techniques. Accurate records about purchases, costs, production volume, and prices were kept, and decisions about matters affecting all members were debated openly. Violators of cartel policies were censured by the curious means of disclosing their names and transgressions to the press.[14] Though clearly of limited effectiveness in restricting hidden action, these techniques were nonetheless significant: they constituted an intermediate step in the transition of the Noda brewers from small, idiosyncratic family enterprises to a large, systematized, managerial bureaucracy coping with the diverse interests of many stakeholders.

Facilitating the change, and lending social legitimacy to it, was a remarkable exploitation of the Japanese concept of family. In a brilliant stroke, Meiji reformers promoted modernization in the name of tradition and used the concept of family as a simile describing the nation and its leadership. Pithy slogans reflected a national ideology of progress for the sake of tradition. People referred to "industrial patriotism" and "business for the nation and for profit."[15] The nation was likened to a large family with the divine emperor as its patriarch.

The new ideology promoted from above was quickly employed by Meiji industrialists as the handmaiden to change. Ancestral authority could be used to justify organizational change to family members, and material success to society at large. Years later there would emerge a more formal corporate structure in which family and enterprise were no longer synonymous, but Shichizaemon Mogi would apply the family simile being used at the national level to the company itself. In December of 1919, he is quoted as saying:

> . . . the enterprise is made up of three classes: owners, office workers, and laborers, and . . . each of these must consider their position in relation to the others and strive to maintain harmonious relations with them. Within the factory, the factory manager should be considered as the father, the

---

14. Ibid., p. 56.
15. See Hirschmeier and Yui, *The Development of Japanese Business*, p. 127; Fruin, *Kikkoman*, p. 79.

foreman as the mother, and the inspector as the successor
to the father. Thus, everyone is a member of the same family and they should live together harmoniously as a result.[16]

## THE EMERGENCE OF A MODERN JAPANESE INDUSTRIAL ENTERPRISE

By the last quarter of the nineteenth century, joint action
for mutual benefit was already a prominent feature of the Japanese economic landscape. A complex, largely informal network
of "contracts" existed horizontally across some families as well
as vertically within a particular family producing *shoyu*. With
the cartel came both a widening and a formalization of this network of contracts, binding together various stakeholders in the
production of *shoyu*. Supplanting family membership or bilateral family alliances as a basis for cooperative decision making
was a written agreement that stipulated responsibilities of association members to one another (not the least of which was for
each to reveal honestly its production figures) and provided for
an administrative superstructure (with constraints) to govern the
agreement.
Clearly, however, the success of the association could not be
left entirely to a formal, written agreement. The agreement
might require specific behavior by members and impose penalties for failure to conform, but unless considerable resources
were devoted to the monitoring of behavior, hidden action for
private gain would always be a possibility. Furthermore, no written contract could ever stipulate what actions should be taken
by individual members under every conceivable set of circumstances. Such an agreement would be virtually impossible to
write and police; in any event, it would almost certainly have
been unacceptable to a wide array of entrepreneurial families
accustomed to independent action and concerned, at least in
part, with family status and prestige. Implicit, unwritten contracts among members were needed to cope with most contin-

---

16. Fruin, *Kikkoman*, p. 115.

gencies, and mutual trust was necessarily the glue holding the coalition together. Indeed, article three of the association's agreement noted that the association was "based on mutual trust and harmony," required members to "conduct themselves honestly and avoid selling imperfect goods which will destroy our good reputation," and stipulated that brokers proving to be untrustworthy must be repudiated to "protect our profit."[17]

Ultimately, this particular network of explicit and implicit contracts, and the trust on which it depended, proved inadequate in the economic environment of the early twentieth century. Technological advances in the fermenting of *shoyu* had made mass production possible on a scale commensurate with that already possible for purchasing and distribution. The size of the prize up for grabs was made evident with the opening of a railroad line (financed largely by the brewers' association) between Noda and Kashiwa, which made safe, year-round transportation possible throughout all of Japan. For the Noda brewers, the potential *shoyu* market had, in effect, become a national one. Exploiting the wider market required still greater degrees of cooperation and centralized decision making than that afforded by the cartel.

Incorporation and Organizational Growth

The organizational response to the changing economics of the *shoyu* industry was the formation of a joint-stock company and the eventual dissolution of the brewers' association. The Noda Shoyu Company was formally incorporated in December 1917 through a pooling of assets owned by nine individual producing families.

Although the family figured prominently in the constitution of the new company, the *ie* and *dozoku* were no longer the framework of the commercial enterprise. Instead, the family now served more as the basis for inclusion in the company, and inclusion necessarily entailed the loss of much autonomy by the separate *ie*. One leading family brand name, that of Kikkoman, was selected to be the corporation's premier product. It would

---

17. Ibid., Appendix C, "Rules and Regulations of the Noda Shoyu Brewers Association," p. 310.

receive the lion's share of the budget for advertising and distribution. Other family brand names were made secondary to Kikkoman or given up altogether.

Even more formal control systems increased coordination and
centralization of decision making. By 1919, uniform bookkeep-
ing standards were applied in all factories, and input-output
data were compiled to permit efficiency comparisons. Sales and
research committees and a kind of executive committee were
formed to centralize information-gathering and coordinate
managerial action. Significantly, a time log was also kept for
managers, including family members, in 1918. Although a passing phenomenon, it demonstrated a recognition of "company
time" that had never existed when family and enterprise were
synonymous.[18] However minor the potential for abuse, it was
now tacitly acknowledged that managers and even family executives could be tempted to pursue self-interest at the expense of
the corporation through sloth or lack of diligence.

The result was an enormous, diversified company with capitalization of ¥21.25 million, making it one of the 50 largest
companies in Japan at the time. By the 1930s, shareholders of
the Noda Shoyu Company worked through the corporation or its
holding company to acquire controlling ownership interests in
six other firms. By 1936, the capital of the entire group totaled
¥46 million, which was roughly 70% the size of the Furukawa
Group, the smallest of the seven large urban zaibatsu (formal
groupings of interrelated companies) of the first half of the
twentieth century. In effect, the Noda Shoyu group constituted a
small zaibatsu, albeit one with more related diversification and
geographic focus than was true of the larger zaibatsu of the period.

Monitoring and Control by Private Banks

Most of the Noda Shoyu Company's growth and related
diversification via merger and acquisition was achieved through
a holding company that originated in an entity known as the
Senshusha, a financial institution founded in 1885 by the nine

18. Ibid., p. 102.

Mogi family heads and one Ishikawa. It functioned as a kind of credit union for the member families by accumulating member savings (through the payment dues) and promoting family solidarity. The savings were used primarily to fund future family investments in plant and equipment to replace losses that resulted from calamities; the financing of new investment had to be obtained from other sources. In 1925, the Senshusha was reorganized as an unlimited partnership of the families owning stock in the Noda Shoyu Company, 60% of which was placed in the hands of the Senshusha. Thereafter it functioned as a holding company to facilitate the buying and merging of companies as the group expanded in scale and scope.

A close association between operating companies and sister financial institutions was a common feature of the large urban zaibatsu. It persists even today in looser, modern industrial groupings known as keiretsu. The Mitsui Bank, for example, began humbly as a money exchange counter in a corner of Hachirobei Mitsui's 1683 dry goods shop (the site of which is occupied today by the Bank of Japan). It evolved into the nucleus of the Mitsui zaibatsu and remains today the main bank, owning equity in, and lending to, a broad network of companies that are members of the modern Mitsui group. It often played a pivotal role in the growth of the Mitsui group, as did the private banks of the other major zaibatsu.

These private banks developed in response to the need for large-scale intermediation of credit by the zaibatsu. Late nineteenth- and early twentieth-century Japan had essentially no securities market, and most banks of that era were small local operations with very little capital (¥50,000–¥60,000), tight liquidity, and scant security behind their loans. The zaibatsu banks revolutionized banking in early industrial Japan. They were affiliates of wealthy "name" families, lenders to a diversified portfolio of industrial enterprises, and known for the most part to have good relationships with a government interested in promoting large-scale industrialization. These banks thus became magnets for deposits nationally in a way that independent banks never could in an era of high uncertainty and minimal disclosure of important business information.

Zaibatsu banks not only provided their industrial clients with the usual banking services such as foreign exchange transactions, letter-of-credit financing, and bill discounting, but also supplied long-term capital and made available emergency lines of credit.

Although its field of activities was narrowly circumscribed, the early Senshusha, as a private financial institution, was a fore-runner to the more sophisticated and typical company-bank relationship that later emerged. With the evolution of the Senshu-sha into a holding company, it was the Noda Shoyu Bank, formally acquired in the 1930s, that ultimately remained as the primary financing arm of the Noda Shoyu Company. Like the larger zaibatsu banks, the Noda Shoyu Bank maintained a tight working relationship with the company. The bank was literally around the corner from the company's headquarters and handled all financial transactions for the company down to and including the banking of daily receipts.

Management as Stakeholder

The Noda Shoyu Company became more formal and complex in its organizational structure as it sought to exploit market opportunities, defend against competitive inroads, ensure sources of supply, and preserve distribution networks. Family owner-managers still played a vital role in the governing of the corporation (and do to this day) through control of the holding company. But layers of professional management below the holding-company level inevitably distanced the families from operations. The distancing was far worse with the larger zaibatsu. For them, the separation of ownership from control effectively became complete by the 1930s.

Contributing to this separation throughout Japan was the transformation of many companies into joint-stock corporations. These emulated the Western model as far as corporate governance was concerned. Company control was vested in a board of directors elected by the owners to appoint and supervise key senior managers. A major shareholder, usually from the owning family, was appointed president and chairman of the board, thus ensuring, in principle, that shareholder interests would be guarded.

As industrial scale and scope increased in Japan, however, the function of president and chairman of the board gradually receded to that of a figurehead. Accompanying the general devolution of family control was the emerging position of "executive director," typically a well-educated manager with a successful track record. Selected from either within or without the company's management structure, he was vested with the real authority and responsibility for running the firm. Eventually, as average corporate size and complexity increased still further, this authority and responsibility were held jointly by a group of executive directors, differentiated from one another largely on the basis of seniority.

As executive directors became more dominant in Japanese board leadership, outside shareholder directors were displaced by other senior managers. By the early 1930s, the entire board, except the figurehead chairman and president, was made up of senior company managers, each under the supervision of the senior executive director. In effect, the typical Japanese board was totally absorbed by the top management of the company it was supposed to govern.[19]

Potentially troublesome about this shift was that the top managers were not major shareholders in the firms they served, nor were their shareholdings in the companies they managed an especially large part of their personal wealth. Share ownership was minimal and provided only to fulfill nominally one of the requirements for being a board member. Thus the incentive to attend to shareholder-wealth considerations was also minimal.

However, top-management compensation systems emerging during this period made up for the lack of share ownership. Mitsui Bank's executive director, Hikojiro Nakanrigawa, successfully established a precedent that executive directors should receive about 10% of the company's total profits. This convention spread to other companies and became accepted to the point that most executive directors actually received 15–20% of profits.[20]

Such a rich compensation scheme might be viewed as goug-

19. Hirschmeier and Yui, *The Development of Japanese Business*, pp. 199–201.
20. Ibid., p. 201.

ing the outside shareholders, an inevitable outcome of a corporate governance system that seemingly left the fox in charge of the chicken coop.[21] A more favorable interpretation is that executive directors held, in effect, a quasi-equity claim on their companies, receiving high remuneration when their companies did well and less when they did poorly. It was not, of course, a true equity claim; based on current-period profits, it was a system that could easily bias managers toward near-term gains at the expense of shareholder wealth. Nevertheless, flawed though it may have been, the system was a powerful means through which to focus senior executive attention on profitability, and it stemmed tendencies to dissipate corporate resources on activities not having a favorable bottom-line impact.

## STAKEHOLDER CONFLICT: LABOR VERSUS MANAGEMENT

Highly motivated, performance-oriented workers devoting their lives to their companies is very much a *modern* phenomenon in Japan. Certainly, these labor force characteristics did not prevail at the founding of *shoyu* production in seventeenth-century Noda. Throughout the Edo period, until large-scale production began to evolve after the middle of the nineteenth century, *shoyu* production was a seasonal activity undertaken primarily by unskilled, temporary and/or part-time workers executing dull and repetitive tasks. Because they held little or no loyalty to the families that owned the production facilities, problems such as labor turnover, performance control, absenteeism, and worker discipline were constant.[22] Indeed,

---

21. Evidently, however, a tacit understanding limited managerial gains through such a compensation scheme. Hirschmeier and Yui (*The Development of Japanese Business*, p. 201), for example, report that the senior executive director of Fuji Spinning Company was once to receive the tremendous sum of ¥300,000 and the other directors ¥150,000 each as a result of the company earning an extraordinary profit of ¥3 million. Sensing the resentment that such an award would cause, he voluntarily reduced his bonus to ¥100,000 and distributed the balance to employees.

22. Fruin (*Kikkoman*, p. 43) presents a list of work rules promulgated in 1853 by Noda factory owners and *toji* that is revealing of the sorts of problems encountered in the breweries. Apparently, drinking, gambling, moonlighting, refusal to accept work assignments, and consorting with transients in the factories were among the more common transgressions.

merely hiring an adequate work force in an agrarian economy without a well-organized labor market was a perennial problem.

Labor Contracting

A standard solution to the recruitment problem was to pay workers a substantial cash advance on contracting for work—between half and three-quarters of their total promised wages—as well as to provide basic human needs such as food, shelter, and clothing. Of course, such a substantial prepayment of wages and what amounted to monthly subsistence thereafter created an immediate owner-worker conflict of interest, for the worker's incentive to complete the terms of the contract diminished considerably. This problem was addressed by two means: the payment of a small bonus on completion of the contracted work, and the securing of guarantor for a worker's services. In small companies, a worker's parents or guardian might serve as guarantor. In the case of larger operations, where workers and craftsmen did not have personal, face-to-face contact with the owner, a labor recruiter known as an *oyakata* would assume the role.

Other terms of the employment contract were negotiated directly between the *toji* and the *oyakata*, and a prospective employee could either accept or reject them. Typically, all employees were paid the same wage regardless of age, experience, job description, or seniority with the hiring firm. (By the 1900s, the Noda Shoyu Company did institute a step increase in the wage rate for *honnin*, workers who had been with the company for four years or more; thereafter, workers received no further promotions or raises.) Contracts for the Japanese rank and file contained no provisions for annual pay raises, performance incentives, pension benefits, or severance indemnities.[23]

Clearly, the potential for abuse on the part of the *oyakata* and *toji* was considerable. They had far superior knowledge of labor supply and demand conditions and the quality of the work force under their oversight, not to mention the brewing process itself, the control of which had long ago been relinquished to *toji* by factory owners. Despite its drawbacks, however, the labor con-

---

23. Ibid., p. 164.

tracting system undoubtedly took root because, at the outset, its benefits exceeded its costs.

These costs became less acceptable as time progressed, however. In the latter half of the nineteenth century, *shoyu* production volume increased substantially (as did volume in most other industries) and was taking place year-round. By the twentieth century, advances in fermenting technology and factory operations had reduced throughput time considerably and contributed to a greater specialization of job tasks. Under these circumstances, the advantages to employers of the old labor-contracting system paled in comparison to the advantages from more direct, central control of a given factory's labor force (particularly the transfer of employees within and among factories during peak production periods).

Restructuring Maladjusted Contracts

Replacing semiautonomous gang bosses with line management on the shop floor was no mean task. As traditional authority figures for workers, it was difficult either to dismiss them or to ignore them. Consequently, Noda Shoyu management chose to absorb them. In 1919, the company founded the Noda Placement Company to deal directly with the local *oyakata* for labor contracting, thus severing ties between *oyakata* and the separate factory *toji*. The *toji*, meanwhile, were co-opted into a series of studies conducted by several of the company's senior management committees and eventually became part of a new personnel department set up in 1922.[24]

Finally, a new wage and work-structure proposal was drafted in the summer of 1919. However, it contained far-reaching changes that could not be implemented quickly without risking worker dissatisfaction and production drops. The proposal would give headquarters greater control over labor costs and labor deployment in the factories, but this change would translate into economic benefits only after production methods were completely rationalized and new job routines implemented. This in turn would require the cooperation of the *toji*, yet it would take

---

24. Ibid., p. 169.

time to turn these independently minded bosses into disciplined line managers. Not surprisingly, therefore, the company waited roughly three and a half years before attempting to implement the plan.

In the meantime a vacuum in the representation of labor interests was created, since the links between *toji* and *oyakata* had been effectively severed. This, in conjunction with a recession following World War I that saw widespread unemployment and labor unrest in Japan, made the Noda Shoyu Company a ripe target for union organization efforts. Evidently, many workers were unwilling to trust patriarchal management to act in the best interests of the "family" of corporate stakeholders, for a Noda local of the Nihon Rodo Sodomei (Japan General Federation of Labor) was founded in December 1921 and claimed a membership of about 800 by 1923.

A modified version of the 1919 wage and work plan was finally implemented in January 1923. Included were provisions for an eight-hour work day (a problem for workers who wanted to be full-time farmers in growing seasons, when more than half the force would leave the factory within six and a half hours of reporting for work) and a division of the production process into 62 distinct steps, each with its performance standard. Wages were to be tied to these standards.

These provisions in particular were the cause of much worker skepticism and resistance. The company stuck to its position, however, and as production fell due to labor resistance, so did wages. Production fell further, complaints became widespread, and organized protests led to suspensions of ringleaders. Positions hardened, and reinstatement of the suspended employees became a further issue to be resolved. By March 16, 1923, a successful work boycott was called.

A month later, the dispute was resolved through a negotiated settlement, aided by a mediation committee that included civic and other political leaders. The company agreed to a modification (but not negotiation) of the work plan and a rehiring of the suspended workers, provided those suspended admitted their offensive behavior. Sealing the deal was a memorandum from the company's executive committee to the prefectural governor that

effectively surrendered company control over future labor disputes to political authority.[25]

Conflict and Resolution

What triggered the Great Noda Strike of 1927–1928 was
actually a dispute between the Noda Shoyu Company and one
of its subcontractors, the Marusan Transportation Company.
This local firm was formed in 1910 to service some of Noda
Shoyu's shipping needs and had been sustained by the company
since then. But in the 1920s, Marusan rebuffed its patron by
refusing to bring its labor contracting system into line with the
reforms taking place at Noda Shoyu. Later, after they had
unionized, workers at Marusan refused to handle output from
one of Noda Shoyu's factories because it was an open shop that
had resisted unionization efforts. As its long-standing contractual relationship with Marusan began to break down, Noda
Shoyu expanded its own container and purchasing departments
and began to rely more heavily on two new transportation subsidiaries that had been formed in 1924 and 1925.

Noda Shoyu's inability to come to terms with one of its major
subcontractors because of union-related activity became the
touchstone for further worker agitation there. Agitation led to
union demands that signaled protracted negotiations. Concomitant drops in production, brought about at least in part by general economic conditions, triggered cuts in wages. At this juncture, any semblance of goodwill between the company and the
union evaporated and a strike action began in September 1927.
By this time the dispute had moved far beyond the Marusan
service delivery issue to the bread-and-butter concerns of benefits and wages.

As usual, the company responded to the strike with dismissals
and the hiring of temporary workers. Production quickly returned to normal levels. From this position of strength, the company sought a complete repudiation of worker demands. The
union refused, and the antagonists settled in for a long and bitter
strike that ended only when the union's financial resources had

---

25. Ibid., p. 191.

been spent and considerable pressure from political and civic authorities had been placed on it.[26] The union formally capitulated in April 1928, having given up essentially all the demands with which they had started the action. As before, a mediation committee was involved in the settlement, but more as a device for allowing the union to save face than as a genuine vehicle for reaching compromise.[27]

## CORPORATE PATERNALISM: A MODERN COVENANT AMONG STAKEHOLDERS

Although the Great Noda Strike crippled the union as an effective mouthpiece for workers, the conflict ultimately did precipitate a change in attitude about the claims of labor (and other stakeholders as well) on the firm's wealth-generating power. To be sure, true power was not shared. But the economic rents of the firm were.

### A New Social Contract

Shortly after the conclusion of the strike, Noda Shoyu was able to rationalize its production processes and thus improve its cost structure. At the same time, revenues were enhanced and stabilized by agreements among manufacturers and distributors aimed at controlling market shares and prices. Production rose more or less steadily thereafter (a trough occurred between 1932 and 1933) with the market share of Noda Shoyu maintaining itself at about 12–15% by the mid-1930s. Another trough in the late 1930s resulted in further consolidation of the industry: Noda Shoyu acquired four breweries between 1937 and 1939. Throughout this period, with the exception of the first half of 1931, the company's shareholders were able to extract between 57% and 87% of the company's earnings as a semiannual cash

26. Contributing further to union leadership demoralization was the failure of a major strike at Dai-Nippon Spinning Company and the mass arrests of leftist radicals in March 1928 (Fruin, *Kikkoman*, p. 205).
27. Fruin, *Kikkoman*, p. 205.

dividend payment (a level well in excess of the median payout by Japanese manufacturers during the early 1980s).[28]

Whatever their level, such economic rents as Noda Shoyu could generate were distributed among other company stakeholders beyond the shareholders. Although labor did not secure an explicit contract in the form it sought at the start of the strike, it did get a fairly solid *implicit* contract that ushered in an era (1930–1960) of corporate paternalism typical of what we today identify as the "classic" Japanese employment system. The new social contract spanned the private as well as the vocational aspects of an employee's life. Employees were trained by the company (in what appear to have been company-specific activities related to Noda Shoyu's particular fermenting technology and *shoyu* recipe) at company expense and then encouraged to remain for life through a system that paid them little at the outset but increased wages with seniority, culminating in a bonus at retirement. In effect, labor received a quasi-debt claim against the company and maintained a long-term interest in it. Other employee benefits included medical treatment, company-operated retail cooperatives with bargain prices, mutual savings and loan programs, company housing, travel clubs, and special subsidies for marriage, births, deaths, and other major household events.[29] Corporate largess extended to the community as well. Noda's water system was constructed by the company, as was much of its housing. Local religious shrines were subsidized by corporate funds. The town's railroad, bank, fire station, hospital, elementary school, library, athletic and recreational facilities, and cultural center were all either company-owned and operated or company-sponsored and supported.[30]

As before, the Japanese "family" was used in the service of recontracting among stakeholders. This time, however, the application of the family simile went beyond mere appeals to patriarchal authority as a justification for organizational change. Indeed, even though there was still a clear genealogical linkage

---

28. Ibid., pp. 230–238.
29. Ibid., p. 216.
30. Ibid., p. 217.

between owning families and company management, the concept of the "company family" was broadened considerably. As Fruin describes it, the relevant family was

> . . . defined by those working together in a spirit and structure of common industrial purpose. Whereas the former definition of family was biological-genealogical, the latter was strictly ideological.

> The new definition of family and the new common purpose that joined labor and management were symbolized by the company ideal of "*Sangyo-damashii*," the "spirit of industry" (spirit in the sense of animation and determination), which was coined and popularized within the company after the Great Strike.* "Sangyo-damashii" proclaimed a new social contract with labor, one rooted in a conviction that mutual respect and interdependence were required for management and labor to get along better in the future than they had in the past.[31]

### A New Ownership Structure

The war years were stormy ones for the Noda Shoyu company, but did little in and of themselves to disrupt the stability of relationships among the company's primary stakeholders. Shipments fell to one-third their normal levels in 1946–1947, and the company's market share was cut in half. But by 1952, market share had been fully recovered and a new record for shipments was set.

What did begin to change stakeholder relationships dramatically, however, was the subsequent occupation and democratization of Japan. One stakeholder that benefited enormously was labor. A series of laws passed in 1949 by the Japanese government and favored by the Supreme Command of the Allied Powers (SCAP) provided a firm legal basis for labor union formation and activity. The same year saw the formation of the Noda

---

*Ichiyama Morio, ed., *Noda Shoyu Kabushiki Kaisha Sanjugonenshi* (Tokyo: Toppan, 1955), pp. 619–624.
31. Fruin, *Kikkoman*, p. 213.

Shoyu Labor Union, which represented 80% of the blue-collar work force at Noda.

Rather than depend on family rhetoric, top-down paternalism, or implicit contracting to secure work benefits, the new union acted in an overtly self-interested fashion, carefully tying compensation and benefits received to the workload.[32] It proactively sought and received power and material benefits through a wide range of concessions explicitly provided in written contract form. The Labor Agreement of 1950 created a 30-person Labor Council with a broad mandate to discuss, negotiate, and approve almost all matters related to employment within the company, effectively making it an organ of management.

Corporate wealth as well as managerial prerogatives were also appropriated by the union. The agreement provided for the building and use of company facilities for union purposes without charge, and for the company to pay the salaries of up to nine employees who would devote full time to the management of union affairs. Shortly after the union was formed, wages were increased by more than 50%. In addition, these gains were codified and formalized to an extent unthinkable in the prewar era. Articles in the Labor Agreement giving the union considerable say in the hiring, firing, retirement, and re-employment of workers effectively turned a mere *expectation* of permanent employment with steady salary increases tied to seniority into a near-contractual *obligation* backed by the force of law.

Accompanying the ascendancy of self-interested union activism was a weakening of family control over Kikkoman (as the Noda Shoyu Company was renamed following World War II), a coincidence that undoubtedly contributed somewhat to the union's enhanced ability to appropriate a larger share of corporate wealth. As part of its democratization efforts, SCAP sought to diminish the status and legal stature of Japanese household heads, which it considered inimical to the egalitarian principles being promulgated in postwar Japan. It did so in part by repu-

---

32. Fruin, *Kikkoman*, p. 255, notes that "it is the very juxtaposition of self-interest between the company and the employee that distinguishes prewar and postwar working attitudes" [in Japan].

diating the legal standing of the household head and male-centered inheritance, and by making the individual, as opposed to the family, the locus of legal responsibility.[33] In addition, an imperial edict forced all companies capitalized in excess of ¥5 million to divest themselves of equity interests held in other companies. This, in conjunction with an article in the commercial code that outlawed holding companies, resulted in the liquidation of the Senshusha, which controlled nearly two-thirds of Kikkoman's stock on behalf of the Mogi and Takanashi families.

Collectively, these actions severely limited (though did not eliminate altogether) the ability of families to concentrate wealth, equity ownership, and thus corporate control. For those very large Japanese corporations that had not already experienced a complete separation of family ownership from control, the process of separation accelerated with the occupation. In the final analysis, however, equity ownership and control were never completely severed in postwar Japan. The private banks founded just before and after the turn of the century stepped in to absorb much of the equity disgorged by the dissolving holding companies. This absorption, coupled with their prominent role as providers of scarce debt capital required to fuel Japan's recovery, strengthened the banks' already close relationships with client companies and made them Japan's new "private" investors, ushering in an era of bank-dominated control of Japanese industrial companies.

## SUMMARY

Clearly, like those in other industrialized nations, Japanese companies have undergone profound changes since the mid-nineteenth century. Furthermore, despite extended periods of relatively slow, incremental evolution, episodes of accelerated change have taken place in response to macroeconomic shocks, major technological advances, or potentially fatal competitive threats. In general, these episodes involved a reconfiguration of

---

33. Ibid., p. 247.

production and distribution to capture economies of scale. These in turn required ever higher degrees of centralized decision making, which could be achieved only by major restructurings of maladjusted contracts among stakeholders. The cartelization of the Noda Shoyu producers in the 1880s, the movement toward incorporation in the 1910s, and the rationalization of production and distribution in the 1920s represent such episodes.

Rapid change did not always involve open conflict among stakeholders, as was the case during the 1920s, but neither was it particularly smooth and harmonious; requisite changes often took years to implement. The reason for such lag appears to have been organizational inertia resulting from the suspicion with which some stakeholders viewed change and the high degree of reluctance on the part of managers and owners to breach implicit contracts.

Even if a reconfiguration of the organization and its production activities could be construed ex post to have been a move by all primary corporate stakeholders toward a more efficient allocation of resources, it was seldom viewed as such ex ante by everybody. More often than not, proposed changes were viewed by some as being inimical to their welfare—an appropriation of their economic rents rather than a realization of economic efficiencies; hence existing contractual arrangements were typically adjusted very slowly. Consequently, pressure to change began to mount only when a legitimacy for the proposed alterations could be found (as in the appeal to patriarchal authority and the company-as-family simile in the late nineteenth century); change was forced by pruning away all alternative courses of action (as in the strengthening of labor and creditor interests and the restructuring of capital and ownership forced by occupation government reforms); or a rupture of relations occurred (as with the labor strife of the 1920s). One way or another, however, if the gains to be had by a particular stakeholder group were large enough, old contracts would be discarded eventually and new ones put in their place.

The reality of organizational change, the capacity for accelerated change when circumstances warrant, and the occasional role of conflict in promoting that change might be observations about Japanese companies too obvious to draw but for a persistent belief that corporate features observed today have more or less always existed and more or less always will. There is little evidence in the case of the Noda Shoyu Company to support such a conclusion. In fact, most of the policies commonly associated with Japanese corporations today have roots extending no further back than the 1920s. Indeed, many are the result of a recontracting among stakeholders as recent as the 1950s. To the extent that Japan experiences yet another realignment of stakeholder interests as a result of further shocks to the political-economic system, any prediction of future Japanese corporate behavior that is but a linear extrapolation of the recent past is likely to be wide of the mark.

My interpretation of the evolution of Japanese companies assigns a central role to the exercise of economic self-interest in the interaction of stakeholder groups. Other things being equal, people everywhere will prefer more wealth to less, will prefer to receive it sooner than later, and will prefer to bear less risk than more regarding the size of that wealth. Given these fundamental preferences, individuals can be expected to behave in a predictable, self-interested way.

Japan and the conduct of Japanese business is often thought to defy economic models based on these axioms, in large measure because the axioms are thought to be inaccurate with respect to Japan. A "culturalist" school of thought holds that *culture* and social structure is as—or more—important a determinant of the organization of human economic activity than is economic self-interest. In the case of Japan, for instance, Confucian principles that make a virtue of obligation to others and submersion of self-interest would seem at complete variance with these axioms. Thus the modern Japanese corporation's apparent inattention to current profitability, low pay differentials among workers, permanent employment, and close attention to quality, to name but a few commonly cited attributes, are thought to be primarily cultural phenomena.

The powerful influence of culture and social structure on economic activity and organizational change cannot be denied.

Certainly, there is nothing in the history of the Noda Shoyu Company as presented here (nor in Fruin's more exhaustive treatment) to refute that influence categorically. The cultural and sociological reality of the Japanese family-as-enterprise in the Edo period was deftly transposed in the Meiji period to create the company-as-family simile, which served as a powerful force in providing social legitimacy to the reorganization of economic activity within firms. Clearly, Japan's culture played a vital role in shaping attitudes about economic activity; thus it facilitated the evolution of the institutions through which economic activity was coordinated.

The importance of culture notwithstanding, the history of the Noda Shoyu Company also reveals that fundamental economics stimulated the change, and the pursuit of self-interest by company stakeholders with different priorities that shaped it. Culture was an essential element in the crucible of industrial change and contributed critically to the creation of an alloy that could bend and adapt itself admirably to a changing political-economic environment. But it was the conflicting interests of diverse stakeholders that were the hammer and anvil used to shape the final corporate form. In this regard, the modern Japanese corporation shares a heritage with corporations of other industrialized nations. It is, in the end, still an economic institution whose behavior is susceptible to explanation and prediction by models rooted in classical microeconomic axioms of purposeful, self-interested action by individuals. So too is its evolution.

# 3
# JAPANESE CORPORATE GOVERNANCE

As a means of coordinating economic activity among many separate individuals, the modern corporation is a social marvel. This is especially true in view of the delicate balance of claims that must be maintained to keep it from being torn asunder by the competing self-interests of various stakeholders. The evolution of Kikkoman Corporation from a handful of rural family breweries to its present multinational status is a study in how that balance was established, maintained, occasionally lost, and eventually renewed in a continuous cycle for more than a century. Although considerable stress and even open conflict were endured as obsolete ties among stakeholders were broken and replaced, the process must be viewed over the long run as having been fundamentally constructive. One is reminded of Joseph Schumpeter's description of capitalism as a process of "creative destruction."

The corporate governance system that has evolved in Japan is distinctly different from the system that has evolved for the typical Anglo-American corporation. Japanese corporate governance relies much more heavily on reciprocity in equity ownership and commercial trade, the use of flexible implicit contracts founded on trust, selective intervention by major equity-owning stakeholders to correct problems before they become unsurmountable, and the alignment of managerial incentives toward growth and away from wealth transfers among stakeholders.

The overall effect of Japanese corporate governance is to foster tremendous efficiencies in the execution of business transactions by making it easier to build and maintain long-term business relationships. These relationships have enabled Japanese companies to function with lower degrees of asset-ownership integration than do most of their counterparts in the West despite high degrees of interdependence in the transactions supported by those assets. So close are these relationships that it sometimes becomes difficult to distinguish the administrative boundaries separating one corporation from another. Because of these enduring business relationships and the somewhat purposeful blurring of administrative lines across organizations transacting with one another, Japan has not required an active market for corporate control at home and operates with different motives in the Anglo-American market abroad.

## RECIPROCAL SHAREHOLDING AND TRADING AGREEMENTS

One of the most prominent and enduring characteristics of the Japanese industrial corporations that I studied is their tendency to engage in tight, long-term commercial relationships with other Japanese companies. Executives in these corporations often explained current company policies and practices by reference to obligations created as long ago as two or three decades through favors performed by other companies, or to future business they hope to transact with the same parties. This particularly characterized their banking relationships, but also their dealings with suppliers, subcontractors, and large corporate customers. Many of these in turn have long-standing relationships with one another, resulting in an intricate network of companies connected by formal and informal commercial and financial commitments.

Today this corporate networking achieves its highest expression in the Japanese keiretsu—a group of companies federated around a major bank, trading company, or large industrial firm. An old and well-known keiretsu is the Mitsubishi group. A partial schematic representation of this group is shown in Exhibit

3–1. Although the complexity of business relationships in Japan can frustrate the precise delineation of various keiretsu and an exact determination of membership, there appear to be at least 16 major industrial groups encompassing over 1,000 corporations (a list is provided in Exhibit 3–2). The Mitsubishi, Sumitomo, Mitsui, and Fuyo groups are actually modern descendants of the pre–World War II zaibatsu. Others are new groups that have sprung up around industrial corporations such as Hitachi and Nippon Steel, or around a major bank such as the Industrial Bank of Japan.[1]

Companies belonging to keiretsu account for only one-tenth of 1% of all incorporated businesses in Japan, but group members are generally much larger than the median Japanese firm. They account for roughly a quarter of total sales and paid-up capital of all Japanese corporations, and just over half of all listed corporations in Japan are members of an industrial group. Most of the Japanese competitors encountered by North American and European companies are likely to have a group affiliation. Even those that do not are likely to have entered into various reciprocal shareholding and trade agreements with other Japanese firms.

Participation in a keiretsu entails more than sharing a common name such as Mitsubishi, Sumitomo, or Mitsui. Among other things, affiliation generally implies extensive reciprocal ownership of common stock within the group. For example, in 1987 Mitsubishi Bank owned 4.6% of Mitsubishi Heavy Industries, which in turn owned 3.5% of Mitsubishi Bank. A selected cross section of other reciprocal shareholding within the Mitsubishi group is tabulated in Exhibit 3–3.

Although such cross-shareholdings are small on a bilateral basis, they are substantial for the group at large. In the aggregate, more than 20% of all the outstanding shares of Mitsubishi group companies are held by other companies within the group.

---

1. The Fuji Bank around which the Fuyo group was organized is the modern successor of the former Yasuda Bank. The modern Fuyo group actually consists of companies from the former Yasuda, Asano, Mori, and Nissan zaibatsu.

Exhibit 3-1 *The Mitsubishi Group*

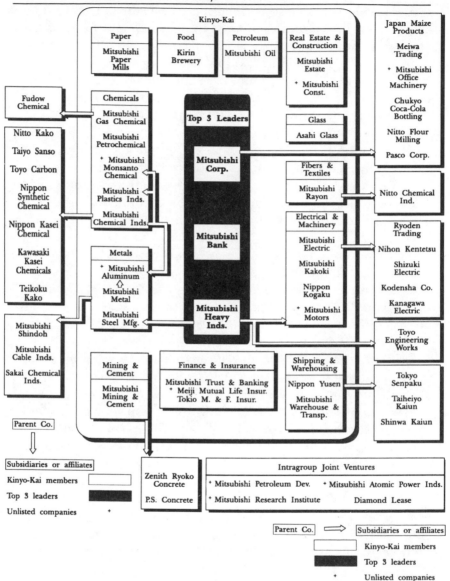

Source: *Industrial Groupings in Japan,* 7th ed., 1986–1987 (Tokyo: Dodwell, 1986), p. 48.

Exhibit 3-2  *Major Japanese Industrial Groups*

*Former Zaibatsu*
Mitsubishi
Mitsui
Sumitomo
Fuyo

*New Bank-Centered Groups*
DKB
Sanwa
IBJ
Tokai

*New Manufacturer-Centered Groups*
Nippon Steel
Hitachi
Nissan
Toyota
Matsushita
Toshiba-IHI
Tokyu
Seibu

Still more stock is in the hands of other reliable shareholders consisting of peripheral group companies now shown in Exhibit 3–3 and nongroup financial institutions that lend to the Mitsubishi group. In 1987, for example, Nippon Life Insurance Company and Mitsui Trust and Banking, respectively, owned 2.5% and 2.0% of Mitsubishi Heavy Industries. The *Nihon Keizai Shimbun* estimates that, for the nation at large, nearly ¥200 trillion of stock is held under reciprocal shareholding agreements.[2]

Accompanying these cross-shareholdings are implicit but widely understood and rigorously observed mutual agreements not to sell shares held reciprocally. These agreements create a cadre of banks and other manufacturers that function as a core of "stable" shareholders. On average, about one-third of a Japanese corporation's stock is owned by financial institutions, pri-

---

2. Kenji Nagano, "Moving to a Common International System," *Nihon Keizai Shimbun* (Tokyo: May 5, 1990), p. 30.

Exhibit 3-3  *The Mitsubishi Group Cross-Shareholdings (%)*

| Member Companies Shareholding Percentage | M. Bank | M. Trust & Bnkng | Meiji Mutual Life Ins.* | Tokio Marine & Fire Ins. | M. Corp. | M. Heavy Inds. | Kirin Brew- ery | M. Rayon | M. Paper Mills | M. Chem. Ind. | M. Gas Chem. |
|---|---|---|---|---|---|---|---|---|---|---|---|
| M. Bank | | 3.1 | | 5.0 | 5.4 | 4.6 | 4.4 | 5.9 | 5.0 | 4.6 | 4.8 |
| M. Trust & Banking | | | | 2.5 | 4.1 | 4.0 | 2.7 | 4.9 | 4.3 | 3.4 | 5.1 |
| Meiji Mutual Life Insurance | 6.1 | 6.1 | | 4.7 | 5.6 | 3.8 | 4.5 | 7.1 | 5.6 | 7.7 | 4.4 |
| Tokio Marine & Fire Insurance | 4.7 | 2.0 | | | 6.5 | 2.6 | | | 3.4 | 2.6 | 2.1 |
| M. Corp. | 2.2 | 3.5 | | 2.3 | | 2.1 | | | 3.4 | | |
| Subtotal | 13.0 | 14.7 | | 14.5 | 21.6 | 17.1 | 11.6 | 17.9 | 21.7 | 18.3 | 16.4 |
| M. Heavy Industries | 3.5 | 3.0 | | 1.9 | 3.8 | | | 1.9 | 1.8 | | |
| Kirin Brewery | | | | | | | | | | | |
| M. Rayon | | | | | | | | | | | |
| M. Paper Mills | | | | | | | | | | | |
| M. Chemical Ind. | | | | | | | | | | | |
| M. Gas Chemical | | | | | | | | | | | |
| M. Oil | | | | | | | | | | | |
| M. Plastic Ind. | | | | | | | | | | | |
| M. Petrochemical | | | | | | | | | | | |
| Asahi Glass | 1.5 | 2.5 | | 1.8 | | | | | 2.5 | | 2.8 |
| M. Mining & Cement | | | | | | | | | | | |
| M. Steel | | | | | | | | | | | |
| M. Metal | | | | | | | | | | | |
| M. Kakoki | | | | | | | | | | | |
| M. Electric | 1.5 | 1.8 | | | | | | | | | |
| Nippon Kogaku | | | | | | | | | | | |
| M. Estate | | 1.9 | | | | | | | | | |
| Nippon Yusen | | 1.3 | | | 2.1 | | | | | | |
| M. Warehouse & Transportation | | | | | | | | | | | |
| Total | 19.5 | 25.2 | | 18.2 | 27.5 | 17.1 | 11.6 | 19.8 | 26.0 | 18.3 | 19.2 |

marily banks (see Exhibit 3–4). Another third is generally in the hands of other corporations.

However, stability does not imply complete passivity or indifference to return on investments. Generally paralleling reciprocal cross-shareholding agreements are implicit reciprocal trade agreements as well. Mitsubishi Bank, for example, is both a major lender to Mitsubishi Electric and a purchaser of its electronic equipment. Mitsubishi Steel simultaneously sells steel to Mit-

Exhibit 3-3 *The Mitsubishi Group Cross-Shareholdings (%)* (continued)

| | | | | | Member Companies | | | | | | | |
|---|---|---|---|---|---|---|---|---|---|---|---|---|
| M. Oil | M. Plastic Ind. | M. Petrochem. | Asahi Glass | M. Mining & Cement | M. Steel | M. Metal | M. Kakoki | M. Elec. | Nippon Kogaku | M. Est. | Nippon Yusen | M. Warehouse Trans. |
| 5.0 | 2.6 | 5.9 | 5.4 | 5.0 | 5.0 | 4.2 | 5.8 | 2.9 | 6.5 | 4.4 | 3.7 | 4.9 |
| 3.3 | 1.8 | 2.9 | 3.8 | 4.9 | 3.7 | 5.8 | 3.3 | 2.1 | 6.5 | 5.1 | 3.0 | 5.7 |
| 2.8 | 2.6 | 5.3 | 5.8 | 9.1 | 5.8 | 6.0 | 5.5 | 4.5 | 5.1 | 4.4 | 4.6 | 7.7 |
| 5.0 | — | 5.7 | 5.1 | 1.9 | 3.1 | | 2.5 | | 2.7 | 3.7 | 5.6 | 6.2 |
| 20.0 | | 3.5 | — | 1.8 | 3.9 | — | 5.4 | — | — | — | — | — |
| 36.1 | 7.0 | 23.3 | 20.1 | 22.7 | 21.5 | 16.0 | 22.5 | 9.5 | 20.8 | 17.6 | 16.9 | 24.5 |
| 2.0 | | | | 2.1 | 6.9 | | 5.4 | 1.7 | | | 5.4 | |
| | | | | | | | | | | | | 2.2 |
| | 48.1 | 6.0 | | | | | | | | | | |
| | | 6.8 | | 1.5 | | | | | | 2.6 | 1.8 | 1.9 |
| | | | 2.0 | 2.2 | | | | | | | | 4.0 |
| 2.0 | | | | | | | | | | | | |
| — | — | — | — | — | — | — | — | — | — | — | — | — |
| 40.1 | 55.1 | 36.1 | 22.1 | 28.5 | 28.4 | 16.0 | 27.9 | 11.2 | 23.4 | 19.4 | 22.3 | 32.6 |

Note: M. stands for Mitsubishi.
*Not a listed company.
Source: *Industrial Groupings in Japan* 7th ed., 1986–1987 (Tokyo: Dodwell, 1986), pp. 152–187.

subishi Heavy Industries and buys the latter's equipment and construction services. Mutual trade credit agreements also accompany these commercial trading arrangements.

Thus, within a Japanese keiretsu, a typical corporate stakeholder is likely to possess a rather complex "blend" of claims against other group companies in which it has invested—a com-

Exhibit 3-4 *The Ownership of Japanese Corporations, 1987*

|  |  | *Percentage* |
|---|---|---|
| Government |  | 0.9% |
| Financial Institutions |  | 43.5 |
| All Banks | 20.5 |  |
| Investment Trusts | 1.8 |  |
| Annuity Trusts | 0.9 |  |
| Life Insurance Companies | 13.3 |  |
| Nonlife Insurance Companies | 4.4 |  |
| Other Financial Institutions | 2.6 |  |
| Business Corporations |  | 24.5 |
| Securities Companies |  | 2.5 |
| Individuals and Others |  | 23.9 |
| Foreigners |  | 4.7 |
| Total |  | 100.0% |

*Source:* Tokyo Stock Exchange "Fact Book," 1988.

bination of equity, credit, and trading contracts. The stakeholder may well accept subnormal rates of return on one component of its blend, such as equity, provided it is able to compensate with supranormal returns on another part, such as the trading relationship.

For most Japanese corporations, the long-term *trading* relationships with companies in which they invest constitute the chief value of their overall dealings with those companies. The value is derived not so much from the exercise of unequal market power by one party in the relationship, or anticompetitive collusion between the two (although some permitted reciprocal trading arrangements in Japan would be precluded by U.S. antitrust laws). Rather, value comes from the transaction efficiencies generated by creating and maintaining a long-term trading relationship. Within the context of such stable long-term dealings, mutually beneficial trust relationships between managers can be forged and cooperation fostered. Contracting can take place on a much less formal, more implicit basis, often an advantage when it becomes necessary to adjust rapidly to a changing environment. Adjustments in implicit agreements can be made much faster and in a more highly nuanced way by managers dealing at the trading interface than they can by lawyers wrestling over formal written contracts.

If the business relationship lasts long enough and becomes close enough, the trading firms can become virtual extensions of one another in a vertical or horizontal production and distribution system, though without some of the management control problems that plague large operations integrated under a single corporate hierarchy. Since the relationship is arm's-length and equity ownership is restricted to minority positions, market incentives are preserved and bureaucratic disabilities held to a minimum.

The Japanese auto industry is exemplary in this regard. Japanese automakers typically rely more heavily on outside suppliers for parts (70% purchased outside) than do their U.S. counterparts (50% purchased outside by Ford, only 30% by General Motors). The same is true even for larger subassemblies such as instrument panels, suspension systems, and seats. Nevertheless, reflecting their preference for stable long-term relationships with trusted suppliers in which they own a bit of equity, Japanese automakers deal with far fewer suppliers than do U.S. automakers. Each of the U.S. companies will typically contract one or two years at a time with 2,000–5,000 different suppliers, awarding contracts largely on the basis of price. Japanese companies, in contrast, will typically deal with only 200–300 suppliers with whom they have done business continually for many years. There is no positive assurance that any single relationship will continue indefinitely. Suppliers can and will be replaced if they fail to remain cost competitive. But compared to U.S. practice, there is less frequent and less intense competitive bidding for supply contracts. The assembler tends to distribute business based on a supplier's reliability in providing high-quality parts on a timely basis and its ability to respond quickly to requests for product changes even in the middle of a model run.

Because Japanese suppliers are heavily involved in the early design and development stages of new parts and subassemblies, they are, in effect, extensions of the engineering divisions of the companies they supply. Within the context of the famous Japanese kanban ("just-in-time") delivery system, suppliers are also important managers of inventory for automakers. The careful synchronization of parts production and delivery helps both automaker and supplier save on inventory-carrying costs.

Success, however, depends on the supplier being intimately familiar with the automaker's needs, and the automaker equally aware of the supplier's capabilities. Success also depends on the transacting parties' highly refined ability to contract informally and implicitly and to adjust such contracts rapidly in response to a changing economic environment. This ability in turn depends heavily on a firm foundation of trust between the companies involved. Without these features, long-term relationships with a few independent suppliers would eventually give way either to formal, short-term procurement contracts with many suppliers or outright ownership of the upstream assets. The outcome would hinge on the uniqueness of assets and the volume of business in question.

## TRUST AND IMPLICIT CONTRACTING

Despite the magnitude of existing contract law, the profusion of practicing lawyers, and the number of contract documents that change hands, much of the world's business is actually conducted on the basis of unwritten—sometimes even unspoken—agreements between transacting parties. Implicit contracting is often easier and less costly than explicit contracting. When parties have been doing business more or less continuously for a long time, their clear mutual recognition of bilateral responsibilities may justify forgoing the trouble and expense of writing a formal contract. In fact, it might be impossible for them to conceive and reduce to writing all the responsibilities of each in every possible future contingency. Beyond some point, transacting parties must simply depend on a mutual understanding of how each will behave in an unforeseen circumstance and assume that any disputes can be resolved without legal recourse.

Because implicit contracts are easier to adapt to changed circumstances, they are particularly valuable when long-term continuity in a trading relationship is desired. By their very nature, implicit contracts are held less between organizations as legal entities than between individual managers operating at the trading interface. It is here that reputations for reliability are built, trust relationships are forged, and mutual expectations regarding the future are established. It is managers who ultimately adapt contracts to changed circumstances and, out of consideration for their professional reputations, can act prophylactically against any ill-advised tendencies toward opportunism elsewhere in their organizations. Assuming a foundation of mutual trust and shared expectations, implicit contracting among individual managers better enables companies to make rapid, informal, and highly refined adjustments in the terms of trade to preserve the spirit and substance of a business covenant rather than the letter of a written agreement. Their inherent flexibility allows implicit contracts to withstand greater stress and promotes the longevity of the commercial relationship.

Given these advantages, it comes as no surprise to learn that implicit contracts, often referred to in Japan as *anmoku no ryokai* (unspoken understandings), are used extensively there, particularly among companies within an industrial group. Certainly, written contracts are drawn up in Japan, and from time to time court enforcement is necessary. But the spirit and substance of a contract between Japanese companies go beyond the letter of the agreement, more often and to a greater extent than among firms elsewhere.

The very nature of implicit contracting makes this a difficult fact to document, but the extent to which the Japanese rely on legal counsel gives some circumstantial support. Although the United States has roughly twice the population of Japan and 1.4 times as many corporations, it has 30 times as many licensed lawyers. The legal departments of Japanese corporations (euphemistically called *bunsho-ka*—archive section) are typically staffed by fewer than a dozen regular employees who have learned corporate legal practice through their experience with the company. The primary job of the section is to prevent litigation. When litigation becomes unavoidable, outside practicing attorneys or law teachers are retained.[3]

The efficacy of implicit contracting ultimately depends on trust between the transacting parties. As used here, trust in a commercial relationship means assuming that, when faced with the capacity to undertake hidden action or utilize hidden information, one's counterpart in an ongoing business relationship will pursue actions that are to one's material benefit, and will likewise refrain from opportunistic behavior that results in one's material detriment. This does not necessarily mean that one's counterpart will act strictly in one's own best interests under all future circumstances. Some situations will be so extreme that strict compliance with an earlier agreement would be unreasonable. It merely implies a sufficiently high likelihood of responsible behavior over a range of normal circumstances to warrant a degree of cooperation on an informal basis.

Trust and thus implicit contracting is engendered in several ways. Japanese ethnic homogeneity is certainly one factor. Well-defined and widely adhered to social and religious norms regarding obligations to others make it easier to form reliable expectations about the behavior of counterparts in an exchange relationship. The virtual absence of significant non-Japanese stakeholders in Japanese corporations creates a culturally homogeneous business community inside Japan. Keiretsu and other industrial groupings of firms may be likened to clans within that broad community. These tend to have their own subcultures that further enhance the formation of trust relationships with the group.

As important, if not more so, than culture and religion is economics. Put simply, it pays to be trustworthy. Trustworthiness pays (in a narrow economic sense) because it supports implicit contracting, which is often more efficient than explicit contracting. The efficiencies will be greatest, and therefore the rewards for trustworthiness highest, when transactions with a particular party are recurrent. Under these circumstances, the long-run

---

3. Robert J. Ballon and Iwao Tomita, *The Financial Behavior of Japanese Corporations* (Tokyo: Kodansha International, 1988), p. 55.

advantage of cooperation with that party will outweigh the immediate gains of self-interested opportunism. As a result, a high value is placed on trustworthiness and extensive voluntary compliance with implicit agreements.

The importance of trust as a foundation for long-term implicit contracting with corporate stakeholders in Japan also results in great emphasis being placed on preserving continuity in the identity of specific managers interacting at the trading interface. This is achieved in part by an active attempt to entrench corporate managers. As pernicious as this might seem (for truly entrenched managers might abuse their positions), there is a rationale for it. Because of the important role played by implicit contracts with corporate stakeholders, Andrei Shleifer and Lawrence Summers suggest the following:

> . . . shareholders will find it value maximizing to *seek out* or *train* individuals who are capable of commitment to [other] stakeholders, elevate them to management, and entrench them. To such managers, [other] stakeholder claims, once agreed to, are prior to shareholder claims. . . .
>
> It is probably most likely that prospective managers are trained or brought up to be committed to stakeholders. In a family enterprise, for example, offspring could be raised to believe in the company's paternalism toward all the parties involved in its operation. Alternatively, a person who spends 20 or 30 years with the company prior to becoming a CEO will have spent all that time being helped by the stakeholders in his ascent, and he therefore becomes committed to them. . . . stakeholder welfare now enters their preferences, and thus makes them credible upholders of implicit contracts.[4]

The early Mogi house rules exhorting family managers to act sincerely and harmoniously in their dealings with one another

---

4. Andrei Shleifer and Lawrence H. Summers, "Breach of Trust in Hostile Takeovers," in A. J. Auerbach, ed., *Corporate Takeovers: Causes and Consequences* (Chicago: University of Chicago Press, 1988), p. 40.

cultivate precisely those attitudes toward other stakeholders mentioned by Shleifer and Summers.

In more recent times, the Japanese practice of lifetime employment with a single corporation and seniority-based compensation has contributed to managerial entrenchment. Among the corporations I studied, Japanese managers are usually recruited straight from college (or possibly accepted in mid-career from other stakeholder firms) and effectively entrenched for life by a widely practiced reward system that makes it unattractive to quit the company.

Typically, young managers start at base salaries below that of their counterparts in other countries. In exchange for below-average pay, they receive broad general management training and an implicit commitment from the company to employ them for "life" (including a commitment to place them in a "second-career" management position on retirement from the company). They receive steady promotions accompanied by nearly automatic pay increases that will bring them into parity with management elsewhere in Japan and the rest of the world by the time they have reached middle age. As the corporate pyramid narrows, opportunities for promotion shrink and the tenure-earnings gradient begins to flatten. But the incentive to stay with the same company remains strong for two reasons: (1) opportunities to move laterally outside one's own corporation are severely limited because of lifetime employment and internal promotion practices elsewhere; and (2) a substantial number of retirement benefits are contingent on achieving further chronological seniority with one's current employer. The latter are provided through a lump-sum severance indemnity on voluntary retirement, generally equal to a month's wages at the current rate for every year of service (larger allowances are provided in the event of involuntary retirement).[5] For accounting purposes, retirement bonuses are treated as deferred wages.

Buttressing these incentives to keep management in place are cross-shareholding arrangements. The extensive ownership of a

---

5. Although the use of pension plans is expanding rapidly in Japan, only about 30–40% of all employees are covered under such plans; the bulk of retirement benefits typically have been paid through lump-sum settlements.

corporation's equity by other companies with which it does business provides a formidable defense against a hostile takeover. These shareholders, of course, might one day discover that they could obtain a premium by, say, tendering their shares in a hostile bid. But they would be unlikely to do so if a change in ownership threatened to disrupt a lucrative business relationship or otherwise lower the value of explicit and implicit nonequity claims against the target company.

Reciprocal shareholding arrangements further moderate temptation to tender shares owned in a target company. According to the executives I interviewed, any visible cooperation with a hostile bidder would reveal the selling company to be an "unreliable" shareholder. This would almost certainly lead other corporations to dispose of their shares of the unreliable firm, and widespread defection from trading relationships with it would follow. The selling company might ultimately find itself a crippled pariah in the Japanese business community. At the personal level, top executives of the selling firm might find themselves bereft of the status normally accorded them as members of Japanese senior management.

## SAFEGUARDS AGAINST OPPORTUNISM

Substantial though they may be, the economic incentives to maintain long-term trading relationships in Japan are not perfect. Because one party to an agreement can undertake hidden action to its own benefit and to the detriment of the other, or make private use of hidden information, the risk of self-interested opportunism corrupting the relationship exists. This is where reciprocal equity ownership comes in. An exchange of equity between two trading parties connects their economic fortunes, which helps mitigate incentives to act opportunistically. The more equity your trading partner owns in your own firm, the less sense it makes to try to take money out of his shareholders' pockets to put in your own. Indeed, in the extreme instance of two corporations virtually owning each other outright, nothing at all could be gained through such transfer.

Admittedly, reciprocal equity ownership between any two Japanese companies is typically small—generally in the range of 1–3% of outstanding shares. By itself, such a bilateral exchange of share constitutes a weak safeguard against abuse of the relationship. But embed two transacting companies in a larger cluster of interacting firms and multiply the percentage of bilaterally cross-held shares by a factor of 20 or 30, and the safeguard becomes potent. For reinforcement, there is the reputation factor: no Japanese company thrives when it is viewed as untrustworthy and unreliable.

Information Sharing

Another feature that helps Japanese industrial groups forestall disputes or other problems that might destroy valuable trading relationships is extensive information sharing. Sitting at the center of a keiretsu are core group members generally consisting of a "main" bank (e.g., a lead lender to the group, such as Mitsubishi Bank), a major industrial corporation (e.g., Mitsubishi Heavy Industries), and/or a large trading company (e.g., Mitsubishi Corporation). These core companies, the bank in particular, form the hub of a vast information-sharing network. Because most companies in the group will borrow at least some of their funds from the group's main bank, which will also own up to 5% of each company's outstanding shares, much financial information about their performance will be funneled to the bank in the natural course of its monitoring activities.

Adding to the information flow will be a number of senior bank "alumni," formally retired from lifelong careers at the bank (usually around age 55) and placed by the bank's president in "second careers" as senior officers and directors of the bank's borrowing clients. At Mitsubishi Steel, for example, three directors in 1985 were former officers at Mitsubishi Heavy Industries, one was an executive at Mitsubishi Corporation, the group's giant trading company, and yet another came from Mitsubishi Bank. Although these alumni officers and directors are formally employees of the companies into which they have been placed, they are also de facto representatives of their former employers.

Information gathered at the core of the group is eventually disseminated through a variety of channels. The network of alumni directors and temporarily seconded officers is one such channel. Another is the various business-interest associations, councils, committees, and clubs in which a large company's senior management will actively participate. Among the major keiretsu, at least six presidential councils meet monthly and are made up of presidents of the companies within the group. Mitsubishi, for example, has a 28-member council of presidents known formally as the Kinyo-kai.[6] Ostensibly, these councils are formed to promote friendship and understanding among presidents of the group. Their resolutions are not binding on members, and they fiercely resist the image of being a group-level policy-setting body. Nevertheless, their activities do extend to the level of coordinating group public relations, controlling the use of group trademarks, managing group joint ventures in research and production, and even discussing top personnel appointments in the group. They are also quick to identify financial trouble spots in the group and assist in workouts under the guidance of the main bank or another group core stakeholder.

Selective Intervention

Perhaps the most effective safeguard is the ability of one or more major share-owning stakeholders to intervene when necessary to resolve conflicts in the coalition or to turn around a company's deteriorating performance. Usually the intervening stakeholder will be the company's main bank, although it might be a large trading company or a major industrial firm constituting the core of an industrial group.

Main banks have historically been the most likely to intervene because of their position as the largest single supplier of capital to the group. In addition to having an equity investment, they have considerable amounts of debt at risk. Nominally, this debt is in the form of senior collateralized short-term loans and 90- to 120-day promissory notes, which are usually routinely rolled over indefinitely. However, in the event of impending financial distress, the character of main bank's loans changes dramati-

6. Other well-known group councils include the Hakusui-kai of the Sumitomo group, the Nimoku-kai of the Mitsui group, and the Fuyo-kai of the Fuyo group.

cally. This is because most main banks voluntarily subordinate their debt to that of other banks lending to the main bank's troubled client. The Dai-Ichi Kangyo Bank, for instance, main bank for the Kojin Corporation, voluntarily repaid all of Kojin's debts to other banks when Kojin failed.

Whereas fear of such equitable subordination keeps most American lenders on the sideline until a loan agreement is formally breached, and even then restrains the degree of intervention, the Japanese main bank effectively assumes such subordination from the outset and takes far-reaching, early steps to limit the damage. The recent handling of the financial difficulties faced by a member of the Mitsubishi group, Akai Electric Company, Ltd., illustrates the point.

Akai Electric is a major Japanese manufacturer of audio equipment and video cassette recorders. Founded in 1929, it was listed on the Tokyo Stock Exchange in 1968. Fifteen years later, it earned ¥2 billion ($8.6 million) on sales of ¥81 billion ($340 million). Better than 85% of its sales was accounted for by exports, particularly to Europe where it had a strong foothold. Its heavy dependence on exports proved problematic when the yen began appreciating against the dollar (and most other major currencies) in 1985. Sales for 1985 dropped 12.5% and a net loss of ¥6.8 billion ($29 million) was incurred.

Little time was wasted in engineering a turnaround, however. Long before the year's final results were known, and just weeks following announcement of the Plaza Accord, in which finance ministers from five major industrialized nations agreed to further the dollar's decline, Mitsubishi Bank and Mitsubishi Electric Corporation announced plans to help Akai out of its deepening slump. At the time, the bank provided 18% of the company's debt and owned 8% of its stock. Mitsubishi Electric also owned 2.5% of Akai's stock and relied on Akai as an original equipment manufacturer (OEM). The rescue plan was remarkable not only for the speed with which it was put together, but for the degree to which these parties were able to intervene without engendering widespread conflict and defection among other lenders to Akai.

The plan called for injections of new debt and equity capital into the troubled company, partial integration of Akai's world-wide marketing network with Mitsubishi Electric's, and sharing production activities between the two manufacturers. Most important, the plan also called for Mitsubishi Bank and Mitsubishi Electric to introduce new management into Akai. The bank was to insert three officers: one as "chief secretary to the president" (in effect, the temporary de facto president), another as head of international business operations, and the third as head of international finance. Mitsubishi Electric was to add four or five directors to Akai's existing board of ten (originally, two of Akai's directors were former officers of Mitsubishi Bank and two were former executives at Mitsubishi Electric). Later, Mitsubishi Electric would send seven of its top engineers to help Akai develop and produce a line of digital audio tape recorders.

Significantly, the injection of new capital into Akai did not await the extraction of concessions from other stakeholders or the general restructuring of loans. Within months of the rescue plan's announcement, Mitsubishi Electric bought enough new shares in Akai to raise its equity ownership to 7.7%. Other direct investments were made by Mitsubishi Electric in Akai's European subsidiaries. For its part, Mitsubishi Bank quadrupled its loans to the company. None of Akai's 11 other major Japanese lenders withdrew from the credit.

Given the rush of new capital into the troubled company, there was little need to engage in massive asset sales to generate cash for debt repayment. Those assets that were disposed of were done so in a manner appropriate to the system by which Japanese industrial groups govern themselves. Assets were not so much sold as they were treated as collateral placed in trust with other Mitsubishi group companies. In the spring of 1986, for example, Akai sold its VCR plant in Tokyo to some Mitsubishi group members, which then shut down operations. A year and a half later, these same companies sold the plant back to Akai when a condominium builder, Hasegawa Komuten Company, expressed an interest in buying the property for ¥8.3 billion. Hasegawa was 4.5% owned by the Mitsubishi Trust Bank, one of Akai's lending banks.

More far-reaching transactions were carried out through the

AM Trading Company. This corporation was set up as a joint venture among Mitsubishi Bank, Mitsubishi Electric, and Akai Electric. Among other functions, it became the new equity owner of Akai's American and Canadian subsidiaries, and also purchased some valuable Tokyo real estate on which stood Akai's business offices and women's dormitory. Other joint ventures between Akai and Mitsubishi group members included the Akai-Tech Company, to which Akai's Yokohama plant was sold (resulting in a reported pretax gain to Akai of ¥4.2 billion), and a parts procurement center in Singapore set up jointly with Mitsubishi Electric.

Finally, although not executed through a formal joint venture per se, Akai and Mitsubishi Electric developed a new joint brand name, "A & D" (for Akai and Diatone, the latter being Mitsubishi Electric's brand name). Twenty new products were eventually developed under this brand name, with collective first-year sales estimated at approximately ¥12 billion.

Because Akai has still to show recurring operating profit or restore its cash dividend, the last chapter of its story has yet to be written. Extraordinary gains have kept net income in the black since 1987, however, and substantial strides toward a favorable conclusion have been made. Sufficient cash was generated to reduce its net debt by ¥7.7 billion and lower its book debt-to-capital ratio from 83% to 60% by 1988. After bottoming at ¥290 per share in 1986, its stock price recovered to trade in the ¥750–¥850 per share range for most of 1989. Although Akai eventually withdrew from the North American market, shrunk its asset base by 20%, and nearly halved its personnel, the total market value of its equity has actually expanded by 43% over and above the level attained in 1986, subsequent to the injection of new capital by Mitsubishi Electric.

No doubt some, but certainly not all, of the gain was helped along by the booming Tokyo stock market between 1986 and 1989. But for a deeply troubled company like Akai, the lion's share of credit must go to the overall effectiveness of the rescue effort mounted by the Mitsubishi group. And it was a group effort in every sense of the word. Although the bank may have been the prime mover at the outset, the actual execution of the rescue plan was customer/vendor led. Consequently, the fundamental thrust of the restructuring was less one of generating cash in the short run to satisfy creditor demands than one of preserving Akai's role in the Mitsubishi group's global network of trading relationships. Rather than restructuring financial claims against the firm, effort was focused on restructuring Akai's function as a purchaser, supplier, and owner of assets used to support transactions occurring in a vertical chain of electronics production and marketing inside the Mitsubishi group.

Typical of this Japanese approach to corporate restructuring is that assets and even entire businesses were not so much disposed of by Akai as simply reconfigured in their ownership and management in the group. Those activities in which Akai held a comparative advantage (primarily production) were left under its control, albeit with managerial support from others. The links in the vertical chain of production not well managed by Akai were removed from its administrative control so that the requisite components and services had to be procured from related vendors in the group's internal market. The activities removed from Akai were either put under the direct control of another (e.g., the management of international marketing and distribution by Mitsubishi Electric) or set up as independently managed entities with which Akai, Mitsubishi Electric, and other group members could continue to transact on an arm's-length basis.

Importantly, and quite characteristically, Akai often maintained minority equity positions in the assets that were spun off. This may be the distinctive hallmark of Japanese restructurings. Thanks in large measure to the blending of claims against the troubled firm held by many of its trading partners, interventions are directed from the start to searching for an optimal means of governing transactions among all the interacting stakeholders, rather than resolving first, and possibly too late, the competing self-interested aims of corporate stakeholders holding entirely different sets of claims.

Akai's story is by no means unique in the annals of Japanese company-bank relationships. Similar interventions involving injections of managerial talent as well as capital have occurred at the hands of virtually every other major Japanese bank, with the Industrial Bank of Japan (IBJ) especially active in this capacity. IBJ played critical roles in the turnaround of numerous Japanese companies, including Nissan Motors, Yamaichi Securities, Chisso Chemicals and, most recently, the giant shipper, Japan Lines, Ltd. In two of the situations, IBJ went so far as to help engineer mergers to strengthen the troubled companies. Nissan was merged with Prince Motors in 1965. Japan Lines eventually combined with Yamashita-Shinnihon Steamship Company in 1989.

Selective intervention by banks is not confined to situations involving financial distress. Tokai Bank, for example, stepped in to resolve a bitter dispute between labor and top management of the Okuma Machinery Works over the appointment of the founder's son as the new company president. An executive vice president of the bank assumed the position of president in place of the son. Even under normal conditions, Japanese main banks use their clout to assist client companies in which they own equity. Sumitomo Bank's financing of nongroup companies such as Nissan, Mazda, and Matsushita Electric allowed the bank to act as a go-between in arranging sheet-metal supply contracts for one of its group clients, Sumitomo Metal Industries.[7]

In short, the main bank acts as a vigilant monitor of performance and begins to act like a private, controlling shareholder well in advance of the time when problems become acute. One effect of this intensive monitoring with early selective intervention is to reduce some of the costs normally associated with the hazards of lending. Opportunities to borrow money and then take extraordinary risks that might benefit shareholders at the expense of lenders are reduced when banks own some equity and are able to intervene early when problems are spotted. So, too, are incentives to borrow money long term and then walk away from investments that will have the primary effect of upholding the value of debt without adding much value to equity. The costs normally associated with financial distress are reduced to the extent that problems are identified and corrected early—

---

7. Michael Gerlach, "Business Alliances and the Strategy of the Japanese Firm," *California Management Review* (Fall 1987), p. 129.

before haggling among creditors and other stakeholders begins to dominate management's time at the expense of operations.

## GROWTH AND THE PARITY OF STAKEHOLDER CLAIMS

The paramount objective of the Japanese companies I studied was growth.[8] For many of these companies, no doubt, growth was a useful proxy objective for the maximization of the value of the firm. Given the wartime destruction of much of Japan's industrial capital and substantial economies of scale in many basic industries, there was a strong fundamental profit incentive underlying strategies oriented toward high rates of investment and high market shares.

However, the bias of Japanese corporations toward growth preceded the war and has extended well beyond the period of reconstruction and the realization of modern economies of scale. This suggests a wider role for growth than as a proxy for value maximization. It may be a means by which management might entrench itself. Managers might proactively seek to secure their positions in the firm by investing heavily in those assets that they have a special expertise in managing, even to the point of expanding beyond the point justified by profit maximization considerations. Alternatively, by pursuing unrelated diversification strategies, some managers may create highly complex organizations that perhaps only they understand well enough to manage effectively. This makes them highly important, human-specific capital to the firm, thus increasing the likelihood that they will be kept in their positions and amply rewarded.[9]

Certainly, some Japanese companies have achieved very large scale in certain industries, some have pursued unrelated diversification strategies, and Japanese managers as a group are at

---

8. See also James C. Abegglen and George Stalk, Jr., *Kaisha: The Japanese Corporation* (New York: Basic Books, 1985) for further evidence of the importance of growth as a corporate objective in Japan.
9. See Andrei Shleifer and Robert W. Vishny, "Management Entrenchment: The Case of Management-Specific Investments," *Journal of Financial Economics* 25, no. 1 (November 1989), pp. 123–139.

least as secure in their jobs as managers elsewhere. But it is not clear whether these facts bear a causal relationship to one another or are merely associated. It may also be argued that growth and managerial entrenchment are desired because they support the continuity of valuable long-term relationships. Growth in particular may forestall potentially costly stakeholder disputes while maladjusted contracts are realigned to changed economic circumstances. Recall that in the evolution of the Noda Shoyu Company, the split between the *shoyu* producers and the distributors on whom they depended for access to the Tokyo market occurred during the depression of 1881–1885. Steady growth in the previous decade had been important in maintaining a strained but workable trading relationship between the two groups.

As suggested, considerable ambiguity surrounds Japanese organizations with respect to the boundaries separating various stakeholder groups. Major lenders are also major equity owners. So, too, are key suppliers and customers that extend trade credit to, or receive it from, the company in question. Because lump-sum retirement benefits are typically an unfunded claim by employees backed only by the net total assets of the firm at any given point, employees are also implicitly in the position of long-term unsecured lenders to the firm. Compounding the ambiguity, moreover, is the fact that all these stakeholders are connected by an intricate network of largely implicit reciprocal trading agreements allowing each to extract returns from his or her "investment" in the corporation through myriad indirect means.

The typical large Japanese corporation does not have clear, bright lines distinguishing stakeholders from one another with carefully delineated rights and responsibilities between them. Rather, it is a coalition of stakeholders—suppliers, lenders, customers, shareholders—holding a complex blend of senior and junior, short-term and long-term, conditional and unconditional, implicit and explicit claims against the company.

Because of the extreme hazards of expropriation to which equity claims are exposed when ownership is separated from control, corporations around the world are typically governed by boards of directors elected by shareholders to act in their best interests. Profitability, or shareholder value maximization, is the presumed goal of the board and the managers it oversees. However, when a majority of shares are distributed among a variety of stakeholders, each holding different senior claims and able to extract returns by various means other than dividends and capital gains on stock, strict shareholder value maximization can be problematic as the dominant corporate objective. Different stakeholder groups owning voting shares may be pursuing their own goals. Some opportunities to add to shareholder value, such as prematurely repaying a high fixed-rate bank term loan, for example, may cost one of the shareholders (e.g., the lending bank) more than it stands to gain from a pickup in the value of the stock it owns.

Unbundling the debt, equity, and other claims is one way of restoring the dominance of the profit objective. But to the extent these complex bundles of claims evolved as successful, cost-efficient ways of tying companies together in ex ante profitable long-term relationships, this may not be desirable. Under these conditions, corporate growth tends to emerge as the common denominator among the stakeholder groups—the one objective that nearly everyone can agree on as having a potential benefit. When the shareholders are also valuable long-term creditors, suppliers, and customers, focusing management's attention on growth may, paradoxically, better serve the goal of ex ante value maximization than would explicit profit maximization, particularly if the latter entails being self-interestedly opportunistic after entering into commercial agreements.

Growth also tends to attenuate disputes among stakeholders by relieving pressures to compare one group's gains to the gains of another from a zero-sum perspective. It is interesting to note that when contracts become uneconomical in Japan, explicit price adjustments are seldom the initial response to the change, in part because of the clear "winner" and "loser" labels such adjustments imply. Instead, Japanese companies tend to modify other aspects of the transacting relationship. Thus Nippon Steel (among many other large industrial corporations) coped with excessively high labor costs by using forced vacations, "worker loans" to affiliates, and early retirements rather than direct layoffs or wage rollbacks. Adjustments in compensating balances or volume adjustments in other services obtained from a bank often substitute for frequent, direct resetting of interest rates on loans. When growth is rapid, the impact of such quantity adjustments can be muted and maladjusted contracts realigned with less overt conflict among stakeholders.

Within the context of the Japanese stakeholder coalition, good management is measured not so much by its ability to maximize the welfare of any one isolated stakeholder as by its ability to maximize the aggregate size of the revenue pie and maintain the stability of the coalition. Certainly the training, promotion, and reward systems for Japanese managers are aligned with these objectives. As Shleifer and Summers suggest, other corporate stakeholders' preferences do indeed become part of a Japanese manager's preferences. By the time a Japanese manager has become a senior managing director, he is fully cognizant of the implicit contracts governing behavior both within the organization and externally at the trading interface. This preparation tends to predispose him to make decisions that will generate primarily efficiency gains from which all stakeholders stand to benefit (or at least in which no one loses) rather than primarily redistributive gains in which one or a few stakeholders gain at the expense of others.

The typical Japanese reward system reinforces this predisposition by not aligning management's interests with those of any one corporate stakeholder. Instead, management's interest is aligned with the preservation of the entire coalition of stakeholders by a system that fosters risk aversion and rewards people for achieving size, stability, and corporate longevity. Bonuses are a particularly good example. Whereas Western incentive compensation systems feature profit sharing, stock ownership, stock options, or "phantom stock" rewards, the Japanese system offers virtually none of these. The companies I studied more commonly paid all regular employees semiannual cash bonuses equaling two or three times their monthly pay. Since unions negotiate pay annually on the basis of prior-year company profit, bonuses bear a detectable but weak lagged relationship to overall corporate performance, not individual merit. In many respects, bonuses are like preferred dividends. They might be declared, yet withheld as deferred wages until such time as the company can make payment. In any event, most employees have come to depend on them as a fairly steady and important source of income, accounting for between a quarter and a third of their annual earnings. The motivating influence of such bonuses clearly relates to companywide performance, broadly construed, and not to individual performance against specific targets.

Given a reward system consisting of steady promotions, seniority-based compensation, regular semiannual cash bonuses, lump-sum severance indemnities, and placement in "second careers" with affiliated companies at the time of retirement, management's well-being depends on the company's longevity, growth, and the preservation of its relationships with other firms. These achievements will ensure an ever-expanding set of opportunities for promotion coupled with salary advancement and a source of income on retirement. Indeed, among the large corporations in my sample, there appeared to be virtually no incentive for personal risk taking for the sake of career advancement or wealth creation by other means. Career and salary advancement, up to a point, take care of themselves, provided only that the corporation continues to exist and expand in a reasonably healthy state. In a market for professional management characterized by lifetime employment and little opportunity for lateral movement, failure due to personal risk taking will likely be met by ostracism by colleagues and lifetime penalization through career stagnation—a worse fate, perhaps, than separation from the firm, which in other markets for management at least brings with it the chance for a fresh start elsewhere. It is safer and economically rational for Japanese managers to avoid individual risk taking. Risks are best taken as part of a broad-based group in pursuit of the common goal of corporate expansion.

In effect, Japanese managers are agents of the entire coalition of stakeholders rather than of the shareholders or any other single group. Consensus decision making starting from the bottom, for which Japanese companies are well known, is at least partly explained by this general corporate identity and the responsibility perceived by management to minimize conflict. Slow, deliberate, and sensitive to the needs and expectations of many stakeholders, it is the style of management least likely to upset the contractual equilibrium of the stakeholder coalition.

## JAPANESE INDUSTRIAL GROUPS: HALF COMPANY, HALF MARKET

Many of the features of a typical Japanese corporation considered remarkable by Westerners are, in fact, vital elements of a successful corporate governance system (or an inevitable by-product of it). The Japanese company, no more and no less than others, is a complex network of explicit and implicit contracts among many different stakeholders. Besides specifying which goods and services are to be provided at what prices, this network necessarily embodies a design for the control of hazards associated with self-interested opportunism. In Japan, the design depends heavily on the use of highly adaptable implicit contracts, trust, reciprocity in share ownership and trade among a relatively small number of key stakeholders, and early intervention by a key stakeholder to correct problems before costly haggling destroys the stakeholder coalition comprising the corporation.

In a sense, the Japanese corporate governance system can be viewed as an attempt to secure the best of two worlds. By tying themselves to one another in groups, yet eschewing outright ownership and control, Japanese corporations have been able to exploit some of the high-powered incentives of the market that derive from independent ownership of assets, while relying on selective intervention by key equity owners to adapt contracts to new circumstances as needed. Judging from its extensive replication throughout Japan, and the economic success of Japanese corporations in product and capital markets around the world, this system of corporate governance evidently is a viable one. It depends critically, however, on the possibility of selective intervention by a well-informed stakeholder such as a main bank. Consequently, any deterioration in company-bank relationships will be inimical to such intervention and could result in break-downs in the system.

Standing in the middle of this intricate network of stake-holder relationships is management. Good managers in Japan understand the interests and priorities of stakeholder groups, are keenly aware of the nexus of implicit as well as explicit con-tracts that exists between the corporation and these groups, and can be trusted to uphold them over time through changing cir-cumstances. Alan Fox's characterization of top corporate execu-tives as a "high-trust fraternity" seems especially appropriate to Japanese management.[10] To some extent, no doubt, voluntary forbearance from self-interested action by management, rooted in Confucian ideals, has been part of the basis for this behavior. But equally—if not more—compelling is the absence of close identity between managers and any one stakeholder.

Because of their commitment to the coalition of stakeholders, Japanese managers have perceived their job to be one of increas-ing the overall size of the economic pie while allocating gains among stakeholders in such a way as to avoid conflict among them. The blending of debt with equity claims, and of commer-cial trading relationships with the supply of capital, has made growth a corporate objective that could be agreed upon with rel-ative ease. Happily, too, for many Japanese companies recon-structing or starting up after World War II, rapid growth in scale was an objective consistent with ex ante value maximization. As long as growth could be sustained, virtually all stakeholders benefited, and conflict could be held to a minimum. When con-flict did occur, or when growth was threatened or interrupted, early intervention by key corporate stakeholders—main banks in particular—rectified problems or adapted old contracts to new circumstances.

---

10. Alan Fox, *Beyond Contract: Work Power, and Trust Relations* (London: Faber & Faber, 1974), pp. 170–171.

# 4
# THE JAPANESE MARKET FOR
# CORPORATE CONTROL

Contrary to popular belief, the sale or merger of companies in Japan is not a rare occurrence. Numbering about 500 a year in the 1950s, combinations have risen dramatically, exceeding 2,000 a year since 1985. While fewer in absolute numbers than sales and mergers in the United States, which experienced about 3,000 combinations of all types in 1985, the relative frequency of Japanese combinations is not remarkably different. Between 1980 and 1986, Japan had 8.8 combinations per 10,000 incorporated businesses. The comparable rate in the United States was 8.2 per 10,000.

The important difference, is that the deal flow in Japan involves combinations of much smaller size. According to Japanese Fair Trade Commission data, more than 60% of all types of combinations between 1981 and 1985 resulted in companies with total equity capitalization of less than ¥1 billion (about $4 million at then-prevailing exchange rates). Better than 80% were capitalized at ¥5 billion (about $20 million) or less. A sample of 186 publicly announced acquisitions between 1982 and 1987 for which the size of the target was disclosed (see Exhibit 4–1) showed an average target size of only ¥520 million (between about $2 million and $4 million, depending on the prevailing exchange rate). The range varied from as little as ¥3 million to as high as ¥13.1 billion. During the same period in the United States, the average disclosed purchase price was $112 million. Whereas the United States since 1981 has witnessed over 200 transactions valued at $1 billion or more, Japan has seen only two domestic deals of that magnitude: the 1989

Exhibit 4-1 *Summary Statistics of Domestic Japanese Mergers and Acquisitions for Which Prices Were Disclosed*

|  | 1982 | 1983 | 1984 | 1985 | 1986 | 1987[a] | Total |
|---|---|---|---|---|---|---|---|
| Number of deals | 10 | 38 | 38 | 41 | 54 | 5 | 186 |
| Volume (millions) | | | | | | | |
| Yen | 1,714 | 12,162 | 22,787 | 29,877 | 29,030 | 1,120 | 96,690 |
| Dollars | 6.9 | 51.2 | 96.0 | 125.3 | 172.4 | 7.7 | 459.5 |
| Average reported price (millions) | | | | | | | |
| Yen | 171 | 320 | 600 | 729 | 538 | 224 | 520 |
| Dollars | .7 | 1.3 | 2.5 | 3.1 | 3.2 | 1.5 | 2.4 |
| Maximum price reported (millions) | | | | | | | |
| Yen | 950 | 3,558 | 6,750 | 13,074 | 3,500 | 845 | 13,074 |
| Dollars | 3.8 | 15.0 | 28.4 | 54.8 | 20.8 | 5.8 | 54.8 |
| Minimum reported prices (millions) | | | | | | | |
| Yen | 3 | 5 | 4 | 5 | 5 | 5 | 3 |
| Dollars | .012 | .020 | .017 | .021 | .030 | .035 | .012 |

[a]January through September only.
*Source:* Daiwa Securities, Merger and Acquisition Department.

merger of two large financial institutions, the Mitsui Bank and the Taiyo Kobe Bank, and the 1990 merger of the Mitsubishi Metal Corporation and the Mitsubishi Mining & Cement Company.

Above this broad base of small combinations are two other distinct tiers in the Japanese market for corporate control. One is characterized by combinations between companies within the same industrial group, or companies that already function in a quasi-parent/subsidiary relationship. In this tier, a strong firm may seek outright ownership of a weak target company to permit greater control as it attempts to boost sales, lower expenses, inject new management or capital, or simply rescue the target company from outright financial failure. The target companies' main banks are often the primary movers in such instances, particularly in cases where financial distress seems imminent. Depending on the year, between 20% and 30% of total combinations in Japan fall into this category.

The other tier involves horizontal or vertical mergers of two or three major large-scale companies more or less comparable in size. This tier is somewhat more typical of the type of combination that occurs in the Anglo-American market for corporate control. But even these combinations are executed in Japan according to a distinctly different standard—one quite predictable on the basis of the Japanese corporate governance system.

The 1970 merger that produced Nippon Steel Corporation is an example of large-scale horizontal combinations. These types of combinations have been few but significant in their impact on industry structure and performance in Japan. They are also highly instructive of how and why the Japanese corporate governance system influences M&A dealmaking in Japan, even when the powerful Ministry of International Trade and Industry (MITI) is sponsoring the industrial marriage. A close look at the creation of Nippon Steel Corporation illustrates the point.

## THE CREATION OF NIPPON STEEL

Nippon Steel epitomizes Japanese industry and the classic Japanese corporate governance system. With annual crude steel production in excess of 28 million metric tons (more than one-quarter of Japan's total output), it is the largest iron and steel producer in Japan and the largest crude steel producer in the world. It stands at the center of its own industrial group consisting of approximately 33 core companies in related industries, and an estimated 180 companies nationwide. Close relationships are also maintained with the large trading companies, Mitsui & Company and Mitsubishi Corporation, which do not have large steel companies in their groups.

With a leverage ratio reaching 75% of total capital in 1972 and still equal to 60% in 1989, Nippon Steel has been a heavy user of debt from various major banks. The largest lender has been the Industrial Bank of Japan (IBJ), which by itself has provided about 10% of this mammoth industrial corporation's debt. Nippon Steel's top ten shareholders, which are predominantly its major lenders, control nearly 20% of its stock. IBJ alone owns 3.4% (Nippon Steel itself owns 2.3% of IBJ and has significant ownership in at least four other IBJ group companies).

As with a number of larger Japanese industrial corporations, the central government bureaucracy has also played an active role in Nippon Steel's development and has effectively been an influential corporate stakeholder. Numerous alumni officers of both IBJ and MITI have found their way into the steel company's management hierarchy. Nippon Steel's director and honorary chairman, Eishiro Saito, chairs the powerful and prestigious business association, Keidanren (Federation of Business Associations); Yutaka Takeda, the current chairman of Nippon Steel, functions as one of its vice chairmen. They and other senior officers also sit on the boards of other prominent national business associations.

Early History
        The status of Nippon Steel and its intricate web of relationships are rooted in the Japanese steel industry's prewar history. Japan's first Western-style blast furnace was established in Kamaishi (Iwate Prefecture) in 1857 in the waning days of the Tokugawa Shogunate. After the Meiji Restoration, the blast furnace was taken over by the central government in 1873, making pig-iron production a nationalized industry.

Following a government study in 1891, steel was declared to be "the mother of industry and the basis of national security." It was announced that an iron and steel industry would be built, controlled, and operated by the government. The first step was the construction of the Yawata Works, an integrated iron and steel works, in Fukuoka Prefecture located on the Japan Sea close to the coal fields in northern Kyushu and with easy access to iron ore from China.

Despite support from the government and the founding of several other steel works, crude steel production grew slowly during the next three decades. Production was below three million tons, less than 2% of the world total, and unit costs were high. Seeking greater efficiency in production, seven major steel companies were merged in 1934 to form Japan Iron & Steel. Thereafter, with the approach and onset of World War II, steel production grew rapidly, reaching eight million tons in 1943 (5% of the world total). Following the war, the Economic Deconcentration Law resulted in the division of Japan Iron & Steel into Yawata Iron & Steel and Fuji Iron & Steel. These two successors to the prewar, government-controlled company were to remain the first and second largest companies in the industry until their reunification through merger in 1970 to form Nippon Steel Corporation.

Ministerial Leadership

Occupation forces did not encourage the revival of the Japanese steel industry until the outbreak of the Korean War. Within a year, production surged, the industry became profitable, and shareholders began to receive cash dividends. The cost of steel production was still quite high, however. As of April 1951, the domestic price of Japanese steel was 50–100% higher, and of lower quality, than that available in other parts of the industrialized world.

This discrepancy triggered a modernization program that began when a report by MITI's Industrial Rationalization Council was adopted in February 1952. Reflecting the government's long history of monitoring and controlling the steel industry, the report laid out a detailed plan for the rationalization of Japan's steel industry; it even specified small investments in particular plants and terms of finance to be provided by the Japan Development Bank.

No substantial industry expansion took place under this program. Only one new plant, the Chiba Works of Kawasaki Steel, was built between 1952 and 1955. Instead, cost reduction and quality improvement were emphasized. Following MITI's guidance, approximately ¥130 million was spent on capital expenditures between 1952 and 1955, 90% of which came from the largest six companies. The investment was encouraged with tax incentives and government-backed foreign exchange loans to buy machinery from offshore suppliers. Government-owned banks provided about one-third of the external financing necessary on a low-cost, subsidized basis. Long-term credit banks, particularly IBJ (also a state-owned enterprise before the war), were active suppliers of long-term capital to the industry as well. They also became significant equity investors in steel companies following the amending of the Antimonopoly Act in 1953 to permit a doubling in the fractional share ownership allowed by banks in industrial companies to 10% from 5%.

MITI's leadership of the steel industry continued in the last half of the 1950s, though no longer under the auspices of an official modernization program such as prevailed from 1952 to 1955. In the second phase of modernization, capacity expansion was emphasized. This was to be achieved by constructing large-scale integrated steel works utilizing modern basic-oxygen furnaces to lower operating costs and cut dependence on iron and steel scrap.

Considerably more attention was paid to the development of infrastructure to support steel production. MITI encouraged establishing long-term purchase contracts with suppliers and building giant ore and coal ships by consortia made up of steel companies, shipping companies, and the government itself. This fostered the sort of business alliances that became so characteristic of Japanese industry. Less direct financing by the government took place during this phase, but tax subsidies continued and MITI wielded its influence in determining the distribution of the Japanese Export-Import Bank's appropriations and in supporting loan requests made to the World Bank.

By 1961, Japan had constructed 20 basic-oxygen furnaces, and Japanese steelmaking capacity had more than doubled to 22.1 million tons annually. A highly oligopolistic industry structure had also emerged in which the six largest firms controlled modern facilities and produced 80% of total national output. Surrounding them were several hundred smaller companies with older technology. These firms became part of the Japanese keiretsu system by aligning themselves with major producers, purchasing semifinished steel from them, and filling small orders for low-quality products.

The dramatic success of the Japanese steel producers and the stable coalition of stakeholders that emerged by the 1960s were not achieved without conflict, however. The promotion of unions by the occupation government in 1949 led to rapid organization of steel plants by aggressive, even radical, union leaders. Not yet part of the governing coalition of corporate stakeholders, the new unions pushed hard for substantial wage increases despite high national unemployment, rampant inflation, and the fact

that steel workers were already the highest paid industrial workers in Japan. Unions also opposed plans for rationalization and
fiercely resisted any attempt to lay workers off. In 1950, Yawata
Iron & Steel was hit with a 20-day strike in protest of a piece-
rate compensation system and a reduction in pay incentives.
Four more strikes occurred in 1952 along with an industrywide
lockout by management in resistance of union demands. Further strikes were experienced annually, eventually reaching a
peak in 1957 when Yawata Iron & Steel suffered 11 separate
strikes, and Fuji Iron & Steel experienced a 49-day strike in protest over a decision not to raise wages that year.

Labor unrest eventually was eased when union members increasingly identified with management and other stakeholders
of the firm. Starting in 1958, blue-collar workers in Yawata Iron
& Steel could be promoted to management. Foremen gained
more authority, and a new "senior foreman" position was created. Most important, a new compensation system was introduced in 1962, tying pay to a combination of seniority, job difficulty, and corporate performance. By tying pay to corporate
performance, creating tracks leading to management, and offering lifetime employment with a retirement bonus at separation,
Yawata Iron & Steel undermined the appeal of radical union
leaders. Worker loyalty gradually shifted from the *Sohyo* (the
national labor confederation) and the steel union federation to
the local company union and even the company itself. The rank
and file elected more moderate leaders who promised them
greater gains through cooperation rather than confrontation
with management. By 1965, the strikes had ceased at the Yawata
and Fuji steel companies.

The Path to Merger

As labor unrest came to a close, potentially destructive
competition among the major producers threatened to dissipate
the gains achieved in the prior decade and a half. The goals
MITI established, the modern technology used in the production of steel, and the emphasis on growth as a corporate objective created such a drive to increase scale that industry overcapacity soon developed. Although domestic consumption of steel
doubled during the 1960s, Japanese production capacity more

than quadrupled from 22 million tons annually in 1960 to 93 million tons by 1970.

MITI attempted to control Japanese steel prices through administrative guidance and sanctioning a voluntary "price-maintenance" cartel, which the Fair Trade Commission approved as an exception to the Antimonopoly Act. Collaboration was difficult to establish, however, given the high fixed costs of production and the industrialists' fear of losing corporate control to MITI bureaucrats. The latter concern was intensified by MITI's past involvement in the steel industry. Both Yawata and Fuji had been part of Japan Iron & Steel, which had been under the supervision of MITI's predecessor, the Ministry of Commerce and Industry. Management of the two descendants of Japan Iron & Steel was filled with former MITI officials. Not surprisingly, other steel makers claimed MITI discriminated in favor of Yawata and Fuji. Sumitomo Metal Industries, Ltd., the only one of the major six steel producers without a MITI officer on its board of directors, went so far as to assert that MITI had become the *Kasumigaseki* (Tokyo) office of Yawata Iron & Steel.[1]

In late 1962, the price-maintenance cartel collapsed and was eventually replaced with informal price leadership by Yawata Iron & Steel. Yawata would announce prices for its steel and others would follow suit. Once again, however, pricing discipline could not be maintained for long. Sumitomo continued its dissent from industry practices and openly defied MITI's administrative guidance.

To reassert the role of central planning in Japan's industrial development, and ostensibly to prepare for Japan's joining the Organization for Economic Cooperation and Development in 1964 (a move expected to expose Japanese industries to heavier international competition), MITI developed a legislative proposal known as the Bill for the Promotion of Specific Industries. Among other things, the bill designated specific industries to be helped in improving their international competitiveness. Companies in these industries would be exempt for five years from

---

1. Chalmers Johnson, *MITI and the Japanese Miracle* (Stanford: Stanford University Press, 1982), pp. 246–248.

the Antimonopoly Act and would be extended various investment incentives in the form of special tax privileges and long-term, low-interest loans.

The bill was ultimately opposed by all quarters, including a sister ministry, the Ministry of Finance (MOF). Debate in the Japanese Diet reflected fears of excessive concentration of economic power and a further fusion of interests among high-ranking MITI bureaucrats and senior executives of large corporations. Some of MOF's opposition was undoubtedly rooted in interministry rivalry, though much of it represented MOF's advocacy of the nation's financial institutions.

Interestingly, the banks put up some of the fiercest opposition to the bill. Their opposition is understandable, however, in light of Japan's system of industrial groupings in the mid-1960s. The major banks were simultaneously lenders and equity owners in fairly well-defined industrial groups characterized by extensive cross-shareholding and reciprocal trade agreements. This ownership structure and web of contracts permitted stakeholders to earn an attractive return on their overall investment in, or relationship with, a specific company while minimizing conflicts within the larger coalition of stakeholders. The bill MITI proposed threatened this equilibrium. The large banks were concerned they might be compelled to make low-interest loans to firms regardless of those companies' past banking ties. Furthermore, being forced to make low-interest loans without owning any of the equity or having other means of extracting gains in consideration for the advantageously priced debt would clearly benefit existing stakeholders at the expense of the new lenders.

Although the Diet defeated the bill, MITI's push for further industrial reorganization did not cease. What it failed to accomplish by broad legislative means was sought piecemeal through a series of mergers among major companies. In 1965, MITI engineered the merger of Japan's second- and fourth-largest automobile companies, Nissan and Prince. Further mergers and joint ventures in the synthetic fiber, chemical, and petrochemical industries followed. Finally, in 1968, two major mergers were announced. One was the combination of Japan's three major paper producers, Oji, Honshu, and Jujo. The second was the reuniting of Yawata Iron & Steel and Fuji Iron & Steel to form the Nippon Steel Corporation.

In contrast to the other MITI-sponsored mergers, these two would result in combinations that controlled more than 30% of their respective domestic markets (36% in the case of the steel combination); hence they required Fair Trade Commission approval. Fearing inimical effects on competition, the FTC turned both mergers down. In 1969, however, it was forced to reconsider the steel companies' proposal after the Tokyo High Court ruled the merger could proceed if Fuji and Yawata sold some assets to competitors. With ultimate FTC approval, the Nippon Steel Corporation became an official entity on March 31, 1970.

The forging among managers, workers, shareholders, lenders, and government bureaucrats of the alliance that became Nippon Steel is a case study in the importance of recognizing and preserving implicit contracts in Japan. Whereas a broad government plan to rationalize certain industries centrally was rejected by nearly all parties concerned, the somewhat more decentralized approach of rationalization via selected combinations achieved a degree of success. This was particularly true for Nippon Steel. Long-standing relationships that predated the Second World War and were maintained throughout Japan's reconstruction facilitated the reaching of consensus and aided implementation of the Yawata-Fuji combination. The presidents of the two merged companies, Yoshihiro Inayama of Yawata and Shigeo Nagano of Fuji, were former officers of Japan Iron & Steel, as were numerous other members of top management in both companies. Annual alumni gatherings had been held ever since the breakup of Japan Iron & Steel in 1950, and both management groups had close ties with officials of MITI, the modern counterpart of the Ministry of Commerce and Industry. The same was true of relationships with IBJ. IBJ had been Japan Iron & Steel 's primary lender prior to its breakup and continued to be the main bank for Yawata and Fuji afterward.[2]

---

2. In fact, despite the banks' general reluctance to support the Bill for the Promotion of Specific Industries, IBJ's past chairman, Sohei Nakayama, took a leadership role in the *Sanken* (the Industrial Problems Research Association) in building support for the steel

Exhibit 4-2  *Top Management Composition of Nippon Steel at the Time of Merger*

Shigeo Nagano (Fuji), Chairman of the Board of Directors*
Yoshihiro Inayama (Yawata), President
*Executive Vice Presidents* (3 from Yawata and 3 from Fuji)

H. Fujii (Yawata)
R. Hirata (Fuji)
T. Hirai (Yawata)
T. Tasaka (Fuji)
N. Kaneko (Fuji)
S. Fujiki (Yawata)—promoted from senior managing director

*Senior Managing Directors* (3 from Yawata and 3 from Fuji)

T. Fujiki (Fuji)
E. Saito (Yawata)
H. Tokunaga (Fuji)
K. Takeda (Yawata)
Y. Takeda (Fuji)—promoted from managing director
D. Imai (Yawata)—promoted from managing director

*Managing Directors:* 7 from Yawata and 7 from Fuji; 2 from Yawata promoted
from director

*Directors:* 4 from Yawata and 7 from Fuji

*Nagano, being the senior to Inayama, became the chairman.
Source: *Japan's Iron & Steel Industry,* 1970 ed., p. 187.

A high degree of familiarity and trust existed among these tightly interwoven stakeholder groups. This provided a firm basis for engineering a merger with minimal threat to the implicit as well as explicit claims held by various stakeholders of the two firms. Reflecting respect for such claims and the intense desire to avoid even minor distributive effects, top management of the new Nippon Steel was constructed carefully to provide a balance between the managements of the predecessor firms. (See Exhibit 4–2 for the composition of Nippon Steel's top management at the time of merger.) In light of the overcapacity problems that

---

merger and calling for mergers in seven other industries including textiles, machine parts, automobiles, and computers.

triggered the rationalization process leading to merger, it is remarkable that none of the new company's major works was shut down, nor were there any layoffs of the two companies' combined work force of 80,000 permanent employees.


## JAPANESE MERGER MOTIVES

Although large-scale mergers in Japan are relatively uncommon, those that do occur fit essentially the same mold as that of the Nippon Steel merger. That is, they are friendly deals, usually among companies with established relationships of some sort. They are motivated primarily by strategic considerations, and prominent objectives are the achievement of greater market share and growth within the existing business. With the sponsorship of MITI and major share-owning banks, Japan's largest mergers have been deliberate attempts to alter the structure and performance of the industries in which the mergers occurred. Common aims were to reduce excess capacity, avoid potentially destructive price competition, and build domestic firms of a scale capable of competing with major foreign competitors in their home markets. The tendency has been to combine weaker firms with stronger ones. This was the case, for example, when Prince Motors was merged into Nissan Motors in the mid-1960s, and when Fuji Iron & Steel was combined with the industry price leader, Yawata.

Major domestic Japanese mergers typically have not been attempts to diversify away from core businesses. Virtually all large, government-sanctioned mergers have been either horizontal mergers (e.g., the Price and Nissan motor companies, the Fuji and Yawata steel companies, the Dai-Ichi and Nippon Kangyo banks, the Oji Paper and Nihou Pulp companies, and the Maruzen and Kansai oil companies) or vertical mergers between companies that had been conducting business for many years, often within the same industrial group (e.g., the Showa Denko and Showa Yuka chemical companies in the Fuyo group, the Furukawa Electric and Furukawa Metal companies, and Toyota Motor Corporation and Toyota Motor Sales).

Indeed, despite a pronounced drive by many Japanese manufacturers to diversify in the late 1980s, even the mergers of small
to medium-sized firms tend to involve a high degree of relatedness. For the sample of combinations described in Exhibit 4–1,
58% represented acquisitions within the bidding company's existing line of business. Another 29% represented a related diversification. Only 13% represented unrelated diversifications.
Slightly more than half the sample of bidders declared growth
to be the purpose in making the acquisition, and more than
three-quarters of them sought that growth in existing or new but
related markets. The announced reasons for selling by the acquired company were overwhelmingly connected, directly or indirectly, with the need to improve unsatisfactory performance.

## JAPANESE DEALMAKING

The role of IBJ as promoter and adviser to both sides in
the Yawata-Fuji combination is also typical of domestic Japanese deals. Even today, the role of M&A advisers in Japan is
considerably different from that of their counterparts in the
West. The Anglo-American market for corporate control is far
more open and competitive. Prior business relationships between bidder and target often do exist and may be highly desirable in ensuring the success of the combination, but they are by
no means the rule nor are they necessary to close a deal. Western investment bankers routinely shop lists of potential target
companies among prospective bidding clients and often expect
responses in a few weeks if not days. When deals are put together, they are tailored to the needs of the buying and selling
parties, but the transacting parties themselves are not uniquely
matched to each other. If a deal is not consummated, the parties
in question will simply seek out other partners. Given the highly
technical but relatively nonspecific nature of the typical M&A
transaction in the West, it is not surprising that both buyers and
sellers entering the market will engage specialists to advise them
and act as agents on their behalf in negotiations.

This is not so in Japan. Among those deals of sufficient size and complexity to be picked up by M&A specialists, the parties involved generally do have a much more unique, almost idiosyncratic relationship to one another. There is generally at least an ongoing business relationship of some sort and often participation in the same industrial group, reciprocal equity ownership, or partial ownership by common major shareholders. All of these features are displayed in the ¥300 billion merger between the Mitsubishi Metal Corporation and the Mitsubishi Mining & Cement Company, which was scheduled to take place on December 1, 1990. In general, the universe of companies that would be suitable matches for a particular bidder or target is far smaller. Indeed, in combinations engineered to rescue financially distressed clients, the two parties are likely to have been very carefully matched by the target's main bank.

Once the two parties have agreed in principle to combine, then a single bank or securities company will act simultaneously as adviser to both sides in the transaction. Not uncommonly, the bank will also have equity interests in both sides as IBJ did in the Yawata-Fuji combination. Besides offering technical expertise, the financial intermediary assumes the role of go-between or arbiter in the process of completing the deal, transmitting information between the transacting parties and resolving differences of opinion that may arise. It will also act as price-setter by "suggesting" the value to be paid for the target at a level that is deemed fair to both sides. Although such a price-setting mechanism would seem ripe for intermediary bias, there is little evidence of this. In an empirical study of 50 domestic Japanese mergers involving listed companies, Richard Pettway and Takeshi Yamada found a small positive (about 2.4% overall) but statistically insignificant abnormal return earned by the acquiring firm's shareholders. (When the sample was confined to a smaller group of mergers between companies unaffiliated by equity ownership or membership in the same group, similar results were obtained: the acquiring firm's shareholders earned a positive but statistically insignificant abnormal return of 3.2%.)[3]

---

3. Richard H. Pettway and Takeshi Yamada, "Mergers in Japan and Their Impacts upon Stockholders' Wealth," *Financial Management* (Winter 1986), pp. 43–52.

This unique status of Japanese financial advisers is aptly reflected in the organizational positioning of Japanese M&A units within banks and securities firms, and in the titles assigned to the units. Whereas a Western M&A unit is likely to be a separate and distinctly labeled department or group within a bank, such a unit in Japan is likely to be but a small, specialized part of a much larger business information or information development division in a major city bank, or a corporate development department in a securities firm. Japanese professionals in these units will typically carry bilingual business cards that plainly declare their M&A specialty in English, while overtly betraying no such specialty on the Japanese side where they are simply identified as a professional in their bank's business information department.

## LAWS AND REGULATIONS GOVERNING JAPANESE COMBINATIONS

There are relatively few formal, explicit legal and regulatory barriers to merger and acquisition activity in Japan. Those that do exist relate primarily to takeovers by foreign investors and are treated in Chapter 6. For purely domestic combinations, the established legal and regulatory apparatus is essentially neutral with respect to the fostering of business combinations. In some respects it is laxer than in other countries.

Antimonopoly regulations, so often used to block proposed combinations in countries such as the United Kingdom and the United States, are noted for their weak enforcement in Japan. The Japanese Fair Trade Commission, which could block proposed combinations in Japan on antitrust grounds, has long exercised a benign policy on mergers and acquisitions. As illustrated in the Yawata-Fuji combination, it has never ultimately opposed a deal sanctioned by a ministry such as MITI or MOF. A sudden reversal of FTC policy seems unlikely in view of the large domestic market shares enjoyed by many Japanese corporations, the global competition faced abroad, and the industrial restructuring sought at home.

The Japanese Commercial Code makes provisions for two types of mergers and three types of acquisitions. Mergers can take place by an amalgamation of two or more corporations in which only one party to the merger continues to exist while the others are liquidated. Alternatively, all parties may be liquidated and an entirely new corporation created from the merger partners. According to Toshiro Nishimura, the latter approach is costly and rarely used.[4] The rules governing the former approach are similar to those of the United States. Both corporations' shareholders must approve the merger agreement. Dissenting shareholders of the target corporation may require the target to buy them out at fair market value, and loans must be paid off to any creditors that object to the proposed merger.

Acquisitions most commonly occur in Japan through a purchase of shares in the target corporation. They can also take place through a purchase of assets (construed broadly to be a "business rights transfer" in which all business and labor contracts, goodwill, and all other intangible assets are transferred), although this is a much more cumbersome procedure than a purchase of shares. If *all* assets of a target are purchased, *both* sets of shareholders must approve of the sales agreement (a sale of a substantial part, but not quite all, of the target's assets requires the approval of only the target's shareholders; dissenting target shareholders may require the target to purchase their shares at fair market value). New permits and government approvals may be required if the assets are to be used in a new business. Consent may also have to be obtained from other parties such as employees and creditors whose contracts are being transferred with the asset sale.[5]

A less complicated way to transfer ownership is through a subscription to newly issued shares of the target corporation. Such an issue requires only a resolution of the target company's board of directors unless the issue price is deemed to be "specially favorable" (which is generally thought to be any price below 85–90% of market value). If it is specially favorable, then approval

---

4. Toshiro Nishimura, "M&A Law in Japan: Rules of the Unplayed Game," *Mergers and Acquisitions* 17, no. 4 (Winter 1983), p. 24.
5. Ibid.

by two-thirds of the votes of shareholders present at a shareholders' meeting at which more than one-half of the outstanding shares are represented is required.[6]

An easier means (from a legal and regulatory standpoint) to acquire stock is via open market purchase of existing shares. Other than exchange limitations that can be imposed at the discretion of the Tokyo Stock Exchange when trading in a target company's stock becomes too thin and volatile, there are essentially no serious legal and regulatory impediments to takeover via open market purchases of stock (and even trading limitations can be circumvented to some degree by off-market transactions).[7]

The least-used means of acquiring a target company's stock is by a tender offer. Japan had no regulations governing tender offers prior to an amendment to the Securities Exchange Law in 1971. Since that time, only two tender offers have been registered and concluded, both of them friendly. In an attempt to raise its holdings in a Japanese auto parts manufacturer from 15% to 20% for financial reporting purposes, Bendix International Finance Corporation made a tender offer to shareholders of Jidosha Kiki K.K. in 1972. Bendix had been unsuccessful acquiring the shares on the open market, but succeeded with a tender offer supported by door-to-door solicitations. In 1975, the Okinawa Electric Power Distribution Company and the Central Electric Power Distribution Company were also acquired by the Okinawa Electric Power Company through the tender-offer mechanism.

A time line depicting the required steps in a regulated tender offer is shown in Exhibit 4–3.[8] Briefly, a tender offer in Japan begins with the filing of a registration statement that sets forth

6. Ibid., pp. 21–22.
7. The articles of incorporation for some Japanese companies require the consent of the board of directors for any share transfers (see note 6). However, companies that are listed or whose stock is registered for exchange in the over-the-counter market are not permitted to have such consent provisions.
8. Japanese regulation follows the U.S. model insofar as tender offers for less than 10% of the target's outstanding shares are exempted from regulation. See Misao Tatsuta, "Proxy Regulation, Tender Offers, and Insider Trading," in *Japanese Securities Regulation*, edited by Louis Loss, Makoto Yazawa, and Barbara Ann Banoff (Tokyo: University of Tokyo Press; and Boston: Little, Brown, 1983), p. 176.

Exhibit 4-3 *Japanese Tender-Offer Time Line*

the purpose, price, and duration of the offer along with other information pertaining to the number of shares to be purchased and the sources of financing to be used.[9] For a cash offer to be validated, a deposit in the amount of the offer must be made in a Japanese bank (the Japanese subsidiary of a foreign bank would qualify)—the "commissioned agent" for the bidder.

Validation of the registration statement by the MOF initiates a 10-day waiting period during which the bidder can undertake no action whatsoever with respect to the target. Following the waiting period, the registration statement becomes effective, at which point the actual offer can begin by publishing the statement in two or more daily newspapers. First however, the bidder must notify the target of the offer by providing it with a copy of the registration statement. Since the length of such prior notice is not specified in the legislation, a last-minute notification may be appropriate.[10]

Once the offer period begins, the bidder must leave the offer open for at least 20 days but must close it within 30, unless

---

9. Ibid., pp. 184–189, for further discussion of the required content of the tender offer registration statement.
10. Ibid., p. 182.

amendments to the statement have been filed, validated, and publicly announced (the price offered can be increased, but all shares tendered for must be purchased at the higher price). Target shareholders who agree to sell their shares may cancel that acceptance within ten days of the public announcement of the offer or an amendment to the offer, whichever is later. False or misleading statements made in the public announcement of the offer may entail penalties, but are generally thought not to affect the validity of the offer itself.[11]

The 1971 legislation regulating tender offers purports to be neutral with respect to favoring either bidders or targets. However, like proxy regulations, the tender offer rules work more to the advantage of the target company's incumbent management than to the bidder's. Whereas proxy regulations allow for *concurrent* filing and general distribution of proxy materials with no provision for advance review by the MOF, tender offer regulations do require bidders to receive MOF approval and to give the target *advance* notice of the bid.[12] The need to complete a takeover within 30 days may also restrict the ability of bidders to change tactics and renew efforts if insufficient shares are tendered during the original offering period.

Two other aspects of securities law work to the advantage of incumbent management in potential targets and against that of the bidders, at least as far as large companies are concerned: the requirement of depositing sufficient cash prior to the announcement of the offer and the present regulatory preclusion of using so-called junk bonds to finance takeovers (or anything else, for that matter). Indirectly, the Japanese prohibition against repurchasing one's own shares may also inhibit the activity of bidders: repayment of any debt of the bidding company used to finance a successful acquisition with funds subsequently borrowed by the acquired corporation may be construed to be an indirect repurchase of shares by the target corporation itself.[13] Similarly, by making the purchase and sale of companies more cumber-

---

11. Ibid., p. 181.
12. Ibid., pp. 178–179.
13. Ibid., p. 189.

some, the prohibition against forming or effectively functioning as a holding company also retards the activity of potential bidders.[14]

Nevertheless, despite such legal impediments to merger and acquisitions activity in Japan, it is difficult to conclude that either the spirit or the letter of Japanese law is fundamentally more inimical to mergers and acquisitions than is, say, American or British law. In the United States, hostile takeovers manage to thrive despite a growing body of state statutes favoring incumbent management even more strongly than the provisions noted in Japanese law. Furthermore, the Japanese law governing takeover bids will be eased by revisions to be made by March 1991. The revisions are expected to eliminate the 10-day validation period, to extend the offering period to 60 days (identical to that used in the United Kingdom), and to dispense with commissioned agents.

If severe regulatory impediments to domestic Japanese M&A exist, they must do so beyond the mere letter of the law. So-called administrative guidance may more often be used to regulate domestic M&A than is codified law. Owing to the relative paucity of large-scale, nongovernment-sanctioned takeovers in Japan, one can only conjecture about how such guidance is effected, if at all. One avenue that seems possible is through control of bank activity as M&A advisers. If banks were required to consult with the MOF concerning the nature and extent of their M&A operations, both the volume and character of the M&A deal flow might be effectively controlled just as manufacturers' investment activities were in the early days of bank-intermediated financing.

However, interviews of public officials turned up little evidence of a strong will on the part of the MOF or MITI to implement such administrative guidance today. Indeed, if anything,

---

14. Tax laws preclude one of the benefits to a stock acquisition that can sometimes arise when a profitable corporation takes over an unprofitable one. Specifically, Japanese tax law prohibits consolidation of jointly owned companies, irrespective of the percentage of ownership. Even if a group of companies is wholly owned by a single shareholder, each company in that group is liable for corporate income taxes on its income without the possibility of sheltering any taxable income earned by some members with losses incurred by others.

the opinions expressed tended to support the opposite point of view. Officials at both ministries acknowledged that the concept of an open market for corporate control was relatively new to them and presently under study. Tentatively, however, their posture was one of seeking first to determine the direction in which the private sector wished to see merger and acquisition activity evolve and then facilitating movement in that direction.

One key player in this process of inquiry, the highly influential Keidanren, has come down squarely on the side of promoting an open market for corporate control, even to the extent of condoning hostile takeovers. Yoshio Nakamura, senior director of the Keidanren's International Economic Affairs Department, stated forcefully that Keidanren policy today revolves heavily around free competition and private sector leadership in the restructuring of Japanese industry. He saw mergers and acquisitions as part of that process and favored only minimal government regulatory interference in that activity. Later, Kazuo Nukazawa, a managing director of the Keidanren, wrote in the *Japan Times* that Japan's "taboo" concerning unsolicited bids was actually hampering economic efficiency.[15]

This is by no means a universal opinion in Japan. But it is evident that some important opinion-setters likely to gain the ears of MITI and MOF as these ministries develop their positions regarding mergers and acquisitions have begun to swim against the anti-M&A tide. They are doing so, moreover, in a highly visible, organized way by publishing research, organizing seminars, and seeking public forums at which to express their opinions. In contrast, those opposed to a more open market for corporate control within Japan have presented no organized response, appearing instead to bank on inertia to preserve the status quo. Given this balance between the opposing points of view, it seems unlikely that even administrative guidance regarding domestic mergers and acquisitions in Japan will emerge as a severe impediment to Japanese combinations, if in fact it was in the first place.

---

15. Gordon Cramb, "Official Calls for End to Tokyo Taboo on Hostile Takeovers," *Financial Times*, November 21, 1988, p. 3.

## CORPORATE GOVERNANCE AND THE ATTENUATION OF DOMESTIC JAPANESE TAKEOVERS

The picture painted here is that of a fairly active market for corporate control within Japan at one particular level (i.e., the lower tier of very small deals), but not a market in which players can transact in size or with complete freedom. That lack of freedom, however, has relatively little to do with explicit legal and regulatory impediments. Rather, it is a by-product of the Japanese corporate governance system.

Most Japanese M&A activity has been concentrated in the third tier of the market, where bidders and targets are small and unlisted. At that level, anything other than a friendly, negotiated deal is virtually impossible. The top tier has been, in effect, the province of the government in the form of MITI (aided and abetted by a few major banks), a necessary promoter to overcome antitrust concerns and act as a catalyst in bringing together two independent and heterogeneous corporate cultures.

In the middle there has been a tier confined more or less to groups of related companies; transactions occur commonly among companies within a group, but between groups only rarely.[16] At this level, acquisitions or mergers among companies related by reciprocal shareholdings or a common set of shareholders have represented the sort of selective administrative intervention one would expect in large groups when changing circumstances—most often poor performance and impending financial distress—make continued arm's-length transactions with a group supplier or customer all but impossible at anything close to market prices. In such cases, actual or impending financial embarrassment has served as sufficiently strong evidence of a severe malfunction to justify intervention by a major investor

---

16. One significant intergroup combination occurred in the early 1970s when the Dai-Ichi Bank lost one of its trading company affiliates, the Nissho Corporation, when it merged with a Sanwa Bank trading company, Iwai Sangyo. When the giant trading company Sumitomo Corporation simultaneously sought a merger with Dai-Ichi's core trading company, C. Itoh & Co., Dai-Ichi moved aggressively to prevent the merger by buying shares of C. Itoh. A subsequent merger in 1972 between Dai-Ichi and the Kangyo Bank, then the tenth-largest shareholder in C. Itoh, crippled Sumitomo's plans to merge with C. Itoh.

(i.e., the main bank) so ownership could be changed, old contracts broken, and new ones put in their place.

These characteristics of domestic Japanese M&A are entirely consistent with what one would predict on the basis of the Japanese corporate governance system. This system has been unusually successful in resolving conflicts of stakeholder interests—a universal problem shared by economic institutions around the world and throughout time. It is this success that has resulted in an attenuation of large-scale Japanese M&A activity. The attenuation occurs because several of the more common motives for acquiring and merging with other firms are substantially diminished. One such motive is the need to integrate operations in order to secure upstream sources of supply, downstream markets, or distribution in some other locale. The successful containment of self-interested opportunism makes it easier to build and maintain stable, long-term exchange relations with suppliers, distributors, customers, subcontractors, and so forth. Managing such relationships will generally be superior to the imposition of direct administrative control over an exchange partner because of the bureaucratic disabilities and loss of high-powered market incentives that such control normally entails. Thus the incentive to integrate is lessened by the Japanese corporate governance system.

The costs of combining companies, whether vertically or horizontally, may also be significantly higher in Japan than elsewhere. For large companies that are part of an industrial group, a merger or an acquisition inevitably entails the blending of two sets of stakeholder groups (some members of which are likely to be competitors) with their company-specific human assets and intricate networks of implicit contracts. The flexibility of implicit contracts may contribute somewhat to the process of adjustment that typically follows a combination. But likely as not, this advantage will be dominated by the costs of breaching old, well-established agreements: closing plants, eliminating product lines, abandoning selected former suppliers and customers, and reducing staff. Such costs are often essential to the realization of the efficiencies to be gained in a typical merger.

For most professional Japanese managers, those costs loom

sufficiently large to preclude nearly all large combinations except those in which the potential gains are enormous. It was for
precisely this reason that most of the Japanese executives interviewed were pessimistic about the possibility of using horizontal
mergers among large industrial companies as a way of quickly
correcting excess capacity and redundant labor problems. Horizontal mergers would only compound the problems they found
most pressing: meeting the lifetime employment expectations of
their employees and sustaining the network of suppliers and
customers on which they depended. Temporary cartelization of
the industry under MITI's auspices, for which there is both
abundant precedent and a high tolerance in Japan, was preferred as a means of achieving many of the adjustments that
might normally be carried out through horizontal combinations.
As previously noted, most megamergers between major industrial firms in Japan have had at least the encouragement if not
the active involvement of the government—a necessary factor in
not only assuaging any antitrust concerns, but also in overcoming stakeholder resistance to merger created by the Japanese
corporate governance system.

Japanese corporate governance provides little incentive to
undertake conglomerate mergers. Little or nothing can be
achieved by outright ownership and control of many diverse
business units that cannot be obtained with less bureaucratic
cost and greater preservation of market incentives within the
framework of the traditional Japanese corporate governance system. Any private advantages that could be gained from practices
such as strictly enforced reciprocal trading arrangements, cross-
subsidization of businesses, or entrenchment in markets because of the size and financial strength of the combined entity
(all of which may reduce competition and were once reasons for
opposing conglomerate mergers in the United States) are already obtained in Japan through group membership. Genuine
efficiency gains through better allocation of capital in the organization, centralized cash management, or the injection of
stronger management into a weak company may also be valid
reasons for conglomerate mergers. But in Japan, except in ex-
tremis, most of these functions have been adequately met by the
main bank serving a particular group's needs.

Finally, the use of takeovers as a device for replacing a wayward board of directors and disciplining self-serving management is also blunted by the Japanese corporate governance system. Historically, the tight monitoring of client companies by share-owning banks and their control over external funding left relatively little room for abusive self-interested opportunism by management. When such abuses did arise, they were apt to be fewer, less severe, and less costly to correct by selective intervention on the part of main banks rather than by expensive battles for majority control.

In short, current Japanese activity in the market for corporate control reflects the contracting milieu in which Japanese companies operate. A well-established corporate governance system allows Japanese companies to coalesce in large industrial groups that can at once realize many of the adaptive advantages of a centralized administrative hierarchy without sacrificing most of the advantages derived from harnessing the high-powered incentives of the market. Consequently, direct ownership and control over specific assets are less imperative, and combinations involving large companies are less frequent. When they do occur, they are likely to have government impetus or be at the insistence of a few major institutional shareholders such as main banks. Except among very small corporations, the players in the Japanese market for corporate control are few and highly circumscribed in their behavior.

# 5
# JAPANESE CORPORATIONS AS GLOBAL BIDDERS

The traditional Japanese corporate governance system has served to retard international acquisitions by Japanese companies. To a large extent, this reflects a Japanese preference for embracing others with a set of bilaterally self-enforcing contracts rather than owning and operating them outright. In this regard, large Japanese companies attempt to function abroad much the same as they do at home.

However, many of the foreign economic institutions with which they must transact are considerably different in terms of corporate governance and contracting practices. Implicit, relational contracting is less highly characteristic of the Western contracting environment, at least in the Anglo-American economies. Dispute resolution turns more frequently to actual or threatened litigation rather than to administrative intervention. The corporate governance system is more explicitly oriented around the interests of equity investors, which as a group are generally distinct from the other stakeholders of the firm. The Anglo-American market for corporate control itself is much more open and active, involving many potential bidders and targets that are less likely to have had long-term business relations with one another before combining.

Aided by the strong yen and driven by pressures to restructure strategically, Japanese companies have shown an increased willingness to hurdle the institutional gulf that separates them from the West. Not only has Japanese foreign direct investment shifted away from Asia toward the United States (which now absorbs nearly half of Japan's foreign direct investment, up from about a third) and Western Europe, it has also tilted toward out-right acquisition as a mode of investment. In particular, acquisitions in the United States have surged since 1985 (see Exhibit 5–1).

Without doubt this trend reflects the enormous bidding advantage created by the coincidence of high cash balances on Japanese balance sheets, the dramatic appreciation of the yen since 1985, and—for some companies—the ability to raise low-cost capital. But this represents only part of the story. In fact, given the strategic importance of the United States and Europe in today's global product markets, the rapid pace of mergers and acquisitions in both areas, and the tremendous bidding advantage held by Japanese companies, it is surprising to note the relative infrequency of their foreign acquisitions. In the United States, for example, Japanese corporations executed 132 U.S. M&A transactions of all types in 1988 at a total cost of $12.6 billion. This compares to 389 U.S. transactions by British companies in the same year for a total of $31.7 billion. Japan may yet become the largest foreign buyer of American companies, though such an eventuality is more apt to follow a decline in the buying activity of other countries rather than an explosion in Japanese activity. In 1989, for example, Japanese majority acquisitions of U.S. businesses rose about 10% and the announced dollar volume only 8%, with much of the latter coming from Sony's late-year purchase of Columbia Pictures.

To comprehend fully the reasons behind Japanese cross-border acquisitions, one must delve beneath national statistics. One has to study the phenomenon at the corporate level to appreciate the nuances that separate Japanese activity abroad from that of companies from other nations. Such an examination is provided here. I look at four prominent Japanese takeovers that occurred in the United States during the second half of the 1980s: Dainippon Ink and Chemicals' takeover of Reichhold Chemicals, Sony's acquisition of CBS Records, Bridgestone Corporation's successful tender offer for Firestone Tire & Rubber, and Nippon Mining Company's purchase of Gould, Inc. These Japanese bidders run the gamut from being highly traditional Japanese companies run by orthodox Japanese manage-

Exhibit 5-1  Japanese M&A Activity in the United States, 1984–1988

| | Total Number of Deals | Total Number of Deals Disclosing $ Amounts | Total Volume | Average | Median | Minimum | Maximum |
|---|---|---|---|---|---|---|---|
| **1984** | | | | | | | |
| AO | 17 | 13 | $ 1,117.4 | $ 85.9 | $ 6.4 | $ .25 | $ 425.0 |
| DV | 3 | 1 | 31.5 | 31.5 | 31.5 | 31.5 | 31.5 |
| IN | 18 | 12 | 231.3 | 19.3 | 2.0 | 1.0 | 189.2 |
| JV | 1 | 0 | NA | NA | NA | NA | NA |
| Totals | 39 | 26 | $ 1,380.2 | | | | |
| **1985** | | | | | | | |
| AO | 23 | 19 | $ 472.3 | $ 24.9 | $ 8.0 | $ 2.0 | $ 110.0 |
| DV | 5 | 4 | 27.8 | 7.0 | 8.3 | 1.3 | 10.0 |
| IN | 17 | 10 | 113.4 | 11.3 | 1.3 | .2 | 75.0 |
| JV | 0 | 0 | NA | NA | NA | NA | NA |
| Totals | 45 | 33 | $ 613.5 | | | | |
| **1986** | | | | | | | |
| AO | 40 | 36 | $ 1,023.6 | $ 28.4 | $ 5.7 | $ .25 | $ 263.0 |
| DV | 6 | 6 | 652.8 | 108.8 | 20.0 | 7.6 | 550.0 |
| IN | 22 | 15 | 704.2 | 46.9 | 5.0 | .2 | 500.0 |
| JV | 3 | 0 | NA | NA | NA | NA | NA |
| Totals | 71 | 57 | $ 2,380.6 | | | | |

Exhibit 5-1 *Japanese M&A Activity in the United States, 1984–1988 (continued)*

| | Total Number of Deals | Total Number of Deals Disclosing $ Amounts | Total Volume | Average | Median | Minimum | Maximum |
|---|---|---|---|---|---|---|---|
| **1987** | | | | | | | |
| AO | 41 | 22 | $ 877.8 | $ 39.9 | $10.9 | $ .5 | $ 540.7 |
| DV | 13 | 5 | 3,593.3 | 718.6 | 35.0 | 11.5 | 2,000.0 |
| IN | 37 | 28 | 1,999.7 | 71.4 | 5.0 | .25 | 508.3 |
| JV | 4 | 3 | 132.0 | 44.0 | 24.0 | 8.0 | 100.0 |
| Totals | 95 | 58 | $6,602.8 | | | | |
| **1988** | | | | | | | |
| AO | 76 | 49 | $10,087.0 | $205.9 | $37.0 | $ .5 | $2,600.0 |
| IN | 37 | 30 | 1,335.5 | 44.5 | 13.0 | 1.05 | 350.0 |
| JV | 2 | 0 | NA | NA | NA | NA | NA |
| DV | 17 | 15 | 1,233.9 | 82.3 | 30.0 | 4.0 | 325.0 |
| Totals | 132 | 94 | $12,641.9 | | | | |
| **1989** | | | | | | | |
| (January–May) | | | | | | | |
| AO | 80 | 63 | $10,554.5 | $167.5 | $19.0 | $ .2 | $3,400.0 |
| IN | 60 | 44 | 2,134.2 | 48.5 | 10.8 | .3 | 300.0 |
| JV | 8 | 3 | 15.7 | 5.2 | 7.1 | 1.5 | 12.5 |
| DV | 23 | 18 | 1,166.2 | 64.8 | 53.5 | 1.8 | 330.0 |
| Totals | 171 | 128 | $13,870.6 | | | | |

AO = Majority acquisition
DV = Purchase of a division
IN = Investment (under 50% ownership)
JV = Joint venture buyout
*Source:* Ulmer Brothers, Inc., 1989.

ment teams (Bridgestone, Nippon Mining) to less conformist companies led by independent-minded chief executives (Sony, Dainippon Ink and Chemicals). As a group, they also span a wide range of technologies, end markets (consumer versus industrial), and corporate strategies.

For all the differences among these Japanese companies, one finds a considerable degree of conformity in their overseas acquisitions. Not only are their foreign takeovers industrially rather than financially motivated, but they are stimulated to a considerable extent by a perceived need to defend vitally important strategic alliances forged over periods of years. I found that the threat of disruption to ongoing business relationships, most often because of an impending sale of the American company to some other bidder, triggered action by the Japanese to acquire the company outright. Having made its decision, the Japanese bidder generally moved forcefully and decisively to bring its target under control by offering selling shareholders deals they could not refuse. True to Japanese form, however, great care was always taken to preserve harmonious relations with all other stakeholders in the target corporation as well.


DAINIPPON INK AND CHEMICALS

Dainippon Ink and Chemicals (DIC) was one of the first Japanese companies to begin an acquisition program in the United States. Founded in 1908 as a small producer of printing inks, it diversified into a broad array of chemical products following World War II. Although its spheres of business activities now include biochemicals and building materials, printing inks, organic pigments, and synthetic resins still constitute the core businesses of the company.

Like many of today's thriving Japanese firms, Dainippon's modern success is rooted in early alliances with American companies capable of upgrading its product and production technology. As early as 1950, DIC acquired the technology for producing synthetic resins from Reichhold Chemicals Inc. of America. Reichhold also gave DIC an introduction to Sun Chemicals Inc., which supplied DIC with the necessary technology for mixing the synthetic resins with pigments to produce modern inks. Besides establishing DIC as a major producer of the latest high-quality printing inks in Japan, the technology transfer also launched synthetic resins, with many applications in adhesives, paints, textiles, and building materials, as an important new business leg for DIC.

DIC's current president, Shigekuni Kawamura, joined the company in 1959, after marrying the daughter of DIC's former president, Katsumi Kawamura. Prior to joining DIC, he was an officer of the Long-Term Credit Bank of Japan. Having lived in the United States as a child and graduated from New York University's Graduate School of Business, he is viewed by many in Japan as highly "Westernized."

Shigekuni Kawamura assumed the presidency in 1978, when DIC, like many other Japanese companies, was seeking new growth in offshore markets after reaching its maturity in Japan. Because of their chemistry, however, specialized inks and resins developed for use in high-speed offset printing equipment could not be transported long distances. Furthermore, to tailor new inks to the needs of printers, it was desirable to locate research and development activities as close to customers as possible. Consequently, Kawamura sought international growth by furthering an acquisition program that began with the purchase of a small U.S. ink producer in 1976, a smaller Indonesian producer in 1977, and a larger American producer in 1979. At the same time, DIC established a global network of chemicals suppliers, sales offices, and distribution points through joint ventures and other business relationships.

By the 1980s, rapidly evolving printing technology had led to a drastic change in the structure of the printing industry and the printing inks market. Computers stimulated the greatest change. Large, centralized systems integrated prepress operations, handling everything from typesetting to the presetting of ink levels to performance monitoring in the printing process itself. Meanwhile, personal computers and commonly available software facilitated desktop publishing of surprisingly high quality. Satellite transmission further revolutionized the production of newspapers and magazines, allowing centralized newsrooms to be connected with remote printing locations around the world. Major publications reach out to an increasingly sophisticated global market for English-language news and advertising with an increasingly sophisticated printed product; color has been added to their monotone pages.

Such advances have reshaped both the printing industry and the upstream vendors supplying it. Printing itself has become a global industry undergoing considerable consolidation internationally. Large printers are acquiring others around the world and investing heavily in the latest technology. This trend is concentrating electronic prepress and large-scale printing activities in a limited number of geographic locations determined in part by the proximity of satellite downlinks. Ink production has also become a more location-specific and more capital-intensive activity. High-quality and highly specialized inks are now required to accommodate the new digitized printing technologies. The limited transportability of these highly specialized inks and the importance of proximity to customers to stay abreast of their needs have made local production more essential than ever. Furthermore, advances in ink production technology, which now permit the direct, low-cost mixing of pigment slurry with resins, have required greater physical integration of production flow.

In short, technological advances in computers and telecommunications have made possible new products and markets in the publishing industry, which in turn have spawned the development of new, highly specialized inks, papers, and integrated printing processes. The coordinated development and supply of these interdependent products have been increasingly dominated by a few megavendors capable of keeping pace with the cutting edge of technological change.

DIC's billion-dollar overseas acquisition program is aimed at providing it with the location-specific assets needed to become such a megavendor. Acquiring the graphic arts division of Sun Chemicals for $550 million in 1986 represented its first major move in this direction. This division was the largest producer of inks in the United States and controlled 11 production facilities and 36 sales points throughout the country. Kawamura had long

been interested in both Sun's graphic arts division and the Inmont Corporation as potential targets that would permit expansion in the United States, but considered them too expensive to
acquire in the late 1970s and early 1980s.

Inmont's sudden acquisition by BASF AG of West Germany
in 1985 increased Kawamura's sense of urgency, however, since
a competitor's acquisition of Sun Chemicals could effectively
pre-empt DIC's ability to expand quickly in the rapidly consolidating North American market. Negotiations to sell the division
deadlocked over a $175 million difference between DIC's $425
million bid for the division and Sun's $600 million asking price.
Kawamura's fear of losing the graphic arts operation led him to
tender for all of Sun Chemicals for $600 million as a means of
securing the one division. The bid was blocked when Sun's principal family shareholders increased their holdings to more than
50% of the outstanding shares. A 36% depreciation of the dollar
against the yen coupled with an 8% concession in the asking
price by Sun helped make a sale of the division possible by late
1986.

The deal with Sun Chemicals was followed by the acquisition
of Reichhold Chemicals in the summer of 1987. Reichhold was
a producer of adhesives and resins used in ink production. It had
earlier business dealings with both Sun Chemicals and DIC.
DIC's management considered its resin production to be out-
moded but easily upgradable with DIC's technology. Its addition
to DIC's U.S. operations would permit vertical integration of the
ink operations acquired from Sun, which was not self-sufficient
in the production of synthetic resins. Moreover, Reichhold
would bring to DIC's North American operations some very attractive plant locations in the Northeast near established satellite downlink stations and major printed media markets.

But as in the earlier deal with Sun, Reichhold's management
was in no mood to recommend a sale to DIC. Following the retirement of its founder in 1982, Reichhold's board recruited new
management outside the company to convert it from a volume-
driven, commodity chemicals company to a profit-driven, specialty chemicals company.

The new team undertook an extensive restructuring that entailed the closing or sale of 21 operations, reducing sales from roughly $1 billion annually to $800 million. Although improved performance elevated the stock price from $11 per share to $43 in early 1985, disappointing performance thereafter reduced expectations of further improvement and caused the price to settle in the $28 to $38 range in 1986. Nevertheless, management (which owned 10% of the common stock) remained bullish on the company's future prospects, as did some industry analysts.[1] Expectations for the future were brightened in part by a possible joint venture combining Reichhold's resin production with that of Hercules. In principle, the combination would permit large-scale, low-cost production of resins using the latest processing technologies, and would allow the pursuit of new markets in inks and papers.

Kawamura opened negotiations with Reichhold with a bid of $42.50 per share at a point when Reichhold's stock traded in the open market for $38. With the advice of Dillon, Read, Reichhold countered with an offer to sell at $80 per share. DIC's response was to drop its initial offer and tender publicly for 100% of the stock at $52.50 per share.

Reichhold's board immediately engaged First Boston to defend it and recommended against the tender, arguing that the stock was worth at least $70 per share. Meanwhile, it sought other bidders in the United States and abroad but found no one willing to pay substantially more for the company. Another foreign buyer was rumored to be interested at a price of $65 per share, but conditional on the results of further inspections and discussions with Reichhold's management. A management buyout and a breakup and piecemeal sale of parts of the company were also said to be under active consideration by Reichhold's board of directors.

Fearing loss of the company to another bidder or the sale of

---

1. Prudential-Bache Securities Inc. rated the stock a "buy" and stipulated $60 as a long-term target price (L. Bosner, "Reichhold Chemicals—Company Report." Prudential-Bache Securities Inc., March 13, 1987).

the resin operations to a competitor, and also wishing to salvage at least the semblance of a friendly combination that would help keep American management in place, Kawamura agreed to sweeten DIC's offer to $60 a share just before it was to expire. Satisfied with the value offered and seeing no alternative bidders, Reichhold's board voted to support the bid at this level.


SONY CORPORATION

On October 28, 1987—just days after the Black Monday stock market crash—it was reported that CBS would soon announce the sale of its long-treasured CBS Records division to the Japanese consumer electronics corporation, Sony.[2] At the colossal price of $2 billion, the sale then represented the largest cross-border acquisition by a Japanese company in America (see Exhibit 5–2 for a list of major Japanese acquisitions in the United States). Because it involved the sale of a unit virtually synonymous with modern American music and culture, a unit once thought to be an untouchable legacy of CBS, the deal was all the more startling to many Americans.

In 1986, Laurence Tisch, a major stockholder of CBS who had become concerned about the company's languishing performance, took active control of CBS's operations. Cost-conscious and strategically conservative, he sought to reduce expenses and refocus the company on what he saw as its core business of broadcasting. The 1986 sale of its music publishing unit, CBS Songs, seemed to signal CBS's willingness to divest businesses. Triangle Industries responded by inquiring about CBS's willingness to sell its record company as well. The Walt Disney Company also expressed some interest. To the surprise of many, not least of whom was CBS Records' head Walter Yetnikoff, an offering price of $1.25 billion and a closing before the end of 1986 were fixed as terms for a possible sale. The high asking price caused Triangle to balk and study the deal further.

Meanwhile, fearing loss of control and jobs at CBS Records,

---

2. The sale was formally announced on November 18, 1987.

Exhibit 5-2 *Major Japanese Majority Acquisitions in the United States*

| Date | Japanese Acquirer/Investor | U.S. Acquisition/Investment | Amount ($ million) |
|------|----------------------------|-----------------------------|---------------------|
| | | A. Nonfinancial Corporations | |
| 12/86 | Dainippon Ink and Chemicals, Inc. | Graphic Arts Material Division (Sun Chemicals Corp.) | 550.0 |
| 8/87 | Dainippon Ink and Chemicals, Inc. | Reichhold Chemicals Inc. | 540.0 |
| 10/87 | Aoki/Bass Corp. | Westin Hotel and Resorts (Allegis Corp.) | 1,530.0 |
| 11/87 | Sony Corp. | CBS Records, Inc. (CBS, Inc.) | 2,000.0 |
| 3/88 | Bridgestone Corp. | Firestone Tire & Rubber Co. | 2,600.0 |
| 4/88 | Paloma Industries, Ltd. | PACE Industries, Inc. (Rheem Manufacturing Co.) | 820.0 |
| 9/88 | Seibu/Saison Group | International Hotel (Grand Metropolitan) | 2,300.0 |
| 9/88 | Nippon Mining Co., Ltd. | Gould, Inc. | 1,100.0 |
| 9/88 | Settsu Corp. | UARCO Inc. (Printing Holdings, L.P.) | 400.0(E) |
| 9/89 | The Dai-Ichi Kangyo Bank, Ltd. [a] | CIT Group (Manufacturers Hanover) | 1,280.0 |
| 9/89 | The Daiwa Bank, Ltd. | U.S. Commercial Banking Division (Lloyds Bank, plc.) | 1,646.0 |
| 2/89 | Hitachi, Ltd. | National Advanced Systems (National Semiconductors) | 398.0 |
| 3/89 | Yamanouchi Pharmaceutical Co., Ltd. | Shaklee Corp. | 395.0 |
| 7/89 | Kyocera Corp. | Elco Corp. (Wickes Companies, Inc.) | 250.0 |

Exhibit 5-2 *Major Japanese Majority Acquisitions in the United States (continued)*

| Date | Japanese Acquirer/Investor | U.S. Acquisition/Investment | Amount ($ million) |
|---|---|---|---|
| | | *A. Nonfinancial Corporations* | |
| 9/89 | Sony Corp. | Columbia Pictures | 3,400.0 |
| 9/89 | Sony Corp. | Guber-Peters Entertainment Co. | 270.0 |
| 9/89 | Secom Co., Ltd. | HMSS Inc. | 250.0 |
| 10/89 | Mitsubishi Estate Co., Ltd. | Rockefeller Group | 846.0 |
| | | *B. Financial Corporations* | |
| 1/84 | The Fuji Bank, Ltd. | Walter E. Heller & Co. | 425.0 |
| 6/84 | The Mitsubishi Bank, Ltd. | Bancal Tri-State Corp. (holding company for Bank of California) | 282.0 |
| 2/86 | The Sanwa Bank, Ltd. | Lloyds Bank of California | 263.0 |
| 11/86 | The Sumitomo Bank, Ltd. | Goldman Sachs | 500.0 |
| 12/86 | IBJ Schroder Bank & Trust | Aubrey G. Lanston & Co. | 234.0 |
| 4/87 | Nippon Life Insurance | Shearson Lehman Brothers (unit of American Express Co.) | 538.0 |
| 12/87 | Yasuda Mutual Life Insurance | PaineWebber Group Inc. | 300.0 |
| 2/88 | The Bank of Tokyo, Ltd. | Union Bank (Standard Chartered PLC) | 750.0 |
| | (California First Bank) | | |
| 9/89 | The Dai-Ichi Kangyo Bank, Ltd.[a] | CIT Group (Manufacturers Hanover) | 1,280.0 |
| 9/89 | The Daiwa Bank, Ltd. | U.S. Commercial Banking Division (Lloyds Bank, plc.) | 1,646.0 |

[a]At the same time, DKB also made a minority investment in Manufacturers Hanover for $120 million.
*Source:* Ulmer Brothers, Inc, 1987–1989.

management of the subsidiary began to structure a leveraged buyout of the unit for the announced offering price. When this appeared impossible, it called Sony to see if Sony might be interested in the deal at the same price, conditioned on an agreement to keep management in place.

The solicitation was far from a shot in the dark. Sony and CBS had been partners in a joint venture in Tokyo, CBS/Sony Group, Inc., formed in 1967 to manufacture and sell phonograph records and music tapes. The agreement was reached through direct negotiations between Sony's chairman, Akio Morita, and CBS's Paley, and was drafted by Yetnikoff, then a lawyer in CBS Records' executive ranks. From the two chief executives downward, management of the two companies reportedly regarded each other with mutual warmth and respect.[3]

But it was not for old times' sake that Sony was potentially interested in the combination. The joint venture in Tokyo had been enormously successful, generating pretax profits estimated at ¥12.5 billion on sales of ¥63 billion in 1987. Also, like many large Japanese companies, its value was further elevated by valuable real estate holdings in Tokyo. Any changes in the key people managing its partner in this venture could result in considerable haggling over the future disposition of these valuable assets and cash flows. Sony had already had one scare thrown into it when just prior to Tisch taking control, Ted Turner emerged as a potential suitor for CBS.

Of equal or greater concern, however, was the impact that a change of ownership at CBS Records might have on one of Sony's most valuable options for future growth, its digital audio tape (DAT) recorder. DAT is a computerized system for recording sounds with nearly flawless accuracy. Like the Betamax videotape player before it, DAT represents a truly superior advance in mass-marketed recording technology. But also like the Betamax, its commercial success will depend upon the ready availability of compatible software (movies in the case of Betamax; musical recordings in the case of DAT) to use with the hardware. The

3. Pet J. Boyer, "Sony and CBS Records: What A Romance!" *The New York Times Magazine*, September 18, 1988, p. 38.

Betamax failed as a commercial product because of Sony's inability to control the production of videotaped movies in a format compatible with its unique technology. A similar fate might await DAT if owners of musical recording copyrights could not be persuaded to produce DAT-compatible products.

This is no mean task in view of the hardware's superior recording ability, which could potentially result in a proliferation of homemade recordings that would eventually cut into record sales and profits. Even CBS Records, for all its good relations with Sony, was understandably reluctant to support DAT technology given CBS's library of recordings. Once available in DAT-compatible format, this library, to some extent, would take on the attributes of an asset specifically dedicated to the support of DAT sales; most of the benefits would accrue to the hardware, not the software, producer. Given such an outcome, the incentive for Sony to own and control a record company, CBS Records in particular, becomes quite clear.

Not surprisingly, Sony responded quickly and favorably to CBS Records' overtures, agreeing to the basic terms of the deal within 20 minutes of the proposal.[4] Dissent among CBS board members over the proposed sale subsequently scotched the deal, but the company was now in play. Sony again sought greater control over the company by suggesting a widening of the scope of their joint venture to include all of CBS Records. Later, when Tisch began to push once again for an outright sale, Sony agreed to a larger asking price of $2 billion. At roughly the same time, for tax reasons, the CBS board began to consider seriously spinning off CBS Records and selling its stock in the company. Ultimately, the October 1987 stock market crash killed talk of a spinoff and made the offer on the table look better than ever. The deal was done at $2 billion.

Roughly two years later, Sony outdid itself with the purchase of another American cultural icon, Columbia Pictures, for $3.45 billion. Like the acquisition of CBS Records, the Columbia deal was strategically motivated. Again, vertical integration into entertainment software (Columbia's vast library of 2,700 films and 23,000 television shows) that could be combined with Sony's

---

4. Ibid., p. 40.

video hardware (8mm video recorders and laser disks) was the attraction. Sony's planners believed they could learn more about the future of home entertainment hardware sales if they knew more firsthand about consumer demand for the software. Further synergies were envisioned longer term through an eventual convergence of audio and video technology.

Unlike the CBS Records deal, however, the Columbia deal was not preceded by a long history of business relations between the buying and selling companies. Not surprisingly, therefore, negotiations with Columbia's principal owners (Coca-Cola and Columbia's own management together controlled 54% of the stock) progressed rather differently in this case. Despite persistent rumors of other interested buyers in the wings, Sony haggled over price for more than a year before an agreement was reached in September 1989. The 28% premium Sony paid for Columbia, while substantial, was ultimately well below the 60% premium it paid over CBS's original asking price for its record division, and below the 50–60% premiums being paid by other Japanese buyers for American targets like Reichhold Chemicals, Firestone Tire & Rubber, and Gould, Inc.


BRIDGESTONE CORPORATION

The second-largest Japanese acquisition of an American industrial firm took place in March 1988. Bridgestone Corporation, Japan's largest tire company, announced that it had acquired Firestone Tire & Rubber Company, the third-largest tire maker in the United States, for a price of $2.6 billion. Prior to this acquisition, Bridgestone had only a minor presence in the U.S. and European tire markets, although it controlled 50% of the market in Japan. The combination did not change Bridgestone's overall ranking as the world's third-largest tire company behind Goodyear and Michelin. But it did raise Bridgestone's share of the global tire market to within a few percentage points of its two larger rivals. The Japanese company also used the occasion of the acquisition to announce its intentions of becoming the largest tire and rubber company in the world.

Measured in dollars, the global market for tires totaled about

$34 billion in 1986. The largest single national market was that of the United States, which accounted for 38% of worldwide tire demand in that year, followed by Japan (14%), West Germany (7.5%), France (5.4%), and the United Kingdom (4.3%). Concentration in the industry had been increasing steadily throughout the 1980s until, by 1986, the 10 largest producers (which included four Japanese companies) accounted for 84% of worldwide sales.

The industry had also become increasingly globalized in the wake of the globalization of the automobile industry and Michelin's 1975 investment in a U.S. factory to supply the North American market with steel-belted radial tires. That product innovation had a profound effect on consumer demand for tires because the longer-lasting radials required less-frequent replacement than did bias-ply tires. Coincident with these developments were the oil shocks of the 1970s, problems with labor relations among the North American producers, and a change in retail tire distribution away from automobile dealers and service stations to price-oriented tire stores and independent dealers. The upshot of these trends was essentially no volume growth between 1978 and 1987, squeezed margins, and heightened competition internationally as major producers sought sufficient volume to remain profitable.

Virtually all major producers attempted to restructure themselves in this period by narrowing tire product lines, closing plants, establishing joint ventures with other producers, entering into a variety of supply-sales-distribution agreements with auto producers, and embarking on diversification programs. Prodded by corporate raiders such as Carl Icahn and Sir James Goldsmith, all of Firestone's American-based competitors were eventually forced to defend themselves from takeover by either repurchasing stock financed with new debt and cash from divestitures (Goodyear's response) or combining tire operations with another competitor (the approach taken by Goodrich, Uniroyal, and General Tire).

As with other competitors, Firestone's sale to Bridgestone capped an extensive period of restructuring that had begun in 1980 under the stewardship of Firestone's then-new CEO, John

Nevin (the first nonfamily chief of the company since its founding in 1900). Nevin's plan for Firestone was to reduce corporate debt and improve the profitability of tire operations while reducing overall dependence on tires through diversification into products compatible with Firestone's basic rubber technology. With respect to tire operations, Nevin specifically sought to withdraw from the production of truck and off-road radial tires and reorient the firm toward retail sales in the tire replacement market. Thus Firestone closed or sold 13 of its North American plants. By 1987, tires for passenger cars were being produced at only four locations in the United States, and capacity was slightly more than one-third of the 1979 level. Firestone's work force was reduced from 110,000 in 1979 to 55,000 by 1987. Revenues declined from $5.3 billion to $3.8 billion in the same period. Worldwide, however, Firestone continued to operate profitable manufacturing facilities in Europe (sales volume, 15 million units) and South America (10 million units). Its chain of retail outlets was also strengthened to a level of 1,506 by acquiring or building more than a thousand new stores and closing several hundred with poor locations.

As part of the restructuring process, Nevin initiated discussions with several foreign tire producers concerning the advantages of a joint venture for tire production in North America. Bridgestone was among the first of those contacted, having successfully negotiated the purchase of Firestone's radial truck tire plant in La Vergne, Tennessee, for $52 million in 1982.[5] Bridgestone subsequently invested about $100 million to improve the facility and entered into an agreement to supply truck radial tires to Firestone's retail outlets.

Talks with Bridgestone continued sporadically over the next few years because opinion among Bridgestone's senior managers was split. Some felt that Bridgestone's best option for entering the U.S. market in greater volume was to build a new plant once export volume justified it. Others argued that such volume (estimated to be about 8–9 million units annually) could not be

---

5. In arranging the plant's sale, Nevin was introduced to Akira Yeiri, president of Bridgestone, by Akio Morita of Sony.

achieved on an export basis. Demand for passenger tires from auto assemblers, Bridgestone's traditional strength in the tire market, was heavily influenced by the physical proximity of tire plants to assembly locations.

As consolidation of the industry in North America quickened in 1986 and 1987, opportunities for foreign producers to obtain attractive plant locations without building expensive new capacity in an industry already burdened with overcapacity began to diminish. The Pirelli group of Italy, another major tire manufacturer without a U.S. production base, was thought to be interested in Firestone and to have approached the company. At this juncture, the impasse at Bridgestone was resolved in favor of those seeking immediate direct investment in the United States. In early 1988, Bridgestone's president, Akira Yeiri, met with Nevin to discuss the sale of Firestone's U.S. manufacturing facilities.

The deal originally cut was one in which Firestone would place all its tire production assets (including overseas facilities) in a joint venture to be owned 75% by Bridgestone and 25% by Firestone. Bridgestone would pay Firestone $750 million for its interest in the venture. In addition, Firestone would receive the proceeds of a $500 million loan to be taken out by the new venture using its assets (with a book value of $1.5 billion) as collateral. Firestone, meanwhile, would retain ownership and control over its retail network, which would continue to be supplied with tires from the new venture. After paying taxes and funding some employee benefit plans, Firestone intended to distribute approximately $1 billion of the proceeds to shareholders through either a share repurchase or a special dividend.

The new venture between Bridgestone and Firestone was announced on February 16, 1988. Less than three weeks later, on March 6, Pirelli launched a cash tender offer of $58 per share for all of Firestone's 32 million outstanding shares (a total purchase price of about $1.85 billion). The price offered Firestone's shareholders a fairly typical 16% premium over market values. Pirelli also announced that on acquiring Firestone, it intended to sell the retail stores, a Brazilian facility, and certain other nontire operations to Michelin of France for $800 million. Firestone's share price, which had risen to about $50 following the announcement of the joint venture, soared to $63.125 on news of the Pirelli bid.

Although Pirelli offered to discuss alternative terms directly with Firestone's management, Firestone negotiated only with Bridgestone subsequent to the Pirelli bid. On March 17, Bridgestone astonished the financial community by announcing an $80 per-share offer to buy all the common stock of Firestone for a total price of $2.56 billion. At this level, Bridgestone was topping Pirelli's bid by 38% and giving Firestone's shareholders a fantastic 60% premium over pre-tender-offer market prices! Yeiri also stated publicly that Bridgestone would seek to improve the productivity of Firestone's operations but had no plans to close plants, cut employment, or replace management. Decision making for the U.S. market would be left to Firestone.[6] Declaring the offer to be unreasonable, Pirelli abruptly dropped its bid for Firestone. (A month later, Pirelli successfully negotiated the purchase of Armstrong Tire Company from Armtek Corporation for $190 million.)

## NIPPON MINING COMPANY, LTD.

In late August 1988, Nippon Mining Company announced it had agreed to buy Gould, Inc., a diversified but troubled electronics and computer firm, for approximately $1.1 billion. Following the Sony-CBS Records and Bridgestone-Firestone deals, it represented the third-largest Japanese acquisition of an American company. At $23.25 a share, the purchase price represented a substantial 50% premium over Gould's market value. Stock analysts described it as being "on the high side" of expectations for a company in Gould's condition. Nippon Mining countered by observing that the acquisition was motivated "industrially," not financially. The Japanese bidder said that Gould's people and products would allow it to expand in a number of businesses important to its long-run future: copper foil, circuit protectors, and optical electronic components.

---

6. Carla Rappaport, "Japanese Tyre Maker Aims to Become World's Largest," *Financial Times*, May 14, 1988, p. 1.

Earlier in the 1980s, Nippon Mining began a program of diversification to diminish its dependence on its historical base in oil refining and the extraction of base metals. Prior to the Gould acquisition, however, its very gradual approach kept it highly dependent on these two lines of business. Petroleum products accounted for 65% of sales and base metals for 25%. Specialty metals and electronics, the areas to be strengthened by the Gould purchase, accounted for only 3%. The Gould acquisition represented a deliberate attempt by Nippon Mining to preserve its program of change.

From Nippon Mining's point of view, the most interesting piece of Gould was the copper foil business.[7] Used in circuit boards for electronics products of all types, copper foil is an obscure but highly profitable niche in the high-tech field. Gould and the Square D Company were two of the major players in the business, controlling 80% of the world market between them. Analysts estimated that copper foil alone would generate 30% of Gould's $920 million sales expected for 1988, but 75% of its $40 million anticipated profit.

Gould had been undergoing a restructuring since 1967, when William Ylvisaker became chairman of the board. At that time, Gould was a medium-sized manufacturer of batteries, a business that it began in 1910. During his tenure as board chairman, which ended in September 1986, Ylvisaker oversaw more than 60 acquisitions and 70 divestitures. His goal was to transform Gould from a rust-belt industrial manufacturer of batteries into a diversified high-technology concern in the rapidly growing computer and defense industries. By 1983, three-quarters of the company's $1.3 billion in sales and almost all of its $80 million in earnings were derived from advanced electronics products.

Problems began to surface soon thereafter. A prolonged slump in the semiconductor business, the winning of a vastly underbid fixed-price contract to develop a new naval radio, ag-

---

7. In the final agreement, Nippon Mining was granted an option to buy Gould's 50% interest in the two companies' copper foil joint venture for $60 million in the event of a change of control in Gould—a hedge, perhaps, against the possibility that the U.S. government might subsequently reverse the deal for national defense reasons such as were raised in connection with Fujitsu's offer to acquire Fairchild Semiconductor in 1985.

gressive price cutting by competitors in the super-minicomputer business, and the souring of a Florida real estate venture combined to turn the company's fortunes around. Having disposed of the dull but steadily profitable and high cash-generating batteries business, Gould lacked the financial strength to maintain its competitive position in cyclical high-tech markets. By 1985, large write-offs and other charges resulted in a net loss of $175.5 million for the year.

In 1986, James F. McDonald left IBM to become Gould's new CEO and later its chairman. He immediately put into motion another restructuring program, which involved the sales and/or write-off of a number of businesses in which Gould was no longer competitive. Management turnover was extensive. Twenty-two relatively autonomous businesses were reorganized into four tightly focused and more centrally managed divisions. By 1987, total sales were reduced to less than half their 1980 peak of $2.2 billion.

The cash generated from the restructuring helped ensure Gould's near-term survival, but not necessarily its independence. Despite a strengthened balance sheet and a rebound in the semiconductor industry, Gould's stock price continued to trade in the $10 to $20 per-share range throughout early 1988, well below its 1983 high of $43.75. Earlier, Siemens AG of West Germany and Westinghouse of the United States had expressed some interest in purchasing the company, but were reportedly deterred by the magnitude of the problems facing Gould and the sheer difficulty in valuing such a complex company that had restated earnings in five of the previous seven years. Gould's management had tried to engineer a buyout of the company, but failed to arrange the necessary financing. With the collapse of the management buyout proposal, Gould's improved outlook but low stock price made it look again like a prime candidate for a hostile takeover. At this juncture McDonald initiated discussions with Nippon Mining concerning arrangements that might defend Gould from such an outcome.

Management at Gould and Nippon Mining had been getting acquainted for some time. Long and protracted discussions had been initiated nearly 20 years before, when Nippon Mining sought out Gould to discuss the possibility of a joint venture in

Japan to produce copper foil. Nippon Mining had done some research and development in the electronics field, but had no commercial applications. For its part, Gould was having difficulty exporting to Japan. In 1981, they finally came to an understanding and formed a joint venture in Japan to make copper foil for printed-circuit boards. After a rocky start punctuated by some sharp disputes regarding the quality of the product coming from America and the timeliness of delivery, the venture began making money and dominating the market in Japan. A spirit of mutual trust and cooperation characterized the business relations between the two companies thereafter.

The pace of cooperation between them quickened in the mid-1980s as Gould's financial performance declined and Nippon Mining's diversification efforts picked up steam. In 1985, Nippon Mining began importing and marketing Gould fiber-optic components. In April 1988, the two companies set up a joint venture to make copper foil in Hong Kong and in July established another joint venture to sell Gould's super-minicomputers in Japan.

Gould's technology had become vital to Nippon Mining's future, yet Gould's future as an independent corporation seemed very much in doubt. This was of great concern to Nippon Mining's top management, for it had taken years to nurture the relationships and agreements that now existed between the two companies. The possibility of backsliding in the event new owners took control of Gould, or perhaps even outright recontracting of their various agreements, was judged too costly to tolerate. Consequently, a top-level decision was made to explore the possibility of acquiring Gould.

Although large parts of Gould were already quite familiar to Nippon Mining, other parts, particularly the computer and defense-related businesses were not. Months of analysis concerning Gould's products, facilities, competitors, and clients preceded Nippon Mining's final decision to acquire the company. According to Peter Rona, chief executive of the IBJ Schroder Bank & Trust Company (advisers in the deal to Nippon Mining), employees at all levels of Nippon Mining were involved in the vetting process, as were three or four layers of management at Gould. Nippon Mining people would approach their counterparts at Gould directly to obtain answers to questions. As a result, said Rona, "there was not so much of a negotiating game" when the price was finally fixed. Confident in what it was buying and wishing to avoid the disruption of a last-minute bidder appearing on the scene, Nippon Mining felt comfortable offering a price at the upper end of its value range for Gould and sticking with it.

## INDUSTRIAL "WHITE SAMURAI"

The combinations I have examined in this chapter are among the most important and highly publicized deals involving Japanese bidders and U.S. targets. In a number of respects, they are also atypical. Their sizes are unusually large. The more common deals are much smaller, although their average and median size has increased since 1984 (see Exhibit 5-1). The four Japanese bidders discussed here are reasonably well-known names in the United States, whereas in fact most combinations involve Japanese bidders large enough to be listed on the Tokyo Stock Exchange, but generally unknown outside Japan. Two of the four large deals were contested, but most U.S. acquisitions by Japanese companies are uncontested. Finally, in three of the four cases, the management of the Japanese bidders was led by prominent chief executives who controlled stock in their company and had strong personal influence on decision making (DIC and Sony), or who continued to have substantial stock ownership by the founding family (Bridgestone). Only Nippon Mining was a nucleus company in an industrial group (the Kyodo Oil group).

But despite these differences, the cases collectively provide an accurate picture of Japanese motives and tactics in recent cross-border acquisitions. Certainly, one thing these large deals have in common with the smaller mainstream is that they were not primarily financially driven deals, that is, they were not motivated by an opportunity to buy undervalued assets and resell them at a profit, to leverage up an underleveraged company, or to secure a cash flow to finance other investments on cheaper terms than might be available from capital markets. Instead, they were strategically motivated combinations in which target-company management as well as shareholders stood to gain.

The Japanese buyers were not conventional white knights, however, seizing opportunity in another company's adversity. With motives rooted in traditional Japanese methods of corporate governance, they might be more aptly differentiated with the epithet "white samurai" who moved decisively to defend strategically important assets that could not easily be replaced by new investment or a contractual relationship with another party. In all four cases reviewed here, the takeovers were triggered by a threat—specifically, acquisition by another bidder—to the existing ownership and management of those assets. In three of the four cases, the assets in question were part of an important strategic alliance between Japanese and American companies in which valuable trust relationships had been forged through years of interaction. In the fourth case, DIC's takeover of Reichhold Chemicals, it was critical location-specific assets in northeastern United States that were at stake.

Much more so than the present-day domestic M&A deal flow in Japan, foreign acquisitions by Japanese companies are driven by the economic pressures impinging on the Japanese economy. They are an outward reflection of the restructuring process taking place in many Japanese industries. Clearly, individual strategies differ among these companies, as one would expect, given their individual circumstances and unique corporate attributes. Nippon Mining, for example, is a mature Japanese industrial corporation that found itself trapped in stagnant product markets. Its acquisition of Gould reflects a common strategy pursued by many such companies to break out of their markets through unrelated diversification. This strategy had been put into motion long before the acquisition through a series of high-tech joint ventures with Gould, at least one of which (copper foil) had proven to be enormously successful. But Gould's weak overall financial condition, coupled with ownership of one valuable jewel, undoubtedly made it a potential target for other bidders and thus threatened Nippon Mining's promising relationship with it. By acquiring Gould, Nippon Mining acted defensively to protect the relationship and consolidate its control over some valuable growth opportunities in the U.S. electronic parts market.

For its part, Sony felt compelled to undertake a kind of vertical integration by gaining direct control over audio software (records, tapes, and compact disks) and the human capital that produced it (musical performers under contract with CBS Records) in order to enhance the commercial viability of its digital audio tape recorder. A similar motive underlay its acquisition of Columbia Pictures. A licensing agreement linking Sony's hardware with CBS Records' software could have enabled Sony to establish its new product. But writing up a contract that would protect and reward both parties adequately under all possible contingencies would have been difficult. Only one thing seemed clear: the immediate impact of such a marketing linkage would work to Sony's great advantage and to CBS Records' disadvantage as DAT recordings by consumers substituted for retail purchases of records, tapes, and disks.

Presumably, Sony could have compensated CBS for the lost sales as well as shared some of the profits from the enhanced sales of DAT recording systems. But the difficulty of measuring either would have confounded attempts to be fair, which would have been critical to the ongoing success of the agreement. Even with fairness, powerful incentives for either party to recontract in its favor or pull out of the agreement could emerge if, ex post, it appeared that the technology might founder without CBS Records' continued support or, alternatively, its tremendous success obviated Sony's need for CBS. The trust that existed between Sony and CBS Records might have been relied on to minimize such haggling and opportunistic behavior, but even that might be lost if CBS Records came under new ownership. Thus, once it became apparent that the record division was in play, Sony, like Nippon Mining, had little choice but to acquire the division if it wished to preserve the transacting relationship.

Bridgestone's cross-border acquisition arose because it found itself in a market with little new growth as tire longevity increased and Japanese auto manufacturers moved plants offshore. Like tire manufacturers around the world, it had to begin competing globally or face the long-run prospects of being a marginal player in the industry. Firestone, with its strong market positions in North America, South America, and Europe, would allow it to do just that. Its established retail network of 1,500 stores would also provide Bridgestone with new growth opportunities in the North American retail market that would complement its OEM focus.

Consistent with the Japanese style of corporate governance, Bridgestone originally sought to control directly only those Firestone assets that had a high degree of specificity to them—local manufacturing facilities with proximity to OEMs—and to rely on arm's-length transactions with its partner so far as the use of the retail stores was concerned. As in the Japanese industrial group, the latter approach to governing the use of the retail stores exploits the sorts of high-powered market incentives that accompany asset ownership. Presumably, Bridgestone would rely on the knowledge, trust, and understanding that it had established with Firestone over the years and expected to continue in the future to adapt the agreements between the two companies as circumstances changed. The same sort of history and buildup of trust clearly did not exist between Bridgestone and Pirelli, making Pirelli an unsuitable stakeholder in the manufacturing joint venture with Firestone. That, along with the threatened immediate loss of the retail stores to Michelin, forced Bridgestone's hand in undertaking a complete acquisition of Firestone.

DIC's story is similar to Bridgestone's in many respects except that rapid change in printing technology, rather than demand stagnation, is globalizing the industry. The new technology, particularly with respect to satellite transmission of digital color images, creates significant cost advantages for printing ink manufacturers that are vertically integrated at, or near, satellite downlinks. Hence we see the importance of acquiring specific assets in specific locations (versus simply procuring the needed inputs from existing vendors in the production chain) and acquiring them quickly before being pre-empted by competitors. Although DIC's willingness to wrest control of these assets from unwilling hands is probably partly explained by the somewhat Western orientation of its chairman, it is also consistent with strategic imperatives imposed on it by the changing industry.

Despite the different motives underlying each deal, all share the property that future growth and profitability depended on having a degree of administrative control over assets that were highly specific as to location, physical attribute, dedication of use, or personal ownership, or to which particularly valuable growth opportunities were uniquely attached. This necessitated having either direct ownership of those assets or, at the very least, continuity in the assets' owners and managers so that trust relationships and essential agreements between the transacting parties could be suitably adapted to evolving market conditions at relatively low cost. The contractual frame of reference in Japan predisposes Japanese bidders for the latter approach, but this can be difficult to preserve in an active and often hostile market for corporate control. Significantly, in each of these cases, the real or perceived threat of a change in the ownership and control of the target company, with the implied loss of a valuable trading relationship, prompted the Japanese bidder to eschew its traditional preference for arm's-length transacting with selective intervention in favor of outright ownership.

Impending financial distress on the part of a foreign strategic ally can trigger the same response. Consider, for example, Ito-Yokado Company's 1990 agreement to purchase 75% of Southland Corporation in the United States for $400 million when the latter risked defaulting on its $1.8 billion of debt (the agreement was contingent on Southland's ability to restructure that debt). Southland is the owner of the 7-Eleven convenience store chain. Ito-Yokado became its partner in the creation of the Seven-Eleven Japan Company in 1973, which was organized to introduce and manage the 7-Eleven store chain in Japan.

Left to their own devices and allowed to contract at will in their own way, Japanese companies will combine with others only slowly, if at all. The process of combining will often begin years in advance with production or marketing agreements between the two companies, followed by partnership in a joint venture and/or, eventually, a toehold equity position taken by the Japanese company in its foreign partner. In this seasoning period, a considerable amount of trust building and implicit contracting will set the stage for a friendly combination later, if necessary. The combination will take place if and when competitive pressures, coupled with the threatened change in ownership of the foreign partner, dictate such a move.

This is precisely what happened, for example, in the acquisition of International Computers Ltd. (ICL) of the United Kingdom by Fujitsu, announced in July 1990. ICL has been a major purchaser of semiconductors from Fujitsu since 1983. The two companies have also operated under a technology-sharing agreement involving ICL's mainframe computers since 1981. Although ICL was profitable in 1990, profits were shrinking and cash flow was under pressure. Rising R&D expenses, growing capital expenditures, and burgeoning competition from a host of European and American competitors called into question ICL's long-term survival as a wholly owned subsidiary of STC PLC in Britain. Discussion of a plan to combine ICL with Nixdorf of Germany and Olivetti & Co. of Italy, which has a strategic alliance with Hitachi, helped trigger a decision by Fujitsu to buy an 80% stake in its British customer for ¥743 million (approximately $1.35 billion).

Western companies finding themselves the target of an unsolicited bid may find a white knight in a Japanese company. But this role is unlikely to be a mercenary one motivated simply by idle liquidity and the prospects of striking a quick, financially advantageous deal. Instead, the Japanese company's willingness to play this role will depend more on strategic fit and, just as important, relationship preservation. Should it choose to rescue a foreign company from an unsolicited bid (e.g., Bridgestone-Firestone) or simply deem it necessary to acquire its foreign associate for strategic purposes (e.g., DIC-Reichhold Chemicals), the Japanese bidder can behave quite aggressively to secure its target. Indeed, the evidence so far indicates that the Japanese buyer is unlikely to engage in auction-like bidding for the target or to tolerate for long any further interference from other unwanted bidders. The huge premiums paid for Firestone, Gould, and Reichhold, and Sony's willingness to increase substantially its bid for CBS Records over an already high asking price (and to maintain that bid despite the stock market's crash), clearly reflect a no-nonsense approach to the implementation of a product market strategy rather than artful dealmaking or bottom-fishing for cheap assets.

# 6
# FOREIGN BIDDERS AND JAPANESE TARGETS

The number of Japanese companies acquired by foreign bidders has been inconsequentially small. Foreigners have taken numerous minority stakes in Japanese companies, and Japanese and foreign companies have established many joint ventures. But it is rare to observe majority equity ownership of a pre-existing Japanese company leaving Japanese hands. In an article on this topic, Walter Ames and Michael Young were able to identify only 32 such deals between 1955 and 1984—19 of them executed by American corporations.[1] Since 1984, American companies have purchased majority interests in 24 Japanese corporations. Eleven of these, however, were simply buyouts of partners in Japanese joint ventures, and two were just the sale of a Japanese subsidiary by one American company to another (see Exhibit 6–1).

Of the 32 deals identified by Ames and Young, only 15 occurred between 1955 and 1980. During this period, foreign acquisitions of Japanese companies were controlled and ultimately discouraged by Japan's highly restrictive Foreign Exchange and Foreign Trade Control Law, and Foreign Investment Law. Prior to 1980, these laws prohibited in principle the direct investment in Japanese companies by foreigners, with exceptions. Foreign investors had to apply to the Ministry of Finance for a special license before undertaking such investment.

Liberalization of the laws began in the late 1960s. More and

---

1. Walter L. Ames and Michael K. Young, "Foreign Acquisitions in Japan: Hurdling the Ultimate Barrier," *The Journal of the American Chamber of Commerce in Japan* (January 1986), pp. 10–29.

Exhibit 6-1  *American Acquisition of Japanese Businesses, 1985–1989*

| Date | American Buyer | Japanese Buyer | Target's Business | Type of Transaction |
|------|----------------|----------------|-------------------|---------------------|
| 7/89 | Telenet Communications Corp. | Telenet Japan, Inc. | Telecommunications | JV |
| 5/89 | Warner Communications | Warner-Pioneer Corp. (Pioneer Electronic Corp.) | Compact disc mfr. | JV |
| 12/88 | Federal Express Corp. | Daisei Co., Ltd. | Trucking | DV |
| 8/88 | R.R. Donnelly & Sons Co. | Dowa Insatsukk | Printing | AQ |
| 7/88 | Kentek Information Systems | Haster Co. | Printers | AQ |
| 6/88 | E-Z-EM, Inc. | Toho Kagaku Kenkyushi | Diagnostic imaging systems | AQ |
| 2/88 | SmithKline Beckman Corp. | SmithKline & Fujisawa K.K. | Pharmaceuticals | JV |
| 2/88 | Ashton-Tate, Inc. | Nippon-Ashton Tate Co., Ltd. (Japan Systems Engineering) | Software mktg. & devel. | JV |
| 12/87 | Thermo Instrument Systems, Inc. | Nippon Jarrell-Ash Co., Ltd. (Yanagimoto Mfg. Co. & Kinsho-Mataichi Corp.) | Emissions measurement inst. | JV |
| 12/87 | Chevron Chemical Co. (Chevron Corp. and Normura Jimusho, Inc.) | Karonite Chemical Co. | Lubricating oil | AQ |
| 11/87 | Coulter Electronics | Japan Scientific Instruments | Medical devices | AQ |

| Date | U.S. Company | Japanese Company | Industry | Type |
|---|---|---|---|---|
| 10/87 | Dun & Bradstreet Corp. | Teikoku Data Bank Ltd. | Credit agency | AQ |
| 6/87 | PruAsia Ltd. (Prudential Life Insurance Co.) | Simmons Japan Ltd. (Wesray Capital Corp.) | Spring mattresses | AQ |
| 5/87 | Fluorocarbon Co. | Nitta-Moore | Hydraulic cables | JV |
| 12/86 | Amax, Inc. | Mitsui & Co., Ltd. and Nippon Steel Corp. | Aluminum producer | JV |
| 11/86 | Coleco Industries | Tomy Corp. & Tomy Canada, Ltd. | Toys | AQ |
| 10/86 | Economics Laboratory, Inc. | Chisso Corp. | Cleaning chemicals | JV |
| 6/86 | Dow Chemical Co. | Funai Pharmaceutical | Pharmaceuticals | AQ |
| 6/86 | General Electric Co. | Yokogawa Medical Systems | Medical equipment | JV |
| 4/86 | Mead Corp. | Pulp Asia, Ltd. | Paper | JV |
| 3/86 | Associates Corp. of North America (Gulf + Western Industries, Inc.) | Japan Avco Finance Services (Textron, Inc.) | Consumer finance | AQ |
| 12/85 | Eastman Kodak Co. | Kusuda Business Machines Co. | Imaging systems | DV |
| 3/85 | Cummins Engine Co. | Komatsu, Ltd. | Diesel engines | JV |
| 3/85 | Cooper Vision, Inc. | Takada Optometric Instruments | Importer, retailer | AQ |

Note: AQ = acquisition; DV = purchase of division; JV = buyout of joint venture
Source: Ulmer Brothers, Inc., 1987–1989.

more exceptions were made in the face of international pressure to open Japan's financial markets. This trend climaxed in 1980 with the enactment of a new Foreign Exchange and Foreign Trade Control Law that swept away the old restrictions and bureaucratic approval processes. Direct foreign investment in the equity of Japanese companies became permissible in principle, with exceptions. It reached a "free-in-principle" status with regard to foreign investment. Investments that would elevate total foreign ownership of a Japanese company to a level in excess of 25% required review by the Bank of Japan, but only prior notification of the investment was needed rather than prior approval on a case-by-case basis. By 1984, even this prior notification was relaxed to the extent of requiring notice only when a single foreign investor intended to acquire more than 10% of a listed company's stock. Foreign investment continues to be limited, however, in a few specific industries (agriculture, forestry, fishing, mining, petroleum, and leather and leather products).[2]

Although liberalization of the Foreign Exchange and Foreign Trade Control Law was associated with a sharp upturn in acquisitions by foreigners (nearly as many occurred between 1980 and 1984 as in the prior 25 years), the deal flow into Japan has remained remarkably slow. Evidently impediments other than explicit regulations are inhibiting foreign-majority ownership of Japanese companies. As has been true for domestic combinations, extralegal barriers such as industrial group membership, reciprocal shareholdings among Japanese companies, and the opprobrium associated with M&A activity in Japan have doubtlessly impeded cross-border acquisitions involving Japanese companies as targets. In addition, there is the element of unfamiliarity on both sides of cross-border deals. Potential Japanese

---

2. Until July 1984, 11 "sensitive" companies were also protected from foreign ownership above a certain amount. They are listed here, noting parenthetically the industries in which they operate and the percentage of foreign ownership allowed: Arabian Oil Co. (oil, 25%); Fuji Electric Co., Ltd. (defense electronics, 26%); General Sekiyu K.K. (oil, 49%); Hitachi Electronics (defense electronics, 30%); Katakura Industries Co., Ltd. (silk, 25%); Koa Oil Co., Ltd. (oil, 50%); Mitsubishi Oil Co., Ltd. (oil, 50%); Sankyo Co., Ltd. (narcotic pharmaceuticals, 25%); Showa Oil Co., Ltd. (oil, 50%); Toa Nenryo Kogyo K.K. (oil, 50%); and Tokyo Keiki Co. Ltd. (defense aircraft, 32%).

sellers often fear abusive mismanagement by foreign owners ignorant of the unique Japanese contracting milieu. For their part, foreign buyers are frequently deterred by the impression that potential Japanese targets will be expensive to buy and difficult to control, not to mention untouchable by a foreign interest.

The impediments and corporate governance differences are not insurmountable, however. Moreover, as the Japanese economy matures and turns toward consumer-led growth, the incentives for foreigners to acquire Japanese companies will increase. In this chapter, I examine the 1983 acquisition of Banyu Pharmaceutical of Japan by Merck & Co., Inc. for its insights on motives for acquiring control over a Japanese company, the strength of forces resisting that control, and the exercise of control once acquisition takes place.

Merck's long history of business relationships with Banyu (and that of other foreign pharmaceutical companies with Japanese partners) suggests that takeovers are neither the only nor the best means of penetrating Japanese markets. However, as with Japanese acquisitions of Western business allies, takeovers in Japan may become essential in response to a heightening of the trading hazards intrinsic to arm's-length business relationships or other threats of business disruption. Merck's eventual acquisition of Banyu demonstrates that if and when acquiring control of a Japanese company becomes necessary, it is possible to do so *provided* the foreign buyer understands and plays by the local rules. Indeed, the carefully measured steps in this deal provide a virtual blueprint for success that other foreign bidders can adapt to their own circumstances. Merck's acquisition also reveals that a thorough appreciation for all the components of a Japanese target's value is the key to bridging the enormous price-earnings multiple gulf that separates Japan from the rest of the global market for corporate control.

## THE MERCK-BANYU COMBINATION

In August 1983, Merck stunned the world with the announcement that it had acquired 50.02% of Banyu Pharmaceutical, a major Japanese producer of ethical drugs.[3] The acquisition was the largest controlling interest in a Japanese company listed on the First Section of the Tokyo Stock Exchange ever purchased by a foreign buyer. That alone was news enough in Japan. What shocked the rest of the world was Merck's willingness to pay roughly 30 times earnings for a weakly performing Japanese company while its own blue-chip stock was selling for only 15 times earnings in the United States. At the time and for months thereafter, the deal was roundly criticized in the press as folly on the part of America's star pharmaceutical company.[4] Today, it is seen in a more favorable light as an important and successful step in Merck's attempt to become the world's leading manufacturer of ethical drugs.

## Merck's Strategy

Merck is one of the world's largest producers of prescription drugs. Just prior to its acquisition of Banyu Pharmaceutical in 1983, Merck earned $415 million on total worldwide sales of $3.1 billion. Its modern success is founded on an extensive research and development program. In the 1970s, a decade that saw many large U.S. pharmaceutical companies diversify into medical equipment, cosmetics, and other consumer products, Merck continued to focus on pharmaceuticals by devoting a substantial fraction of its sales dollar to research and new product development. With the industry spending an average of 5.8% of sales on R&D during the 1970s, Merck spent 8.5%. By 1982, Merck was spending $330 million (9.4% of sales) on R&D and was expected to increase this level to 11% in 1983.

Merck's rising R&D expenditures reflected in part an important strategic decision made about 1975, when current CEO Dr. P. Roy Vagelos was hired as the new president of Merck Sharp & Dohme Research Laboratories. Research efforts were

3. An extensive description of Merck's acquisition of Banyu is provided by Timothy A. Luehrman, "Merck-Banyu," No. 288–127. Boston: Harvard Business School, 1987, rev. 1988. In addition to interviews with executives at Merck, I have benefited substantially from Professor Luehrman's research.
4. See, for example, Lee Smith, "Merck Has an Ache in Japan," *Fortune*, March 18, 1985, pp. 42–45.

concentrated on the pharmacological application of break-throughs occurring in life sciences such as biology, biochemis-try, and genetics rather than on the more conventional "hunt-and-peck" approach of screening new compounds developed through basic chemical research. Merck's decision also reflected (as did the diversification efforts of other pharmaceutical com-panies) a rise in real R&D costs associated with increased regu-lation of the drug industry. In 1962, U.S. legislation gave the Food and Drug Administration the responsibility of determining the safety and efficacy of new drugs, and broad authority to reg-ulate every phase of the drug approval process. One outcome of the legislation was an increase in the time and expense involved in bringing a new drug to market. It was estimated that by 1980 the cost of developing a major new drug in the United States had reached $70 to $90 million, and the time frame ran from seven to nine years. (These figures were roughly twice those of Japan.)

Once past the regulatory screening process, a successful new drug could be enormously profitable. Highly successful drugs might have annual sales well in excess of $100 million and pre-tax operating margins of 60–70%. However, for pharmaceutical companies basing their development efforts on traditional chemical research, roughly 10,000 compounds had to be screened to yield a single marketable (and not necessarily highly successful) drug. Mounting regulatory expenses ate into the profitability of many approved drugs, reducing their returns to a level barely justifying the risks incurred in the initial sunk in-vestment costs. Lengthening approval processes further reduced new drugs' expected profitability by encroaching on the period of patent protection.

Ultimately, the regulatory trends of the 1960s and 1970s dis-couraged many smaller companies from taking the risks asso-ciated with substantial expenditures on pharmacological R&D, and stimulated larger companies to redirect investment into other businesses with different risk characteristics. The trends also contributed to the globalization of the pharmaceutical mar-ket. By substantially raising the R&D stakes necessary to remain viable, the increased regulatory burden necessitated the sale of drugs beyond U.S. national boundaries to generate sufficient profits soon enough to justify the huge up-front commitment of resources (the U.S. market for human pharmaceuticals totaled $27.7 billion in 1983, which was 37% of worldwide retail sales).

The industry's new global imperatives were not missed by Merck, which had extensive international operations managed by its Merck Sharp & Dohme International division. Sales outside the United States represented 44% of Merck's consolidated sales for 1982. Its stated long-term goal was to rank first or second in total market share in each of the world's major prescription drug markets. As of the first quarter of 1983, Merck ranked first in North America, fifth in Europe, but only thirtieth in Japan.

The Japanese Pharmaceutical Market

Being nearly insignificant in Japan was of no small consequence in the global pharmaceutical market. With estimated 1983 sales of $12 billion, Japan was the second-largest national market for drugs. In per capita terms, Japanese drug consumption was the highest in the world in 1982. Japan also led the world in aggregate sales of some therapeutic classes of ethical drugs, antibiotics in particular.

Competition in Japan was highly fragmented, however. In the early 1980s, over 2,000 firms competed in this market. Takeda Chemical, the largest domestic producer with worldwide pharmaceutical sales of $1.29 billion, had a market share of less than 7% in Japan. The multitude of producers was strictly regulated by the Koseisho, an agency of the Japanese government. Pricing was set by the Koseisho and drugs were sold by prescribing physicians whose patients would be reimbursed for substantially all of the cost of the prescription under the National Health Scheme (NHI). Because doctors bought drugs from producers at wholesale prices and kept the retail markup as income (a source of earnings that could account for half of a doctor's annual income), there was a pronounced tendency for Japanese doctors to prescribe drugs liberally.

With pricing and product introduction strictly controlled by the Koseisho, competition among pharmaceutical producers took place through intense, personal selling efforts focused on doctors. Manufacturers hired their own sales representatives, known as "propas" (for propagandists), who would call on the company's accounts in a given locale. A typical doctor would be called on at least once a week, with an important prescribing physician being called daily. This was roughly four times more frequent than was typically true in the United States and required a commensurately larger sales force.

In response to rising health care costs, partly related to prescribed drug consumption, and the slow pace of pharmacological innovation in Japan, several important regulatory changes took place in the 1970s. First, in 1975, the Japanese patent law was revised to strengthen patent protection of drugs. Previously, a Japanese company could produce another company's patented drug if it could simply devise an alternative manufacturing process for doing so. This possibility deterred even large companies from undertaking major, expensive research and development projects. The second important regulatory change was the Koseisho's new policy of regularly reviewing and reducing prices of prescription drugs sold under the NHI reimbursement scheme. Older, less-effective drugs and generic drugs were the primary targets of this policy.

The effect of these two changes was to stimulate pharmacological R&D in Japan. By 1983, Japanese pharmaceutical companies led the world in the introduction of new substances. The larger companies, however, were the principal beneficiaries of the changes. Smaller companies, which often depended heavily on sales of a few older products licensed from abroad, were placed under severe pressure by the changes. They also lacked the resources to become serious players in the new R&D-based competition.

Merck's Japanese Connection

Prior to its acquisition of Banyu Pharmaceutical in 1983, Merck's arrangements in Japan ran the gamut of contracting relationships. Because foreign participation in the Japanese pharmaceutical market was highly restricted, licensing agreements and joint ventures with local producers constituted the only feasible means for foreign producers to gain a foothold in the Japanese market.

In the years immediately after World War II, Merck entered into several marketing agreements with Banyu and another Japanese firm to distribute several Merck products including streptomycin and cortisone. Drug manufacture within Japan began in 1954 with the formation of the joint venture, Nippon Merck-Banyu (NMB), which was 50% owned by Merck, 49% by Banyu, and 1% by a Japanese employee of Merck's. NMB acquired a Banyu plant for production and sold its products through both NMB and Banyu salespeople. Actual drug distribution took place through wholesalers affiliated with Banyu. (A parallel set of relationships also evolved between Banyu and Bristol-Myers. Banyu began licensing antibiotics from Bristol-Myers in 1955, established a research laboratory with Bristol-Myers in 1961, and a manufacturing joint venture in 1973.) In 1970, Merck set up a wholly owned subsidiary, MSD (Japan), to monitor and administrate Merck's various Japanese activities. Not until 1982, under the liberalized Foreign Exchange and Foreign Trade Control Law, did Merck acquire a direct 5% equity interest in Banyu and a 30% interest in a much smaller firm, Torii Pharmaceutical, both through purchases of common stock on the open market.

Before the regulatory changes that began in 1975, these arrangements were highly profitable for Banyu and worked at least acceptably well for Merck. For two decades, Banyu relied on foreign products for more than half its sales, maintained R&D expenditures at 2% of sales, and enjoyed pretax profit margins of more than 25%. By this measure, it was one of the best performers in the Japanese pharmaceutical industry.

One reason the Merck-Banyu liaison worked well was that each had something the other lacked in the Japanese market. Banyu controlled a moderately large and highly effective sales force that had well-established relationships with doctors. For its part, Merck offered a number of widely efficacious drugs that could be sold in large volume. These assets had to be combined to achieve commercial success in the Japanese pharmaceutical market, but they did not have to be owned and controlled as an integrated unit in a single administrative hierarchy.

In fact, the incentives were to do the opposite. Because of the high costs of developing new drugs and the weak patent protection in Japan prior to 1975, there was relatively little incentive to invest in product development programs that would depend heavily on Japanese sales to provide an adequate rate of return. It was cheaper to license proven products developed by foreign producers that could amortize their expensive R&D programs over one (i.e., the U.S.) or more large national pharmaceutical markets. By the same token, it was expensive and time-consuming for foreign producers to build the sort of heavily staffed, relationship-intensive sales force and distribution networks that were essential for success in the Japanese market.

Even with several highly successful drugs, foreign producers had difficulty acting on their own to achieve the economies of scale and scope in distribution that could be obtained by a Japanese company holding licenses for many such drugs. Only three (Bayer, Roche, and Sandoz) of eighteen foreign pharmaceutical companies operating in Japan achieved levels of sales per propa comparable to those of the indigenous Japanese producers (these averaged sales of ¥132 million per propa). Only one (Sandoz) had achieved Banyu's level of efficiency of ¥150 million per propa which, by 1982, had been eroded by seven years of declining sales growth in the wake of Japanese regulatory reform.

With respect to the Japanese market for drugs, it was most economical for foreign producers to specialize in product development and for domestic companies to specialize in marketing and distribution. Local manufacture of foreign-owned drugs in Japan through a joint venture made sense if sales volume justified it and if appropriate safeguards were implemented to inhibit the loss of proprietary technology to other competitors having relationships with the same local company.

The Path Leading to Acquisition

Just as the regulatory environment helped shape the structure of the Japanese pharmaceutical industry and the organizations that participated in it, so changes in that environment triggered a change in the relative effectiveness of various types of organizational forms. Specifically, the regulatory changes that began in 1975 made the Merck-Banyu style of contractual arrangements less tenable as a way of structuring transactions, and formal integration of research, production, and marketing more crucial.

The effects of the regulatory changes on Banyu were typical of those on small to medium-sized Japanese pharmaceutical companies in general. Continual price reductions on established bread-and-butter products such as penicillin and other antibiotics cut deeply into profits. Banyu saw its 25% pretax margins at the beginning of the 1970s fall to 12% by 1980. Contributing to this decline was a substantial increase in R&D expenses, which rose suddenly and dramatically from ¥75 million in 1975 (0.4% of sales) to an average of ¥2 billion a year over the next five years (4.3% of sales). The development of new proprietary products was at once more desirable in light of the heightened patent protection, and more imperative in light of the need to replace old product lines with new ones. Indeed, for companies like Banyu whose strategy had been built around cost-efficient distribution of established high-volume drugs, innovation was essential for survival.

Despite these efforts, which included a research joint venture with Kirin Beer, Banyu found it difficult to reverse the decline in its fortunes. Commercially successful new products could not be discovered and introduced fast enough to offset price reductions in its highest-volume products. In fact, not a single new product developed in-house was introduced between 1973 and 1982. Meanwhile, Banyu's existing product lines experienced steep price reductions. In 1981 and 1983 alone, reductions averaged 20% and 25%, respectively. As a consequence, Banyu's after-tax return on sales declined steadily from a level of 10% in 1975 to 3.75% in 1983. Return on equity also declined from a 1975 level of 6.8% to 5.2% in 1983. Both these returns were well below the average for large Japanese firms of 10% for return on sales and 12% for return on equity.

Happily for Banyu, its need to replace old product lines with new ones coincided with the fruition of Merck's R&D push begun in 1975 and its determination to become a leading player in every major pharmaceutical market in the world. By 1983, Merck had 65 new compounds in the clinical stage of testing, 18 to 20 of which were thought to be in their final three years. (Normally, between one-quarter and one-third of the compounds that reach the clinical testing stage eventually receive regulatory approval for sale.) With many potential new products in the pipeline, and the Koseisho seeking the introduction of innovative new drugs that might be used in lieu of more expensive forms of health care such as hospitalization, it remained only for Merck to decide the best means of managing its new product introductions in Japan before a flow of new drugs began. What alternatives made sense?

Licensing agreements were—and remain—a viable means of selling drugs in Japan. By licensing local production in Japan, an American pharmaceutical manufacturer can circumvent U.S. restrictions on the export of non-FDA-approved drugs while meeting strict Koseisho requirements for quality control or laboratory and manufacturing practices. But it is a contracting alternative best suited for drugs made with common, widely understood production techniques. It is less suitable when proprietary production technologies are involved and safeguards against their appropriation by others are difficult to implement.

For new substances produced using life-science technologies rather than conventional chemistry, licensing production in Japan might be tantamount to transferring process know-how to the licensee. In principle, this need not create a problem so long as the licensee can credibly commit itself never to use the technology for producing anything other than the products under license and/or if the licensor can adequately monitor the licensee's use of the technology. But once the process technology is known to the local producer, the genie is out of the bottle. It strains credulity to assume it would not eventually be used to the licensee's advantage.

In short, licensing entails hazards, which increase with R&D expenses and the importance of new process technology to competitive success. Given the growing importance of pharmacological R&D in Japan and the high stakes involved (e.g., dominance in a consolidating global market for pharmaceuticals), it is easy to appreciate Merck's reluctance to continue licensing as a means of serving the Japanese market with its new, state-of-the-art products.

The same conclusion can be reached with respect to the well-established joint venture, Nippon Merck-Banyu (NMB). It too would provide Banyu, which was playing desperate catch-up ball on the R&D field, with a valuable window on Merck's new process technologies. Recall that Banyu, with its own products and a series of other products licensed from Bristol-Myers, was as much a competitor as a partner of Merck in the Japanese market. Therein lies an inherent conflict of interest in joint ventures and other forms of strategic alliances: they have competitive as well as cooperative aspects. It is interesting to note that for all its association with Banyu, the efficiency of NMB's sales force was considerably less than Banyu's (¥50.4 million sales per propa for NMB compared to ¥150 million for Banyu). No doubt this reflected the wider range of products that Banyu's propas had available to sell. Perhaps it also reflected the fact that NMB's propas depended upon Banyu-affiliated wholesalers for actual distribution. Given discretion, these wholesalers may have provided better distribution service to Banyu's propas than to NMB's. In any event, the partial ownership of NMB by Banyu and the below-average performance of NMB's sales force made it a less than completely desirable vehicle for handling Merck's new products in Japan.

With complete ownership and control over whatever Japanese organization handled its new products, Merck could reap the advantages of local production and avoid the appropriation hazards endemic in the rapidly consolidating Japanese pharmaceutical industry. Investing directly to start a new, wholly owned subsidiary would leave it with the problem of building up effective local distribution within a reasonable time frame. Buying out Banyu to take complete control of its joint venture was another option, but this would do little to enhance (and might even hurt) the effectiveness of NMB's already struggling sales force.

Under the circumstances, acquiring outright control of Banyu was an attractive alternative. Between NMB and Banyu, Merck would control a combined sales force of 900 propas, one of the five largest in Japan (with the addition of Torii, the level would rise to 1,200, the second-largest in the nation). Based on 1982 performance figures, sales per propa would also be relatively high at ¥100 million, although Merck's ownership might adversely affect the licensing agreements Banyu had with other foreign competitors. In addition, Banyu would bring with it valuable connections with physicians, wholesalers, and government officials, as well as a reputation in the Japanese pharmaceutical industry (Banyu was founded in 1915), which is critical in Japan for recruiting purposes. None of these assets could be replicated quickly in a brand new venture, nor did NMB possess them to any great extent. In short, provided Merck believed that it could successfully manage a wholly owned, pre-established Japanese company, acquiring a company like Banyu would be a faster, cheaper, less hazardous way to obtain local manufacture and distribution of its new products in Japan.

## CORPORATE OWNERSHIP AS AN ALTERNATIVE TO CONTRACTUAL RELATIONSHIPS

Merck's acquisition of Banyu may have been a pathbreaking deal, but it came only at the end of a well-trodden road that began with basic marketing agreements signed more than 30 years before. Although direct administrative control over Banyu eventually made strategic sense for Merck, this was not true from the start. It was the changed economics of the pharmaceuticals industry (demanding a significant presence in all major pharmaceutical markets around the world) coupled with the exacerbation of trading hazards with Japanese pharmaceutical companies that made the management of alternative contractual relationships (e.g., licensing agreements, joint ventures) unstable at best. Direct control over a Japanese pharmaceutical company was not so much sought by Merck as forced on it by a changed operating environment. In this regard, Merck's acquisition of Banyu was triggered by essentially the same economic circumstances as those stimulating recent Japanese takeovers in the United States.

There are many good reasons for a foreign company to seek out an established Japanese company to spearhead its competitive thrust in Japan. Access to—and guidance through—Japan's complex distribution system, the availability of sound local management, and the avoidance of having to site and build new manufacturing facilities are but a sample of the more prominent advantages. But few if any of these advantages necessarily require direct ownership of a Japanese company in order to be captured. In many cases, they can be obtained indirectly by foreign investors through a variety of other contractual arrangements (marketing agreements, product licensing, joint ventures, and so forth). These have the advantage of requiring less capital and exploiting the high-powered incentives of the marketplace. At the same time, problems of monitoring and controlling a foreign subsidiary operating in a vastly different business environment are avoided.

To the extent that a Japanese subsidiary's value lies in implicit contracting relationships depending heavily upon pair-wise continuity in the contracting parties, acquiring Japanese companies can be fraught with peril for foreign bidders. On one hand, distance and lack of loyalty to (or trust of) a foreign owner may expose that owner to the hazards of hidden action and the opportunistic use of hidden information by local Japanese managers and other stakeholders. On the other, heavy-handed control and the implementation of Western management techniques could disrupt these relationships and destroy much of the value sought in the acquisition in the first place. Managers at Merck, for instance, had an important reservation when they began to consider internally the idea of acquiring Banyu: the extreme difficulty of replacing Japanese management if the existing team should bolt in the wake of a foreign takeover.

Confronting the perils of cross-border acquisition becomes

justified when the hazards of expropriation and/or defection from an alliance begin to loom large in comparison. Generally, this happens when the product or manufacturing process involved is highly proprietary; when highly specific or dedicated assets (tangible, intangible, or human) are used in connection with local production and marketing; or when continuity in the identity of the local Japanese agent/partner is crucial to commercial success.[5] When one or more of these characteristics holds, licensing agreements and joint ventures are likely to offer inadequate safeguards against potential opportunistic behavior by the Japanese partner. Direct ownership and control, management problems notwithstanding, become the preferred alternative for governing commercial activity.

In the Merck-Banyu case, the need to exert tighter control over a Japanese partner developed in the wake of new drug-pricing policies the Koseisho implemented in the late 1970s. Domestic Japanese pharmaceutical companies depending on older drugs licensed from foreign companies faced the prospects of either acquiring new, more advanced (hence more proprietary) products fairly rapidly or being squeezed out of business. By raising the specter of financial failure and increasing the temptation for Japanese licensees to expropriate valuable product and production research from their foreign partners, this choice destabilized many existing alliances between foreign and second-tier Japanese drug companies.

In response to the instability, the Rorer Group acquired Kyoritsu Pharmaceutical in 1979 and Toho Iyaku, another Japanese drug manufacturer, in 1982; Merck acquired Banyu and Torii in 1983; and Dow Chemical Company acquired a majority interest in Funai Pharmaceuticals Ltd. in 1986. In a different move, but one nevertheless aimed at bringing its Japanese drug manufacturing under direct control, Upjohn Company announced in 1985 that it would spend $50 million building a research and

---

5. See Oliver E. Williamson, *The Economic Institution of Capitalism: Firms, Markets, Relational Contracting* (New York: Free Press, 1985, Chapter 2) for discussion of contracting problems associated with asset specificity.

manufacturing facility outside Tokyo, into which drugs then produced by its joint venture with Sumitomo Chemical Company would soon be moved.

## THE LIMITED AVAILABILITY OF ATTRACTIVE JAPANESE COMPANIES

In principle, all but a very few (those considered to be of vital national importance) private-sector Japanese companies are available for possible sale to foreigners under the terms of the new Foreign Exchange and Foreign Trade Control Law. In practice, however, most will remain out of reach for considerable time to come. The only truly viable targets will be companies like Banyu Pharmaceutical, which had a stable, friendly, long-term relationship with its suitor and was under external pressure to integrate with a strong R&D company in its field.

Recall that when Japanese companies combine with others, domestic or foreign, generally they are seeking to protect a threatened commercial relationship (e.g., the loss of supplier, subcontractor, or customer) or striving to honor implicit contracts with some of their stakeholders (e.g., saving employees' jobs, salvaging the value of a main bank's loans). Although the selling company's management may benignly state the motive for the combination to be the need for new capital or new technology, the enhancement of growth prospects, or possibly the strengthening of management, it is the serious erosion of competitive position or the onset of financial distress that underlies the deal.

Hence most targets available for friendly acquisition in Japan are likely to be distressed companies facing financial failure or caught in a stronger competitor's cross hairs. Of this population, many will be part of a well-established industrial group or have long-term commercial relations, reinforced by reciprocal stock holdings, with a larger corporate stakeholder. These are primary candidates for acquisition by another Japanese company under the guidance of a main bank, effectively removing them from the field as far as foreign buyers are concerned.

For most foreign buyers, the typical Japanese company available for sale will be a small, financially and competitively weak company with only loose connections, if any, to other major Japanese companies or banks (a characteristic that may be an underlying cause of poor performance and potentially difficult for a new foreign owner to correct). To this group may be added independent, family-controlled firms facing management succession problems, joint venture corporations established with a Japanese partner, and Japanese subsidiaries of other foreign companies.

Virtually all the Japanese companies in which American corporations acquired a majority interest during the mid-1980s fall into one or more of these categories. Other than its relatively large size, Banyu Pharmaceutical is highly typical as a Japanese target. It was a struggling competitor in its industry, not part of an industrial group, was led by a founding family member who was also a significant shareholder, and a partner with Merck in a joint venture.

## JAPANESE PRICE-EARNINGS MULTIPLES

Merck paid ¥75.8 billion ($313.5 million) for the equivalent of 114 million new shares of Banyu (assuming conversion of the convertible bonds into equity). Having already purchased 6.04 million existing shares on the open market at an average price of approximately ¥625 per share, Merck had paid a total of ¥79.56 billion ($329 million) for 50.02% of Banyu's fully diluted common shares. At the preacquisition market price of ¥625 per share, this figure represented only about a 3% control premium for the newly capitalized Banyu—a small premium by nearly any standard. What startled many observers was that Merck paid approximately 30 times Banyu's annual earnings, while its own stock sold at a multiple of only 15 times. At the time, that seemed to be a vast overpayment for a weak player in the Japanese industry with no attractive growth prospects of its own. What justified such a price?

This same question comes to the lips of nearly every foreign investor looking at the prices of equities on the Tokyo Stock Exchange, especially prior to their sharp decline in the first quarter of 1990. With equities trading in Tokyo at an average multiple approaching 50 times earnings compared to 18 in New York, investing in Japan seems suitable only for the most intrepid. Add to this the recent volatility of the Tokyo Stock Exchange and effects of a strong yen on the home currency cost of Japanese stocks for foreigners, and investing in Japanese equities can seem foolhardy indeed.

Some of the overpricing of Japanese stocks may be more apparent than real, however. Basic accounting differences, high levels of excess cash balances, what the Japanese call "hidden assets" (primarily land and equity investments carried at historical cost on the balance sheet), and the effects of reciprocally held shares on the calculation of price-earnings multiples account for much, if not all, of the difference.[6] Assuming the acquisition of a Japanese company makes strategic sense for a foreign investor and that a suitable target has been identified, foreign buyers should not necessarily be deterred by simple comparisons of Japanese and home market price-earnings multiples. Attention should be focused instead on estimates of the intrinsic yen value of the company in question.

Take the case of Banyu. A breakdown of its intrinsic value into components, the sum of which justifies Merck's acquisition price, is shown in Exhibit 6–2. The breakdown begins straightforwardly with the ¥75.8 billion injection of new capital that Merck made by paying cash for new shares (and in which Merck retained a 50% interest by virtue of its equity holdings after consummation of the acquisition). Shown next is an estimate of excess cash held by Banyu prior to the deal. On March 31, 1983, Banyu held ¥26.8 billion in cash and marketable securities and had no long-term debt outstanding (short-term debt amounted

---

6. For a detailed discussion of Japanese price-earnings multiples and their differences with U.S. multiples, see Paul Aron, "Japanese Price Earnings Multiples: The Tradition Continues," updated as of August 31, 1989 (Daiwa Securities of America, Inc.); and Kenneth R. French and James M. Poterba, "Are Japanese Stock Prices Too High?" (Cambridge, MA: National Bureau of Economic Research working paper, February 1990).

Exhibit 6-2 *Justification of Merck's Purchase Price for Banyu Pharmaceutical (¥ billion)*

| | |
|---|---:|
| Existing excess cash | ¥  20.8 |
| New cash injected | 75.8 |
| Existing business | 22.6 |
| New growth opportunities under Merck's ownership | 39.9 |
| Total | ¥ 159.1 |
| Merck's fractional ownership | × .5002 |
| Price paid | ¥  79.6 |

to less than ¥500 million). This represented 28% of the company's total assets and 56% of its net working capital. Assuming existing operations required only about one month of sales (¥6 billion) held as cash, nearly ¥21 billion can be considered as excess cash.[7]

A valuation of Banyu's existing business begins with its 1983 pretax operating earnings of ¥6.4 billion. At its 1983 average tax rate of 68%, this is reduced to an after-tax level of ¥2 billion. To obtain cash flow from operations, depreciation of ¥414 million must be added to this figure. Also, noncash charges to income associated with various reserves commonly carried on Japanese balance sheets must be added to after-tax operating earnings.[8] In 1983, these charges amounted to ¥260 million. This yields an estimated 1983 cash flow from operations of approximately ¥2.7 billion. If future capital expenditures are assumed to run about even with annual depreciation expense,

---

7. Banyu's excess liquidity may be even larger than this, however. In 1983, notes and accounts receivable amounted to 36% of Banyu's total assets. A more typical figure for Japanese companies would be about 25%. For American firms, the figure is closer to 20%.

8. One of the major factors giving rise to lower reported earnings by Japanese companies (hence higher price-earnings multiples) compared to their American counterparts is the common practice of making charges against current period income to set up balance-sheet reserves of various types. Usually, the largest single such reserve is the "long-term liability" reserve, which relates to a company's severance indemnity plan. Companies are allowed to reduce taxable earnings annually by an amount sufficient to bring the reserve to a level equal to 40% of the liability that would be incurred should all employees voluntarily separate at the same time.

then Banyu's cash flow available for distribution to suppliers of capital is expected to be about ¥2.3 billion. If capitalized as a perpetuity at a 10% rate (at the time of the deal, Japanese government bonds were yielding 6%; thus 10% allows for a modest risk premium on this riskless yield), Banyu's existing operations can be assigned a present value of ¥23 billion. Netting short-term debt of ¥426 million against this leaves an estimate of ¥22.6 billion for the equity.

The sum of existing excess cash, new cash, and the present value of current operations provides an estimate of total value for Banyu of ¥119.3 billion. To justify Merck's total cost of ¥79.56 billion for 50.02% of Banyu's equity, incremental cash flow from the ownership of Banyu must have a present value of ¥39.9 billion ($164.6 million). Given the new products in Merck's development pipeline, the fraction of world pharmaceutical sales accounted for by Japan, and a reasonable estimate for the return on sales of the new products once Banyu is controlled by Merck, ¥39.9 billion can be viewed as a reasonable value.[9]

Although Merck's stock price fell 1.8% on the day the acquisition was announced, the drop was associated with a 1.3% decline in the Standard & Poor's Composite index that same day. If it is assumed that a drop of only 0.5% that day was due to the acquisition announcement, this would imply a loss of approximately $35 million in connection with the Banyu deal. However, by the end of August, Merck's stock price was trading 1.2% above its preannouncement levels. Given the subsequent rise and the general volatility of stock prices, it is difficult to make

---

9. At the time of the acquisition, Merck had 65 new drugs in clinical testing, 18 of which were in their final three years. Assuming that half of the 18 and one-third of the others were eventually approved for sale, Merck could reasonably have expected 25 new products coming on stream in the next five to seven years. If they each generate $50 million in annual worldwide sales (half the blockbuster level of $100 million) and if Japan is assumed to account for one-quarter of those sales, a net return on sales of only 5–6% would be needed to justify the additional value placed on new business in Japan. Although this percentage is more than the 3.5–4.5% realized by Banyu in recent years, it is well below Merck's own 13–17% ROS. Moreover, it is reasonable to suppose that margins would be higher on these new products in Japan than was the case on Banyu's existing product line.

the clear-cut inference that Merck substantially overpaid for Banyu and damaged its shareholder interests.

Not included in this analysis is the extra value associated with the land owned by Banyu and carried on its books at ¥2.6 billion, or long-term investments, primarily securities, valued at ¥8.8 billion. This implicitly assumes that Banyu's operations require it to use all the real estate it currently owns or some substantially similar property, and that the investments are an important part of Banyu's relationships with other corporate stakeholders. If, however, Banyu could sell its securities or its real estate and relocate on less expensive grounds (or could lease back its facilities at attractive rates, a possibility in the eyes of many Japanese real estate experts who assert that property val-

Exhibit 6-3  *Sources of "Hidden Value" on Japanese Corporate Balance Sheets, 1986*

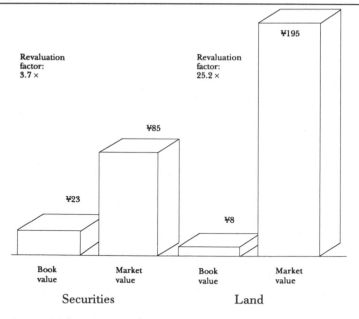

*Source:* Wako Research Institute of Economics, *Quarterly Economic Review* (Winter 1988), p. 25.

ues in Japan exceed the capitalized value of the rents that can be generated by the property), substantial additional value may be found in this part of the balance sheet as well.[10]

Consider the figures shown in Exhibit 6–3. By one estimate, land owned by a large sample of First-Section TSE companies in 1986 had market value 25.2 times the figure at which it was carried on company books. Applied against Banyu's book value of land (most of which was acquired long before 1979), this market-to-book ratio suggests that unrealized gains exceeding ¥60 billion may be possible. Similarly, a revaluation factor of 3.7 on the book value of securities suggests that unrealized gains in excess of ¥20 million may be possible there.[11] These are the so-called hidden assets that contribute to Japanese companies' very high equity values relative to reported earnings. To the extent that latent gains can be realized or borrowed against, the seemingly high prices of many Japanese companies may be justified.

## THE NEGOTIATING PROCESS IN JAPAN

The need to be patient when negotiating with the Japanese, especially over matters as delicate as the sale of a company, has been emphasized and repeated by experienced negotiators to the point of rendering the imperative a cliche. This is sound advice, though somewhat misleading. It is not merely that Japanese consensus decision making takes more time than the top-down Western approach, although certainly Western negotiators should be prepared for a longer bargaining period. Rather, through the exercise of patience one demonstrates qualities such as tolerance, forbearance, steadiness, dependability, and diligence—in short, the qualities that form the mortar of an enduring trust relationship.

With ownership of any corporation comes an affiliation with

10. At the very least, one might expect that these assets would provide good collateral to support debt, which would create additional value through the interest tax shields.
11. Wako Research Institute of Economics, *Quarterly Economic Review* (Tokyo: Wako Securities, Spring 1988).

a large coalition of stakeholders, a coalition that most Japanese managers feel obliged to represent in its entirety in their negotiations with a potential buyer or seller. A foreign company with little or no understanding of that coalition and the delicate network of contracts that binds it together will be viewed as a potential threat. Japanese managers will naturally proceed quite tentatively when dealing with such a company, even if the offered price is attractive. Time during negotiations is needed not so much for its own sake or to allow for a decision-making process to play itself out, but to provide a validation period in which the foreign company can be assessed as a candidate for admission to the high-trust fraternity of Japanese management on the basis of its actions. The process of reaching agreement is as important, if not more so, than the content of the agreement itself. The less experience the Japanese company has with its negotiating counterpart, the more time (and patience) will be required.

Merck's approach with Banyu demonstrates an effective understanding of the purposes underlying the slowly measured pace of Japanese negotiations. To begin, Merck's objectives vis-à-vis Banyu were advanced substantially by a pre-existing business relationship. Merck had nearly 30 years of experience with Banyu when it approached the company for acquisition talks. This in and of itself was a credible demonstration of the sort of steadiness and dependability valued by Japanese stakeholders. Even today, the most likely candidates for acquisition by foreign companies are their native Japanese partners.

Merck also took outright control in stages, an approach that accommodated the process of *nemawashi*[12]—the building of individual relationships, implicit contracting, and consulting of key stakeholders to obtain a consensus—a process essential in Japan to tie a new owner to the target company's other stakeholders. Merck was every inch a typical Japanese stable shareholder when it began its acquisition of Banyu by first purchasing

---

12. Literally, *nemawashi* means "wrapping," a reference to the Japanese nurseryman's procedure for transplanting a tree. Rather than dig up the tree and move it, the normal procedure in Japan is to begin cutting small roots a year or more before the anticipated transplant, wrapping the bigger roots with straw to encourage new hair-root growth. This will give the tree a greater chance of survival when the major roots are cut.

5% of its stock on the open market. Later, when it increased its stake in Banyu substantially, Merck still avoided taking immediate majority ownership position by accepting a convertible debenture (convertible after July 1, 1984 into 16.7% of Banyu's fully diluted common shares) as part of the interest received.[13] For as long as it took Merck to convert its debentures, and at least 11 months in any event, Merck remained a minority shareholder in Banyu. Banyu was still technically, even if only temporarily, a Japanese majority-owned corporation.

Although there was never any doubt who had stepped into the driver's seat as far as control of Banyu was concerned, this deal structure provided an interval even after the formal closing when both sides of the transaction could continue to come to terms about the changes that would be necessary and the likelihood that the combination would work. Since Merck's injection of cash into the company was retained on the balance sheet as just that—cash—the stage was set for a freezing or even an orderly reversal of ownership and control in the event that Banyu's stakeholders discovered they could not work effectively with one another under Merck's majority ownership. By creating a viable exit option, the staged structure of the deal facilitated the *nemawashi* process, thus enhancing the likelihood that the combination would succeed and reducing the likelihood that the exit option would ever be used.

Despite its clout, Merck was careful about the way it managed Banyu after the deal was consummated. As I have noted, excess cash was not drained from the company, a move that fortified relationships with Banyu's banks that received the deposits and/ or managed the funds, as well as signaled Merck's long-term commitment to the company. Implicit contracts of lifetime employment were also honored in typical Japanese style. Although Banyu's 3,300 employees were considered too many by at least one-third, no layoffs occurred. Instead, natural attrition brought employment into line with the newly constituted company's needs.

---

13. General Motors had a somewhat similar staged acquisition of shares in Isuzu. GM first acquired 34% of Isuzu for $56 million in 1971. Later, in 1982, it purchased convertible debentures from Isuzu that on conversion would increase GM's share to 49%.

The point is that successful operations in Japan are likely to depend on the adoption of a Japanese style of corporate governance rather than the imposition of an American style. The reason is more economical than cultural; much of the value of the acquired business will often depend on long-established and evolving implicit contracts with other key stakeholders. The loss of trust that may accompany wholesale breaching of these contracts could be more costly to the new foreign owner in the long run than the burden of excess cash or personnel in the short or intermediate term.

Insofar as many available Japanese targets are likely to be financially weak companies in need of restructuring, this can be problematic. One solution Japanese companies occasionally practice is to agree today to finalize an acquisition a year or two later (a form of acquisition in stages) after the bulk of needed restructuring (designed by the buying company itself) has been completed by the target's incumbent management. Ultimately, however, the best policy for a foreign company is a cautious one. Outright majority control of a Japanese company is best viewed as a substitute for other arm's-length forms of business relationships—a final solution to the business hazards intrinsic to alternative contractual arrangements.

## RECIPROCITY IN THE MARKET FOR CORPORATE CONTROL

For all the financial service capacity being developed in Tokyo to support cross-border merger and acquisition activity, virtually none is being put in place with expectations of a booming business in the buying of Japanese companies by foreigners. Everyone's eyes are on the "in-out" deal flow (Japanese companies buying American targets) and appropriately so. To date, there has been far too little activity of the "out-in" variety to justify additional overhead by itself. Many professionals view its development as a distant final stage in Japan's integration into the global market for corporate control.

Like trade in goods and services, the emerging asymmetry in cross-border acquisitions involving Japanese companies has raised issues of fairness and reciprocity in the opening of markets. In fact, however, today's relative paucity of Japanese targets for foreign bidders has less to do with barriers explicitly thrown up or maintained by the Japanese government than with the system of corporate governance exercised in the private sector. Foreign bidders are not so much being unfairly denied access to the Japanese M&A market as they are simply confronted with a corporate governance system that sharply diminishes the activity in general. Recall that even purely domestic M&A activity is quite thin in Japan for deals much above ¥1 billion.

Acquisitions of a controlling interest in Japanese companies by foreigners do occur, albeit rarely. When they do, they are always friendly and frequently the last stage in an evolving commercial relationship between a pair of foreign and Japanese companies. In fact, a sizable number of what are commonly classified as foreign takeovers are really buyouts of the local partner in a Japanese joint venture.

Merck's acquisition of Banyu (and, as will be shown in Chapter 10, Minebea Company's rebuff of an aggressive foreign bidder) suggests that the typical Anglo-American approach to M&A is not yet a viable means of acquiring a Japanese company. The Anglo-American approach emphasizes the private-property nature of equity ownership wherein one set of equity owners can be relatively easily detached from a stakeholder coalition comprising a company and replaced with another. Considerations such as price and voting control play prominent roles in this approach.

The Japanese approach, in contrast, rests heavily on a community-property concept of the firm as reflected in the complex blend of claims generally held by various corporate stakeholders. Consequently, dealmaking in Japan requires greater emphasis on maintaining the value of a host of implicit as well as explicit claims on the target firm held by members of a stakeholder coalition, all complicated by the fact that cross-shareholding arrangements are part of what supports the contracts already in place. Therefore a gradual approach to transfers of corporate control is required in order to permit recontracting to occur among stakeholders in such a way that important long-term relationships are not ruptured, and the value of the business is preserved. As a rule, foreign companies should not expect to come to Japan and find quick success as a bidder for a target company with which it has no seasoned relationship. The only targets likely to be available to those who use such tactics will be small, undercapitalized companies in weak competitive positions, poorly situated to help the foreign parent achieve its strategic aims in Japan.

# PART II
# Advent of Change

In Part II, my focus shifts from what the Japanese corporate governance system has been to what it is gradually becoming in the wake of profound changes in product and capital markets. Part II looks at the major stresses currently impinging upon the Japanese corporate governance system. The pressure to restructure strategically in the wake of a strengthened yen, rising competition from newly industrialized nations, and slower growth in demand for Japanese goods are discussed in Chapter 7 through an examination of Nippon Steel's massive restructuring efforts over the past decade.

Evidence indicates that events since the late 1970s have placed traditional Japanese shareholder coalitions under tremendous pressure. Companies no longer can rely on growth in existing product markets to satisfy the expectations of all corporate stakeholders. This situation has led to the pursuit of unrelated diversification and a potential transfer of value from suppliers of capital to corporate employees.

The effects of two other major trends, a widening of access to global capital markets and the buildup of cash on Japanese balance sheets, are examined in Chapters 8 and 9, respectively. Collectively, these trends are freeing Japanese corporations from the rigors heretofore imposed by competition in a single industry and dependence on a few large creditor-shareholders for external capital. Excess financial liquidity, eroding control by traditional lending banks, and widening managerial discretion in the allocation of corporate resources have collectively produced some critical fissures in what many had thought to be a solid and virtually seamless alliance among Japanese corporate stake-holders.

It is the opening of these fissures that has made possible, even inevitable, the expansion of certain Anglo-American takeover tactics and Western participation in the Japanese market for corporate control. The overall impact of these developments on the Japanese market for corporate control is discussed in Chapter 10. Accounts of the attack on the large confectioner, Fujiya Company, by Japanese greenmailers and the foreign bid for Minebea Company provide clear illustrations of both developments.

Severe though the stresses may be, these trends are unlikely to bring about the complete disintegration of the Japanese corporate governance system and a true Japanese/Anglo-American integration of the market for corporate control. This is the focus of Chapter 11. A more likely outcome will be limited Japanese adoption of Anglo-American takeover tactics and limited Western entry to the Japanese market, all ultimately in the service of reasserting the power and control traditionally exercised by Japan's large share-owning financial institutions.

# 7
# RESTRUCTURING AND RECONTRACTING

Mergers and acquisitions among large corporations occur less frequently in Japan than in the United States and are more narrowly motivated when they do occur. Large-scale takeovers by Japanese companies are more accurately viewed as extreme steps taken to defend and preserve a valuable pre-existing business relationship than as either spontaneous attempts to create value by capitalizing on a financially attractive deal or as planned initiatives in the execution of a corporate strategy. When one Japanese company discovers that another's business fits its strategy or has some other useful technological, distribution, or marketing fit, it is more likely to set up an arm's-length trading relationship with it, reinforced by reciprocal minority equity ownership, than to seize majority ownership and control.

Part I traced these characteristics of Japanese mergers and acquisitions to the Japanese corporate governance system.[1] More so than culture or law, this system has functioned powerfully to alleviate the adverse effects of self-interested opportunism among corporate stakeholders, thereby helping companies to sustain long-term business relationships and focus on long-term objectives. Integration of asset ownership has been less imperative among Japanese corporations, as has been the need to take over companies in order to reverse the policies of entrenched, wayward managers.

---

1. Two notable exceptions to this general characteristic are Misawa Homes Company, Ltd. and Minebea Company, Ltd., both of which executed explicit strategies of growth by acquisition. Both, however, also concentrated on buying and revitalizing financially weak companies.

169

However, trends that began taking shape in the late 1970s and gained momentum by the mid-1980s are calling into question the integrity of the classic Japanese corporate governance system—and with it, the future of Japanese M&A activity. So admirably suited to high growth, the corporate governance system is being severely tested in this low-growth era. In the case of Nippon Steel, we see management striving to satisfy expectations of lifetime employment for skilled workers in the face of receding growth and threatened profitability of the company's core business. Unrelated diversification plans in progress today are arguably more to the advantage of Nippon Steel's current employees than to the suppliers of capital and could, therefore, set the stage for future stakeholder conflicts.

## NIPPON STEEL

In Japan, as elsewhere, changes in technology and the external business environment have precipitated significant modifications of the corporate governance system, often preceded by overt conflict among stakeholder groups. From the historical perspective offered by the Noda Shoyu Company case, the past decade may be viewed as the most recent of several important watershed periods in the evolution of the Japanese corporate governance system. Again Japanese corporate stakeholders are undertaking the delicate but vital task of adjusting the terms of their involvement in corporations.

Nippon Steel, considered by many to be the flagship industrial enterprise in Japan during the high-growth period, has not been immune from this process. Burdened with implicit contracts of lifetime employment for its workers, wages higher than those paid elsewhere, and a nearly unshakable commitment to the steel industry, the Japanese steel giant has experienced increasing difficulty in the current economic environment. In 1986, following the dramatic rise of the yen and the export thrust of Korean steelmakers, Nippon Steel saw sales drop by 23% and realized a loss of ¥47 billion. Other Japanese steelmakers turned in similar results. Nippon Steel's president declared the situation facing the industry the "worst crisis since World War II," when American bombers destroyed Japan's steelmaking capacity. A vice president said that without cutbacks in personnel there would be no future for Nippon Steel.

In this atmosphere Nippon Steel announced a dramatic new restructuring plan in February 1987—a plan that would profoundly change the strategic direction of the company. By various means, the company intended to reduce employment in its steel operations from 46,000 to 27,000 full-time workers by 1990. At the same time, it would nurture five major new businesses that were expected to contribute half the company's sales by 1995.

Prelude to Restructuring

Nippon Steel's excess labor problem was a latent but clearly recognized problem as early as the late 1960s, when the groundwork for the Yawata-Fuji merger into Nippon Steel was being prepared. Acknowledged overcapacity in the industry prompted both companies to curtail further investment in steel works, thus idling thousands of in-house engineers previously devoted to the design and construction of such facilities. As soon as the combination took effect, the new company embarked upon diversification efforts to maintain the productivity of these employees and avoid having to lay them off.

The upswing in Japanese housing construction and urban development at that time appeared to be activities well suited to the professional talents of Nippon Steel's underemployed engineers. With a vision of "industrializing" home production and creating further domestic demand for steel, Nippon Steel purchased a large tract of land (approximately 108 million square feet) near Tokyo Bay for development purposes.[2] Company engineers were also put to work earning fees in a "technology transfer" program that entailed the construction of steel operations in such developing nations as China, Korea, and Brazil.

---

2. Lack of familiarity with the market for urban real estate and construction resulted in what one executive estimated to be a ¥50 billion loss.

Aggressive penetration of export markets, particularly North American markets, kept capacity and labor fully employed during the 1968–1974 period. But the oil shock of 1973–1974 collapsed the profitability of Nippon Steel by 40% in 1974 and another 50% in 1975. Although Japan's exports of steel remained fairly high in this period (30.8 million metric tons in 1974 and 39.4 million in 1975) domestic demand fell by 23.7 million metric tons between 1973 and 1975. The drop called into question the future viability of Nippon Steel's 47-million metric ton capacity and, with it, the loan agreements, shareholder dividends, management compensation packages, lifetime employment expectations, and various other stakeholder commitments that depended on its high utilization.

True to form, Nippon Steel's management attempted to deal with the crisis by first seeking cost efficiencies from which all stakeholders in the company would stand to gain, deferring the thorny problem of implementing changes that would benefit some at the expense of others. The company's primary operating responses included energy-saving projects such as recovery and reuse of "waste" energy, integration of several processing steps into a continuous sequence, and conversion to cheaper sources of energy. Meanwhile, the buildup of receivables and inventory well in excess of sales growth, coupled with declines in profitability, led to a ballooning debt in 1976. Although the work force was allowed to shrink through attrition, no layoffs were made. Instead, cash flow to service debt requirements was obtained by cutting dividends 40% in 1977 (restored somewhat with a 33% increase the following year) and selling security holdings.

Although Nippon Steel's profitability staged a near-term recovery, the implementation of EEC import quotas, the U.S. trigger-price mechanism, and generally slackening demand for steel kept both Nippon Steel and the Japanese steel industry from regaining their pre-oil-shock levels of output before the onset of the second oil shock in 1979. Efforts to achieve further efficiencies in the use of energy were redoubled, and to good effect: by 1985, the amount of energy consumed in the production of a ton of steel at Nippon Steel declined by 20% relative to the level used in 1973. Nevertheless, the onset of the second shock made it more apparent than ever that capacity—and therefore the work force—would eventually have to be reduced. The construction industry, which accounted for 40–50% of domestic demand for steel, fell into a depression; shipbuilding activity declined similarly; auto producers, the next-largest consumers of steel, made increasing use of lighter-weight steel substitutes such as plastics and fine ceramics; and the demand mix in general began to shift toward higher-quality steel.

Thus, by 1979, with some mills operating at 40% capacity, Nippon Steel found itself saddled with 3,500 workers in excess of personnel requirements for its current annual output level of 33 million metric tons. Given average annual compensation packages of ¥4.28 million per employee (¥2.76 straight salary, ¥.92 annual bonus, and ¥.6 in fringe benefits), this translated into an annual aggregate cost to the company of nearly ¥15 billion—approximately 15% of Nippon Steel's pretax income in 1979. Steel operations themselves could be relieved of this burden through attrition: workers were scheduled to retire at an annual rate of 1,500 a year for the next four or five years. By ceasing to make new hires, management projected that excess personnel would be eliminated by 1982. Through transfers of remaining employees, underutilized mills could eventually be shut down, generating further savings in overhead.

Although such a formula could correct Nippon Steel's manpower problem without requiring layoffs, it entailed substantial excess costs in the interim. Furthermore, there would be a subtle additional cost to the company in the way of suboptimal hiring practices: an internal study indicated that the optimal hiring rate for Nippon Steel was 700 new employees a year. Finally, threatening to negate the normal rate of attrition was the company union's demand in 1979 to increase the mandatory retirement age from 55 to 60. This demand followed the lead of the Japanese civil service. Given the higher wages of senior employees nearing retirement and the normal retirement patterns of the company, such an extension would result in higher annual labor costs of approximately ¥50 billion a year—half of Nippon Steel's pretax income in 1979 and nearly 10% more than its average annual pretax income since the first oil shock.

Management responded predictably. It pursued a variety of temporary and permanent employee outplacement techniques that effectively distributed excess labor costs across a wide number of the company's customers, suppliers, and subcontractors. Several hundred workers nearing retirement were placed early with subcontracting companies that normally hired Nippon Steel's retirees needing further income before complete retirement. The subcontractors would pay their own going rate, about 60% of the annual salary paid by Nippon Steel; Nippon Steel would pick up the balance, along with bonuses and fringe benefits. Several hundred workers were also "loaned" to a major auto company on a rolling three-month basis. Again, the loaned workers performed low-skill jobs and were paid the going rate by the auto manufacturer (about 70% of the wage level at Nippon Steel) with Nippon Steel making up the difference. Nippon Steel also created new jobs in related activities. Some were created by cutting back the volume of work that was subcontracted out to other members of the Nippon Steel group. Less common was the transfer of workers to entirely new jobs in new ventures set up by Nippon Steel.

These means met the immediate challenge of the 1979 energy crisis without dramatic breaches of trust or serious ruptures in the agreements binding together the firm's stakeholders. Nevertheless, the preservation of employees' claims ultimately came at the expense of other stakeholders. Labor had to content itself with some lower-skilled jobs and unwanted transfers, but its monetary wage package and implicit lifetime employment commitments were essentially untouched. It was subcontractors, customers, and shareholders that had to make do with less cash in the form of reduced revenues, higher labor costs, and/or lower dividends. But by carefully spreading the burden of these costs among many different stakeholders Nippon Steel's management successfully diffused the redistributive impact of the restructuring of claims and avoided explicit conflict among stakeholders.

Restructuring in the 1980s

A 14% rise of the dollar against the yen between 1979 and 1982 reduced the dollar cost of Japanese steel and helped boost Nippon Steel's exports. This allowed the company to avoid any further immediate adjustments beyond those described above and gave management time to implement a series of three restructuring plans focused on improving the profitability of steel operations. Each plan by itself was modest, with primary emphasis placed upon improving product yield, reducing unit consumption of raw materials, and achieving various administrative efficiencies. However, collectively they resulted in an annual reduction of crude steelmaking capacity from 47 million metric tons to 34 million by 1986. Four blast furnaces and several rolling mills used to produce wire rod, plate, and hot strip were closed.

But even as these rationalization plans were being completed, the Plaza Accord of 1985, which coordinated and accelerated the dollar's decline, made it apparent that even this degree of adjustment was not enough. As far as current operations were concerned, the advantage of cheaper imported oil, iron ore, and coking coal was more than offset by the disadvantages created by the strong yen.

Competitive advantage in a glutted world market (annual crude steelmaking capacity of a billion metric tons versus annual global consumption of 700 million) was rapidly passing to producers in newly industrializing Asian countries such as Korea and Taiwan. These producers had low labor costs, and their modern large-scale facilities kept operating at close to 90% capacity. The steeper rise of the yen against the dollar in comparison to the currencies of these other producing nations only exacerbated this trend.[3] The collapse of Japanese shipbuilding and the general decline in the fortunes of Japanese export industries further reduced domestic demand for steel.

The combined effect of these developments was to plunge the industry into its worst financial crisis in the postwar period. The five major producers reported 1986 losses totaling ¥187 billion, ¥47 billion of which was borne by Nippon Steel. The immediate prospects for improvement looked bleak. The yen continued to show great strength in 1986 and rising protectionist sentiments in the United States in the face of a growing trade imbal-

---

3. At an exchange rate of ¥150 to the dollar, South Korea's POSCO steel works had a 28% cost advantage over its Japanese rivals.

ance threatened to choke off exports of steel and steel-built products still further. In 1986, all major Japanese steel producers cut their cash dividend payments and eliminated them altogether by September of the next year. By 1987, the government designated steel, among others, a "depressed industry."

The depth of the crisis created by *endaka* (the sudden, unexpected rise in the yen) helped create the consensus needed to undertake finally a major restructuring of the steel industry. By the end of 1986, all five major steel producers made public their plans for strategically restructuring their businesses over the next two to four years (see Exhibit 7–1). The specifics of Nippon Steel's plan are shown in Exhibit 7–2. Briefly, it called for further reductions and concentration of steel production, personnel reductions in steel manufacturing totaling 19,000 by 1990, and extensive diversification. The businesses targeted for entry and target sales for 1995 are shown in Exhibit 7–3. If the plan were achieved, steel sales would account for only 50% of total corporate sales by 1995.

Although clearly different in several important respects, the basic design of Nippon Steel's fourth restructuring plan echoed that of earlier plans, at least as far as employees were concerned. The size of the announced personnel reductions may appear radical in comparison to the past, but as before, relatively few workers were destined for outright layoff. As Exhibit 7–2 shows, most reductions were to take place through attrition, aided by a modest amount of early retirement. A sizable number of employees currently occupied in the steel division were to be redeployed in new businesses by 1990.[4]

Diversification and Job Preservation

Creating new activities to absorb redundant employees was also characteristic of past restructuring plans. What was different in the latest plan was the degree of diversification repre-

---

4. Redeployment into new businesses as part of this plan should be distinguished from past redeployments to other companies in the group. At the time of the announcement of the new restructuring plan, it was estimated that Nippon Steel already had approximately 8,000 employees seconded to other companies, who nevertheless retained their salaries and status as Nippon Steel employees.

Exhibit 7-1  Outline of Rationalization Plans of Japanese Steel Mills

| Steel Mills | Period | | Outline of Rationalization Plan |
|---|---|---|---|
| Nippon Steel Corp. | 1987–1990 | Concentration of production facilities | 1. Reduction of pig iron production from 12 blast furnaces (8 Works) to 8 BFS (4 Works . . . Yawata, Nagoya, Kimitsu, Oita). |
| | | | 2. Shutdown of BF-related facilities. |
| | | | 3. Concentration of rolling mills. |
| | | Work-force reduction | Steel division to reduce 19,000 by end 1990. (50,000 employed at end 1986.) |
| | | New field (nonsteel), etc. | 1. Total sales ¥4,000 billion 1995. |
| | | | 2. To strengthen electronics and communication divisions, and to decrease sales of steel division to less than 50% of total ones. |
| | | | 3. Absorption of 6,000 workers in new sectors. |

Exhibit 7-1  Outline of Rationalization Plans of Japanese Steel Mills (continued)

| Steel Mills | Period | Outline of Rationalization Plan | |
|---|---|---|---|
| Nippon Kokan K.K. | 1987–1990 | Concentration of production facilities | 1. Reduction of pig iron production from 5 BFS to 4.<br>2. Rolling mills—partial shutdowns to concentrate production and streamline operations. |
| | | Work-force reduction | Steel division to reduce 6,000 by end 1990. (19,400 employed at end 1986.) |
| | | New field (nonsteel), etc. | In new field, sales ¥100 billion in 1990 by expanding new materials divisions (e.g., Ceramic). |
| Kawasaki Steel Corp. | 1987–1988 | Concentration of production facilities | Optimum, efficient operation in Chiba Works by shutting down steelmaking plant (partially) and plate mill. |
| | | Work-force reduction | Steel division to reduce 5,300 by end 1988. (19,100 employed at end 1986.) |
| | | New field (nonsteel), etc. | Expansion of new divisions relating to electronics, services. |

| Company | Period | Measure | Details |
| --- | --- | --- | --- |
| Sumitomo Metal Industries, Ltd. | 1986–1988 | Concentration of production facilities | Shutdown of plate mill in Wakayama Works, seamless pipe mill in Amagasaki Works. |
| | | Work-force reduction | Steel division to reduce 6,000 in 1986–1988. (25,200 employed at end 1985.) |
| | | New field (nonsteel), etc. | Sales of new divisions (e.g., new materials, electronics) to ¥90 billion at end 1988 from present ¥60 billion. |
| Kobe Steel, Ltd. | 1986–1989 | Work-force reduction | Companywide to reduce 6,000 by end 1988. (28,000 employed at September 1986.) |
| | | New field (nonsteel), etc. | Sales of new divisions, new products to ¥350 billion in 1989 from present. |
| Nisshin Steel Co., Ltd. | 1986–1989 | Work-force reduction | Companywide to reduce 1,700 by end 1989. (8,600 employed at end 1986.) |

*Source:* Nippon Steel Corporation.

Exhibit 7-2 *Nippon Steel's Restructuring Plan*

A. Restructuring Objectives
    1. Reduce crude steel production to 24 million tons by 1990
    2. Ensure top-level global competitiveness
    3. Improve profit in all aspects of steel business
B. Concentration of Steel Production
    1. Capacity reduction of 34–24 million tons by 1990
    2. Crude steel production—4 steel works (number of blast fur-
        naces): Yawata, 1; Nagoya, 2; Kimitsu, 3; Oita, 2
    3. Plant closure of blast furnaces: Yawata, Sakai, Kamaishi, Hiro-
        hata, Muroran (1988–1990)
    4. Plant closure of rolling mills: Muroran, hot strip mill and cold
        mill
C. Personnel Reduction and Method
    1. Reduce 19,000 workers in steel business (46,000–27,000) by
        1990
    2. Measures: retirement (full year)             9,000
                retirement (1 year less)      2,000
                new business               6,000
                tentative leave            2,000
D. Future Business Composites
    1. Reduce steel sales to 50% of total sales volume
    2. Emphasize new business opportunities for the twenty-first cen-
        tury founded on Nippon Steel's technological capabilities

*Source:* Nippon Steel Corporation.


Exhibit 7-3 *Nippon Steel's Diversification Objectives*

| Domain | | Sales (¥ billion) | |
| --- | --- | --- | --- |
| *Market* | *Business* | *1986* | *1995 Target (% of Total)* |
| Materials | Steel | 1,940 | (2,000) 50% |
| | New materials | 5 | (400) 10% |
| | Chemicals | 230 | |
| Engineering | Engineering | 275 | (400) 10% |
| Electronics Information Communications | Electronics Information systems | — | (800) 20% |
| Social development, Life development | Urban development Leisure development services | — | (400) 10% |
| Biotechnology | Biotechnology | — | (10) — |
| Total | | 2,450 | 4,000 —— |

*Source:* Nippon Steel Corporation.

sented by these new businesses. In the past, the impetus created by the Japanese corporate governance system to avoid changes that redistributed benefits among stakeholders and to allocate resources primarily to realize true efficiency gains meant that expansions into new markets tended to be slow and incremental. Capital was devoted only to new activities that represented an extension of the technical and managerial skills already possessed by the existing human resources (e.g., engineering projects, technical consulting). Thus, in effect, the Japanese corporate governance system contributed to Japanese management's tendency to eschew unrelated diversification as a means of achieving growth and to preserve what Alfred Chandler calls "organizational capabilities." It also created a strong tendency for management's attention to revert to the core business—steel—as soon as the crisis passed.

Nippon Steel's latest restructuring plan painted a radically new picture of the company by 1995. Fully half of the company's sales were expected to come from new businesses in which, at least on the surface, the company had no special organizational capability. Indeed, so radical was the proposed diversification that the company found it necessary to amend its bylaws and statement of corporate purpose to permit multiple-business management. To facilitate the management of such a company, it was also necessary to complete an organizational transformation (begun in 1979) from a functional structure (i.e., sales, production, procurement, finance, and so forth) to a multiunit, multidivisional structure that included separate units to manage new materials, electronics and information systems, biotechnology, and various service businesses. Although these new units are presently operated as cost centers, management expects them to be self-sustaining in four or five years; each will be responsible for its profitability, allocating its capital, and providing a stream of "dividends" to headquarters in a highly decentralized fashion.[5]

---

5. Some Japanese security analysts conjecture that Nippon Steel may be paving the way for an eventual holding-company arrangement in which each of the operating divisions, including steel, would be a separate company. This is similar to the organizational struc-

Management pointed out that the main criteria for selecting new areas in which to expand were the potential for long-term growth and the possibility of applying the skills and know-how of Nippon Steel's human resources. With respect to the latter, however, the relatedness of the targeted businesses appears to have more to do with the technical and research skills of non-managerial employees, which the company is striving to keep fully employed, than the functional skills of management itself. For example, although the company has no experience competing in the communications systems market, it employs more than 3,000 software engineers and other electronics and information systems specialists whose former jobs were to apply electronics technology to steelmaking operations. In the field of biotechnology, the company finds a natural connection stemming from its previous research into areas such as waste disposal and the development of specialized oils (e.g., jojoba oil) for use in its rolling mills. It also cites its "spacious landholdings [another underutilized asset in the slow-growth environment], vast amounts of applicable energy and capable human resources" as contributing to the natural, evolutionary fit between biotechnology and the production of steel. Finally, in what perhaps is the most far-reaching venture of all, Nippon Steel opened a theme park, Space World, on the site of one of the former plants. Among other things, the park provides jobs to local residents formerly employed at the plant, which was a major employer in its remote location.

Nippon Steel views its entry into these businesses as a way of providing new long-term streams of profits and cash flow to replace those generated by steel today. It sees itself as quite legiti-

---

ture of most U.S. steel companies. Besides facilitating the purchase and sale of assets or even companies, one of the benefits of such a structure is thought to be the separation of the steel business—and with it, the union representing steel workers—from the newer businesses. This could help the negotiation of a more competitive compensation contract with steel workers. Under present conditions, one company union represents all employees including those engaged in high-paying, nonsteel activities. The basis of the conjecture is Nippon Steel's move to a multidivisional organizational structure coupled with the Keidanren's support of a proposal to repeal the anti-holding-company clause of the Commercial Code. The honorary chairman of Nippon Steel, Eishiro Saito, became chairman of the Keidanren early in 1986.

mately striving to create options today for tomorrow's growth. But whether those options prove worth exercising in the future clearly depends on management's ability to make informed, intelligent decisions in these diverse fields as well as on a host of market developments beyond the direct control of the company. Given a comparative lack of direct competitive experience in some of these fields, the gamble is a risky one.[6] Meanwhile, the unambiguous beneficiaries of ongoing investment in new businesses are the employees no longer required in steelmaking activities. Indeed, it is clear that finding uses for their skills as a means of satisfying lifetime employment expectations was central to the planning process that led to the restructuring plan. Whether or not suppliers of capital will benefit from these investments is far less clear at the present time.

The recent focus on employees' interests over those of other stakeholders at Nippon Steel may be explained in part by the company's acute sense of social responsibility, a legacy of its close historical ties to various organs of government and the public largesse heaped upon it in the period of reconstruction. Undoubtedly, strong implicit contracts between the industrialists who owned and managed the steel industry and the bureaucrats who regulated it were associated with the early subsidization that it received. Today's managers, many of whom hail from the ranks of MITI, are doing little more than what they perceive is expected of them in this period of economic transition.

Management's focus on employees also reflects industry economics and Nippon Steel's position within it. Given the highly specific attributes of the asset base (primarily steel works appropriate only for the production of steel) and the deep pockets that Nippon Steel is perceived to have as Japan's industry leader and pre-eminent industrial enterprise, the company is highly susceptible to employee demands, especially those of organized labor. This susceptibility is neither new nor unique to Japan. Labor began pressing its demands on the steel industry in Japan quite soon after the legalization of union activities. In the United

---

6. It has already abandoned ventures in an international business communications center and a mail-order business.

States, labor's appropriation of returns to capital has even led to the transference of steel mill ownership to workers, as in the case of the Weirton Division of National Steel in 1984.

But in Japan, following the period of union activism in the 1950s, the classic corporate governance system that eventually evolved (particularly at Nippon Steel) made labor's interests, and those of other employees and corporate stakeholders, largely coterminous with growth. As long as the company grew rapidly and continuously, virtually all stakeholders' interests could be met. Even if employees extracted gains at the expense of others, the distributive impact of such gains could be masked somewhat by the essentially private means through which some stakeholders secured their returns and by the general wave of growth that lifted the welfare of all stakeholders. Only when the tide of growth receded dramatically did it become apparent that future gains by employees and even the preservation of the company's claims might have to come at the expense of others.

Nippon Steel's restructuring efforts throughout the low-growth period highlight several important attributes of Japanese corporations. They illustrate powerfully the strength of the implicit contracts that govern relationships among corporate stakeholders in Japan, particularly with respect to the ideal of lifetime employment, and the apparent high cost that stakeholders associate with the breach of such contracts. Adverse trends in the value of claims some stakeholders (e.g., lenders and/or shareholders) hold tend to be observed and addressed early. But the first impulse of Japanese management is to relieve pressure by expanding sales into new geographic markets, undertaking related diversification, and aggressively pursuing those operating efficiencies that improve overall performance without imposing heavy costs on any one stakeholder. These remedies are favored because they expand *total* corporate value rather than simply redistribute value among stakeholders, which would entail potentially costly recontracting.

This impulse contributes significantly to a tendency to focus on core businesses and make only incremental changes in the configuration of assets, management, and manpower used to conduct those businesses. Usually it takes a crisis to trigger more substantial changes. Even then, management's impulse is to minimize the necessary recontracting among stakeholders. Workers, for example, may be asked to assume new jobs in new businesses with costs possibly imposed in the way of relocation or loss of prestige associated with less skilled work assignments. But the basic implicit contract relating to pay and lifetime employment tends to be kept in force.

These tendencies are by no means confined to Nippon Steel. Numerous other Japanese companies in shipbuilding, textiles, rubber, and chemicals have also undertaken profound strategic restructurings, some of them much sooner than steel companies did. Producers of synthetic textiles, for example, encountered slowing growth and overcapacity as early as the mid-1960s. Two industry leaders, Asahi Chemicals of the DKB group and Toray of the Mitsui group, undertook earlier restructurings quite similar to those of Nippon Steel. Initial threats to profitability in core product markets were met with rationalization plans. These included better inventory control, abandoning unprofitable products, and personnel reductions in fibers and textiles through attrition as well as transfers to subcontractors and other group companies. Related diversification to provide new growth and jobs followed in the wake of continued challenges to core businesses in the late 1960s and 1970s. By the mid-1980s, both companies had reduced their dependence on fibers, textiles, and chemicals to 51% and 60% of total sales, respectively. Asahi Chemical had diversified into plastics, synthetic rubber, construction materials, medical products, and biotechnology. Toray also entered plastics, engineering and construction, electronics, ceramics, and biotechnology.

Specific circumstances may differ, but nearly all major Japanese companies trapped in mature markets in the 1980s share the problem of restoring growth and profitability without breaching long-standing implicit contracts with labor. In Japan, the nearly universal approach to handling this dilemma is to diversify as a means of providing jobs today and, ideally, profitability tomorrow. Although they are often far removed from original core businesses, areas such as electronics, engineering and construction, new materials (advanced ceramics, functional

alloys, magnetic materials), telecommunications, and biotechnology dominate the attention of these restructuring companies.

The near-term costs of entering these businesses are, in the
words of Asahi Chemical's former president, Miyazaki Kagay-
aku, viewed simply as "healthy losses" necessary for the long-
term viability of the organization. Perhaps they are. Certainly, if
any companies can withstand such losses, it is Japanese corporations with their enduring business relationships, patient investors, and focus on the long run. But even as significant changes
take shape on the asset side of the Japanese corporate balance
sheet, profound changes are occurring on the liability side—
changes that threaten to test the patience of at least some important providers of capital. In conjunction with extensive diversification strategies, such changes could pave the way to a more
active Japanese market for corporate control.

# 8
# THE GLOBALIZATION OF FINANCE AND THE NEW PERFORMANCE ORIENTATION OF STABLE SHAREHOLDERS

Close, stable relationships between companies and banks have been essential elements of the classic Japanese corporate governance system. As such, they have contributed significantly to the mitigation of Japanese takeover activity. Today, however, this stability is being shaken by two major changes in the world of finance: the buildup of financial slack on Japanese balance sheets and the globalization of the Japanese financial system. The former change is altering the nature of business that banks execute with their major industrial clients and generally weakening bank control over these companies. Concurrently, the latter change is causing banks and other institutional owners of equity to demand greater returns on their holdings of client-company stock. Together these trends are evoking a creeping instability in Japanese equity ownership and signal a widening of activity in the Japanese market for corporate control.

This chapter examines in depth the recontracting process that is now taking place between Japanese companies and banks in the wake of Japanese financial liberalization. It traces the effects of such liberalization on the financing patterns of Japanese corporations and on the competitive pressures confronting Japanese financial institutions. Displacement of traditional relational contracting between companies and banks by price-driven, deal-oriented financing imposes great stress on the traditional Japanese corporate governance system. Because this displacement is being driven by the inexorable globalization of Japanese financial markets, the stress is not likely to subside.

## THE EMERGENCE OF MODERN CORPORATE FINANCE
## IN JAPAN

Major Japanese companies' widespread use of securities to raise capital externally was largely a phenomenon of the 1980s, but its roots could be traced to transitions that began in the 1970s. Deficit spending by the Japanese central government in response to the first oil crisis was accompanied by a dramatic expansion of secondary markets for government bonds and gradual deregulation of interest rates. By creating a tight credit market, government deficit financing also indirectly stimulated an expansion of the corporate bond market by those companies unable to satisfy external needs with bank loans. Whereas domestic bonds accounted for only 5.0% of external funds raised by large corporations from 1970 to 1974, they accounted for 13.7% of funds raised in the 1975–1979 period.

But the real watershed for Japanese corporate finance came with the amendment of the Foreign Exchange Control Law in 1980. The amendment permitted cross-border capital transactions with only prior notification of the Ministry of Finance rather than the obtaining of a formal permit. This relaxation had an immediate and significant impact. Attracted by the lower cost of funds, less regulation, greater flexibility, and, for some, the benefits of liabilities denominated in foreign currencies, major Japanese companies turned to the Euromarkets as a source of funds. Total funds raised in overseas markets in 1981 exceeded ¥1.4 trillion, nearly triple the 1975–1979 annual average of ¥560 billion. Despite generally slack demand for external funds in the early 1980s, overseas financing by Japanese companies continued to increase to levels approaching ¥3.5 trillion annually by the late 1980s. As a fraction of all securities issued by Japanese companies, overseas issues rose steadily from a level under 20% prior to 1980 to nearly 50% by 1985. Much of the funds so raised were used to repay notes payable and long-term borrowings from banks, resulting in a restructuring of Japanese corporate liabilities in which various types of bonds were substituted for trade and bank credit.

At home, yen loans continued to dominate security financing in domestic markets, although borrowings continued to shrink as a proportion of total funds raised. Moreover, lending practices began to change in the wake of overseas financing by Japanese manufacturers and the continued relaxation of domestic financial market regulation. Continued growth in the CD market and the introduction of large-denomination money market certificates in 1985 contributed to greater variability in banks' cost of funds. This in turn gave rise to spread lending, in which a margin—say 50 basis points—is added to the lender's cost of funds. A relatively new practice in Japan, spread lending was accompanied by lowered compensating balance requirements, which improved the cost of funds to the borrowing company and lowered the yield that would otherwise be earned by banks. The introduction of a commercial paper market in November 1987 provided another viable alternative for large companies in search of short-term funds and further reduced the dependence of corporations on banks. For all practical purposes, lending to large corporations has ceased to be a growth business for Japan's major banks (see Exhibit 8–1).

## THE BUILDUP OF FINANCIAL STOCK

Paralleling the liberalization of Japanese corporate finance has been a dramatic buildup of financial slack on Japa-

Exhibit 8-1 *City Banks Loan Balance by Size of Borrower*
*(¥ trillion)*

|  | End of FY 1983 | | End of FY 1987 | |
| --- | --- | --- | --- | --- |
| *Borrowers* | *Balance* | *Share* | *Balance* | *Share* |
| Large firms | ¥32 | 37% | ¥ 36 | 28% |
| Medium-sized firms | 12 | 15 | 17 | 14 |
| Small firms | 31 | 37 | 60 | 46 |
| Individuals | 9 | 11 | 15 | 12 |
| Total | ¥84 | 100% | ¥128 | 100% |

*Source:* Industrial Bank of Japan.

nese corporate balance sheets. During Japan's high-growth period (1948–1973), Japanese corporations were confronted with a volume of attractive investment opportunities that vastly exceeded their cash flow and the amount of funds most companies could reasonably expect to raise externally. The twin leaders of this growth were inventory and new capital investments by businesses, both of which grew at annual average *real* rates in excess of 10%. Opportunities to invest at attractive rates of return were sufficiently great that the corporate sector experienced chronic and growing shortfalls between uses of funds and internally generated cash. Later, as domestic demand for products slowed, Japanese companies turned to offshore markets where they faced established domestic competition.

Throughout this period, Japanese corporate finance served an enabling function, pure and simple. Factory and product managers determined what the company needed in order to attain and preserve competitive advantage in its markets. Financial managers raised the cash necessary to fund the approved projects. Senior finance executives in my field sample routinely described their challenge in this period as primarily one of securing a sufficient volume of external finance. Minimizing capital costs was a distant secondary concern to most of them.

In any event, the scope of their decision making was tightly confined. For all practical purposes, there were only two major sources of external funds: collateralized loans (both short- and long-term) and trade credit. These, in turn, were supplied by essentially the same institutions—banks, insurance companies, and major suppliers—stakeholders that were also major shareholders in their companies. As noted in Chapter 3, these stakeholders monitored client companies closely, even to the point of occasionally injecting new management to ensure a rational deployment of scarce funds. Thus high growth, the rigors of competition at home and abroad, the heavy use of debt and trade credit, and the ownership of these claims by institutional shareholders that monitored performance closely were sufficient to ensure the deployment of cash in a pattern consistent with the priorities of the suppliers of capital.

Although double-digit real growth in Japan had begun to subside even prior to 1973, the oil shock produced a sudden, dramatic, and essentially permanent reduction in Japanese economic growth. As both a by-product of, and contributing factor to, this slowdown, capital spending growth fell to an annual rate of about 6%. So too did inventory investment, as companies sought to conserve cash. As in the case of Nippon Steel, a drive to achieve operating efficiencies, particularly with respect to reducing energy-related costs, replaced volume growth as the near-term objective of most large manufacturing concerns.

The joint effect of investment reduction and cost improvement was to reduce gradually the external capital needs of the corporate sector (see Exhibit 8–2). For large corporations, internally generated funds as a proportion of the change of total assets rose from less than 20% in the 1960s and early 1970s to more than 100% by the mid-1980s. The latter figure reflects the fact that many large Japanese corporations were using their prodigious cash flow during this period to repay debt and build up liquid assets on the balance sheet rather than to increase dividends or invest in real fixed assets.

As a result, Japanese corporations have accumulated considerable financial slack in the form of unused debt capacity and temporary investments in marketable securities. As Exhibit 8–3 shows, the net debt-to-equity ratio by Japan's largest companies (calculated on a book-value basis and adjusted for cash and marketable securities) has declined more or less steadily since 1978, even becoming negative in 1987.[1] Similarly, interest coverage—an alternative measure of leverage—rose from the already high level of 6.8 in 1978 to 16.7 by 1987. Finally, cash, deposits, and marketable securities, another pocket for accumulating financial slack, were drawn down between 1979 and 1985 as bank debt was being repaid, but eventually ticked sharply upward in 1986 and 1987.

---

1. The unleveraging of Japanese corporations is even more pronounced when equity is priced on a market-value rather than book-value basis. In an earlier study, I found Japanese leverage ratios in 1983–1984 to be statistically indistinguishable from that of a comparable set of U.S. companies (see W. Carl Kester, "Capital and Ownership Structure: A Comparison of United States and Japanese Manufacturing Corporations," *Financial Management* (Spring 1986), pp. 5–16.

Exhibit 8-2  Changes in Balance Sheet Accounts for Large Japanese Corporations*
(% of change in total assets)

| | 1966–1970 | 1971–1975 | 1976–1980 | 1981–1984 | 1985–1987 |
|---|---|---|---|---|---|
| *Assets* | | | | | |
| Cash and marketable securities | 16.7 | 14.9 | 12.4 | 40.9 | 43.6 |
| Accounts receivable | 23.4 | 22.8 | 30.8 | (19.1) | 7.6 |
| Inventory | 12.0 | 22.0 | 3.3 | 30.0 | (0.4) |
| Net fixed assets | 30.3 | 22.4 | 30.3 | 31.9 | (15.6) |
| Long-term investments | 13.3 | 13.5 | 2.7 | (24.5) | 37.8 |
| Other | 4.3 | 4.4 | 20.5 | 40.8 | 27.0 |
| Total | 100.0 | 100.0 | 100.0 | 100.0 | 100.0 |
| *Liabilities and Equity* | | | | | |
| Trade credit | 22.8 | 28.6 | 37.9 | (21.6) | (20.0) |
| Bank debt | 32.2 | 36.9 | (26.6) | 46.9 | (73.6) |
| Bond and convertible debentures | 13.3 | 4.0 | 13.7 | 23.4 | 67.1 |
| Accruals and other liabilities | 7.5 | 9.0 | 28.6 | 10.5 | 34.7 |
| Reserves | 1.9 | 5.8 | 21.3 | 0.2 | 4.1 |
| Equity | | | | | |
| New shares | 6.0 | 3.6 | 2.7 | 8.5 | 11.8 |
| Retained earnings | 16.3 | 12.1 | 22.4 | 32.1 | 75.9 |
| Total | 100.0 | 100.0 | 100.0 | 100.0 | 100.0 |

*Data are average percentages for the 250 largest nonfinancial corporations.
Source: NEEDS: Nikkei Financials (magnetic tape). Nihon Keizai Shimbun, Inc. Databank Bureau Information Service Department. Tokyo, 1987.

Exhibit 8-3  *Trends in Japanese Corporate Leverage and Liquidity*

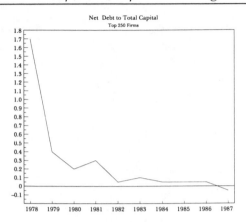

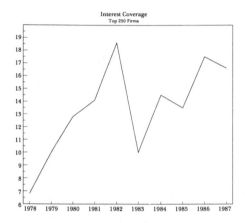

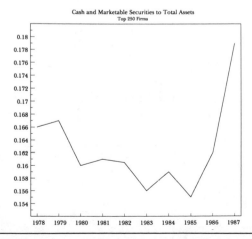

*Source:* NEEDS: Nikkei Financials (magnetic tape). Nihon Keizai Shimbun, Inc. Data-bank Bureau Information Service Department. Tokyo, 1987.

RECONTRACTING WITH FINANCIAL INSTITUTIONS

The buildup of financial slack on Japanese corporate balance sheets, the persistence of excess cash flow throughout the 1980s, and gradual financial deregulation in Tokyo have led to a kind of financial emancipation of Japanese industrial corporations from their traditional lenders. Consider the Daishowa Paper Company. In the spring of 1986, Daishowa Paper surprised Tokyo's financial community by announcing it intended to repay its ¥28 billion of outstanding loans from the Sumitomo Bank when the debt became due in the near future. Timely repayment of debt is not normally newsworthy except, perhaps, when the borrower is a financially troubled concern that has been brought back from the brink of bankruptcy. Such had been Daishowa's situation in the early 1980s after a major expansion program failed to generate sufficient cash flow to service the debt assumed.

But the recovery alone was not the cause of surprise in connection with Daishowa's announcement. What shocked the financial community was that Sumitomo was the bank that in typical Japanese style had helped Daishowa recover by providing a timely infusion of capital and management. Moreover, accompanying the announcement of loan repayment was the declaration that Daishowa intended to repurchase its 805 million common shares (representing a 4.3% equity interest) held by Sumitomo. The repayment, coupled with the announced intention to repurchase, seemed to signal unambiguously a severing of ties with Daishowa's traditional main bank.[2]

The changes now occurring in company-bank relationships are seldom as dramatic as that of Daishowa Paper and Sumitomo. They rarely show up in the press and are difficult to discern in published statistics. But observations made by executives interviewed on this topic indicate that they are widespread. Corporate financial managers and bank officers agree that the

---

2. Evidently, Daishowa did not follow through with its repurchase threat. Sumitomo Bank continues to hold equity in the company.

"main bank system" still exists. But they also agree that the content of the relationship is quite different from that of the past.

Reflecting the national trend among large corporations, the companies I studied borrowed less from banks in the 1980s than they did in the previous decade. Just under half of my sample had little or no need for the bank borrowings at all. The bank debt on their books was usually described as mere "courtesy" loans or unamortized balances of older loans that could have been refinanced on favorable terms, but were being repaid on schedule "out of respect for the main bank."[3] Despite the gains these companies could reap by refinancing immediately, they are apparently eschewing any such ex post opportunism in favor of preserving what were evidently implicit contracts regarding the volume and maturity of loans struck with lenders in an earlier and different economic environment.

The financial policies of Asahi Chemicals were typical of this subset of the sample. Asahi Chemicals has been steadily raising its net worth-to-assets ratio toward its target of 40% (see Exhibit 8–4), repaying bank loans at an increasing rate. It has made no major borrowings from banks in the last five years and is gradually short listing the number of banks with which it will do business. Within four or five years, Asahi expects to have reduced bank borrowings to only ¥50 billion (about 6% of 1988 total assets) spread among 15 major lenders (versus 91 with which it did business at the peak of its bank borrowings).

As the volume and uses of bank financing have changed, so too has the traditional role of banks as monitors of managerial decision making. A manager in one of Japan's largest city banks summarized it this way:

> A decade ago, our relationship with our clients was very old-fashioned. The clients would visit us quarterly to explain their performance, discuss their investment plans, and

---

3. One company noted that most of the bank debt on its balance sheet actually represented borrowings the company undertook on behalf of its employees as part of a mortgage assistance program offered in its benefits package.

Exhibit 8-4  *Asahi Chemical Industry: Trends in Bank Loans and Net Worth Ratios*
(¥ billion)

| | 1978[a] | 1984 | 1985 | 1986 | 1987 | 1988 (Estimate) |
|---|---|---|---|---|---|---|
| Bank loan repayment | NA | ¥23.7 | ¥36.7 | ¥12.4 | ¥78.8 | ¥50.2 |
| Outstanding balance | NA | 352.1 | 315.4 | 303.0 | 224.2 | 174.0 |
| Net worth ratio[b] | 22.8% | 27.3% | 28.4% | 28.9% | 31.3% | NA |

[a]For the year ended March 31
[b] $\dfrac{\text{Shareholders' equity}}{\text{Total assets}}$

*Source:* Asahi Chemical Industry Co., Ltd. (nonconsolidated financial figures).

plead for more loans. Today it is we [the lenders] who must do the pleading. We have to make appointments with them to learn what is happening, and we must now compete with other banks for what little borrowing the company does.

Financial managers at manufacturing companies generally concur with this description of the degree of monitoring and control exerted over their companies by their traditional main banks. Whereas all but one of the companies in the field sample indicated that their corporate plans and investments were closely examined by banks during the 1950–1980 period, *none* reported being subjected to such scrutiny today. Although meetings with lenders are still held semiannually or at least annually to discuss performance, these have apparently evolved into largely perfunctory presentations of past performance rather than substantive discussions of future capital investment. Financial managers in two different manufacturing corporations said they believed that banks were now more interested in tracking the overall return earned on their total investments (debt and equity) in client companies rather than monitoring and influencing managerial decision making.

The exchange of information historically fostered by placing retiring bank officers in senior management positions at client companies also appears to be waning. Two companies in my field sample have been bold enough to refuse bank nominees for managing directors. Evidently the problem has become sufficiently widespread that major banks have begun to experience difficulties in placing retiring employees in second careers— generally a major responsibility of the bank president himself. One of the major city banks stated that this difficulty has reached the point that the normal process for "retiring" an active employee and placing him in a second career has been moved back from the traditional age of 55 to 45. Even then, the bank has found it necessary to place many retiring employees in their own finance subsidiaries rather than in client companies.

As constraints on Japanese corporate finance relax and Tokyo's financial markets deregulate, competition among Japanese banks has further weakened traditional company-bank relationships. The securitization of Japanese corporate finance has made financings increasingly price-sensitive transactions in which past relationships count for little. A company's main bank may win a mandate to lead-manage a deal, but only if it offers a better idea or a competitive quote.

The recent opening of a commercial paper market in Japan represents a good example of this trend. As short-term, unsecured securities sold at a discount, commercial paper is essentially a substitute for bank credit for high-quality issuers—a securitization, in other words, of bank loans. So far, every indication is that price and placing power, not traditional banking relationships, drive this business. Asahi Chemical initiated its commercial paper program in April of 1988 with a ¥50-billion offering. Sumitomo, its traditional main bank, participated in the first underwriting but was closed out of the second because of its unwillingness to offer a competitive bid. Mitsubishi Bank has become a major dealer in this market, not because there are so many more Mitsubishi group companies issuing commercial paper, but because its close relationships with Japan's regional banks create tremendous placing power and allow it to bid aggressively for the paper. Although its volume of commercial paper business was second to Mitsubishi's in 1988, the Bank of Tokyo had actually been awarded more dealerships in that year than any other Japanese bank despite the absence of a clientele of group companies. Indeed, according to corporate financial officers, it was precisely this "neutrality" of the Bank of Tokyo, along with its competitive pricing, that enhanced companies' willingness to award it new business in the absence of attractive bids from traditional main banks.

Nonetheless, although Japanese industrial corporations may be distancing themselves from banks, Japanese banks and other financial institutions still own considerable fractions of these companies' outstanding shares. In fact, the data show this ownership has actually increased slightly in recent years (see Exhibit 8–5). Moreover, however diminished the perceived need by industrial corporations for a close banking relationship, the Japanese bank executives I interviewed all maintain that, from *their* point of view, strong relationships with their industrial clients

Exhibit 8-5  *Share-ownership by Type of Investors, All Listed Companies*
(%)

| | 1980 | 1981 | 1982 | 1983 | 1984 | 1985 | 1986 | 1987 |
|---|---|---|---|---|---|---|---|---|
| Government and local government | 0.2 | 0.2 | 0.2 | 0.2 | 0.2 | 0.2 | 0.8 | 0.9 |
| Financial institutions | 38.8 | 38.8 | 38.7 | 38.9 | 38.9 | 39.6 | 42.2 | 43.5 |
| All banks | 17.1 | 17.3 | 17.3 | 17.6 | 17.9 | 18.3 | 19.6 | 20.5 |
| Investment trusts | 1.9 | 1.5 | 1.3 | 1.2 | 1.0 | 1.1 | 1.3 | 1.8 |
| Annuity trusts | 0.5 | 0.4 | 0.4 | 0.4 | 0.4 | 0.5 | 0.7 | 0.9 |
| Life insurance companies | 12.3 | 12.5 | 12.6 | 12.6 | 12.7 | 12.7 | 13.5 | 13.3 |
| Nonlife insurance companies | 4.9 | 4.9 | 4.9 | 4.9 | 4.8 | 4.8 | 4.5 | 4.4 |
| Other financial institutions | 2.1 | 2.2 | 2.2 | 2.2 | 2.1 | 2.2 | 2.6 | 2.6 |
| Business corporations | 26.1 | 26.0 | 26.3 | 26.0 | 25.9 | 25.9 | 24.1 | 24.5 |
| Securities companies | 2.0 | 1.7 | 1.7 | 1.8 | 1.9 | 1.9 | 2.0 | 2.5 |
| Individuals & others | 30.4 | 29.2 | 28.4 | 28.0 | 26.8 | 26.3 | 25.2 | 23.9 |
| Foreigners | 2.5 | 4.1 | 4.7 | 5.1 | 6.3 | 6.1 | 5.7 | 4.7 |
| Total | 100.0 | 100.0 | 100.0 | 100.0 | 100.0 | 100.0 | 100.0 | 100.0 |

*Source:* Tokyo Stock Exchange.

are still central to the success of their institutions. Even though large industrials no longer rely heavily on intermediated credit to meet financing needs, financial institutions still look to these industrials for access to affiliated middle-market companies for commercial lending, access to employees for retail banking and insurance underwriting, and as customers for new products and services offered on a fee basis.

Commercial Banks

The securitization and globalization of Japanese finance dramatically changed the business of Japan's major banks. With lending to large industrial firms waning, they have aggressively sought to offer product-oriented, fee-based banking services such as currency and interest rate swaps, leveraged lease arrangements, and M&A advisory work. Thanks to deregulation, they have also become secondary dealers in Japanese government bonds and primary dealers in the new Japanese commercial paper market. Services and trading activities like these have brought them into direct competition with securities firms to a degree not previously experienced.

Some of the fiercest competition occurs overseas beyond the reach of the MOF and is being used to erode further the distinction between banks and securities firms. In the summer of 1986, the Sumitomo Bank paid $500 million for a 12.5% partnership stake in Goldman Sachs, the U.S. investment bank. Although prevented by the U.S. Glass-Steagall Act from exercising any role other than that of a passive investor in Goldman Sachs (much to the chagrin of Sumitomo), the fact remains that Sumitomo now owns a substantial stake in an American firm with a seat on the Tokyo Stock Exchange.

Later in 1986, J. Henry Schroder Bank & Trust, a U.K. bank 75% owned by the IBJ, bought Aubrey G. Lanston & Company, a primary dealer in the U.S. Treasury bond market, thus indirectly bringing IBJ into competition with two other Japanese primary dealers in this market, Nomura Securities and Daiwa Securities. In part by using aggressive pricing of swaps connected with nonyen Eurobond financing and providing guarantees on yen-convertible bonds and bond-warrant units, a number of major banks have also become major underwriters of bonds in the Euromarkets.[4] IBJ, the Long-Term Credit Bank, and the Bank of Tokyo frequently appear in the ranks of the top 25 Eurobond underwriters. Offshore subsidiaries of these and other Japanese banks have been used to solicit business from Tokyo-based Japanese clients, and representative offices of these subsidiaries have been set up in Tokyo to sell Eurobonds to domestic institutions.

For their part, Japanese securities firms have fought back by setting up banking subsidiaries in Amsterdam, London, and Luxembourg. Such subsidiaries allow them to arrange swaps, and eventually to take positions in swap markets, without depending upon the intermediation of a Japanese bank. In Japan, the Big Four securities firms have also been authorized to deal in money market instruments previously reserved to banks (e.g., bankers' acceptances and certificates of deposit) and have experimented with various instruments in the domestic market that function like savings accounts or other types of deposits.[5]

The upshot of financial deregulation in the midst of Japan's era of capital surpluses and decelerating industrial investment is that more rivals are now competing more freely in a more slowly expanding market for funding and financial services. The gradual further opening of Japanese financial markets to foreign competitors will only exacerbate this problem. High real growth and strong franchises protected by regulatory fiat, as well as historical relational contracting, were sufficient to sustain the presence of many banks and securities firms in Japan prior to the 1980s. But neither of these sources of continued profitability can

---

4. The so-called Three Bureaus Agreement, an accord reached in 1975 among the banking, securities, and international finance bureaus of the Ministry of Finance (each of which tends to act within the MOF as an "advocate" for the segments of the financial sector that it regulates), allows Japanese banks to participate in the underwriting of securities offshore, but prohibits them from being the sole lead manager of an offering. They can be co-lead managers along with a Japanese securities firm, but their name cannot appear in the more prestigious upper-left position in the list of underwriters appearing on tombstones or cover pages of offering circulars. Also, there cannot be more Japanese banks than Japanese securities companies participating in an offshore underwriting group.

5. Aron Viner, *Inside Japan's Financial Markets* (London: The Economist Publications Ltd. and Tokyo: The Japan Times Ltd., 1987), pp. 23–26.

be depended on in today's more competitive financial markets. An executive of an American bank with a subsidiary in Tokyo observed that in terms of numbers of organizations and human resources, there was now far too much banking capacity in Tokyo (Japan's 12 city banks now report total assets that collectively nearly equal that of the whole U.S. commercial banking sector). He reckoned that only about half the number of large banks in Tokyo today would survive as independent entities in the long run.

Anticipating the possibility of a future shakeout, banks and securities companies alike are competing furiously to increase their shares of the markets on which they have staked their futures, hoping to ensure that they will be among the dominant players in whatever long-run industry structure emerges in the global financial services market. Insofar as most of this market penetration at home and abroad has come from aggressive price competition, Japanese banks have experienced rapid growth at the expense of current profitability. Consider the composition and characteristics of the largest 25 banks in the world, shown in Exhibit 8–6. Quite a few Japanese banks have surged to the top of that list in a relatively short span of time. But they have arrived there with no better than average rates of return on capital and decidedly below-average capital ratios.

The rapid growth and low profitability of Japanese banks has led to concern about their capital adequacy. Foreign banks have sought protection from the onslaught of Japanese competition by calling for Japanese banks to operate with capital ratios comparable to those required in the United States and Europe. In 1986, in response, the MOF promulgated a double set of capital adequacy ratios, one that provided for the vast unrealized gain on long-term shareholdings by banks and one that did not. Within one year, banks were to achieve a 6% ratio of capital to total assets, but were allowed to include 70% of their unrealized gains on long-term investments in their measurement of capital. By 1991, they were to achieve a 4% ratio of capital to total assets without including such gains in their measurement of capital. In July 1987, the pressure to improve capital ratios increased still further when the Bank for International Settlements (BIS)

Exhibit 8-6 *World's 25 Largest Banks*

| Rank | Name | Country | Assets ($ billion) | Estimated Capital Ratios (1988)[a] (%) |
|------|------|---------|--------------------|----------------------------------------|
| 1 | The Dai-Ichi Kangyo Bank, Ltd. | Japan | 270.7 | 2.75 |
| 2 | The Sumitomo Bank, Ltd. | Japan | 250.5 | 3.25 |
| 3 | The Fuji Bank, Ltd. | Japan | 244.0 | 3.25 |
| 4 | The Mitsubishi Bank, Ltd. | Japan | 227.4 | 3.25 |
| 5 | The Sanwa Bank, Ltd. | Japan | 224.4 | 3.00 |
| 6 | The Industrial Bank of Japan, Ltd. | Japan | 215.3 | 2.75 |
| 7 | Credit Agricole | France | 214.4 | — |
| 8 | Citicorp | United States | 198.4 | 4.1 |
| 9 | Norinchukin Bank | Japan | 186.3 | — |
| 10 | Banque Nationale de Paris | France | 182.7 | 4.1 |
| 11 | Deutsche Bank Aktiengesellschaft | West Germany | 168.9 | 5.8 |
| 12 | Credit Lyonnais S.A. | France | 168.3 | 3.5 |
| 13 | The Mitsubishi Trust & Banking Corp. | Japan | 165.9 | 3.25 |
| 14 | Barclays Bank PLC | United Kingdom | 165.6 | 6.3 |

Exhibit 8-6 *World's 25 Largest Banks* (continued)

| Rank | Name | Country | Assets ($ billion) | Estimated Capital Ratios (1988)[a] (%) |
|---|---|---|---|---|
| 15 | National Westminster Bank PLC | United Kingdom | 164.1 | 4.9 |
| 16 | The Tokai Bank, Ltd. | Japan | 161.7 | 3.25 |
| 17 | The Mitsui Bank, Ltd. | Japan | 154.1 | 3.00 |
| 18 | The Mitsui Trust & Banking Co., Ltd. | Japan | 145.5 | 3.25 |
| 19 | Société Generale | France | 145.0 | 3.5 |
| 20 | The Sumitomo Trust & Banking Co., Ltd. | Japan | 144.6 | 3.25 |
| 21 | The Long-Term Credit Bank of Japan, Ltd. | Japan | 138.8 | 2.75 |
| 22 | The Taiyo Kobe Bank, Ltd. | Japan | 138.5 | 2.75 |
| 23 | The Bank of Tokyo, Ltd. | Japan | 136.4 | 3.25 |
| 24 | Dresdner Bank A.G. | West Germany | 130.5 | 4.6 |
| 25 | The Yasuda Trust & Banking Co., Ltd. | Japan | 128.7 | — |

[a] Does not include unrealized gains on securities investments in the measurement of capital.
*Source: Institutional Investor,* June 1988, pp. 143–146; *Euromoney,* July 1988, p. 39.

set 8% as the target ratio to be met by participating banks by 1992.

Four basic means are available to achieve this new ratio: (1) slow down asset growth, (2) increase return on assets, (3) realize substantial gains on equity holdings, and (4) issue new equity shares. So far, alternative 4—issuing new shares—has been the dominant technique employed by Japanese banks. Few are willing to give up what they see as the strategic imperative of rapid growth in an increasingly globally competitive market. Realistically, this implies continued pressure on earnings as banks fight to acquire and preserve market share. Realizing capital gains on equity investments by selling stocks is being done, but its undesirable side effects include incurring large tax liabilities and possibly calling into question the client relationship implied by such equity holdings.

A burst of new equity and convertible bond offerings totaling ¥2.6 trillion between January 1988 and June 1989 brought many banks in line with the BIS requirements. But some of this improvement was undone by the 30% slide in the Tokyo Stock Exchange in the first half of 1990, and the nearly 25% erosion in the value of the yen. Furthermore, given continued double-digit growth in assets, another ¥2.6 trillion of capital is likely to be required over the next four years just to remain even with current levels.[6]

Not surprisingly, therefore, Japanese banks are watching their bottom lines carefully. In contrast to the low-margin, volume-oriented banking practices of the recent past, Japanese banks are now restraining growth and carefully tracking the profitability of their relationships with industrial clients. Today, with the stroke of a few keys, bank officers can retrieve electronically stored data on their bank's open positions with a given client, the return being earned on those positions, and all recent transactions. None of the banks I visited would insist that every transaction with a client be profitable on a stand-alone basis. But they did point out that a cash return on investment calculation was

---

6. Thomas H. Hanley, John D. Leonard, Diane B. Glossman, Ron Napier, and Steven I. Davis, "The Japanese Banks: Emerging Into Global Markets" (New York: Salomon Brothers, Inc., September 1989), p. 24.

made with respect to the bank's overall commitment of capital to the company, including any "stable" stock holdings.

It was not for convenience only that such information was compiled. Increasingly, clients are being ranked by banks according to the profitability of the relationship with them. Just as industrial clients are now short listing the banks with which they do business, banks are now beginning to identify and terminate relationships with clients that do not provide them with sufficiently attractive rates of return. Kyowa Bank, the tenth-largest of the thirteen major city banks, has been the most aggressive in this regard. In 1985, even before the BIS requirements, Kyowa embarked on a new corporate lending strategy aimed at making it the largest lender in the more profitable middle market for commercial loans by 1988. To do so meant committing at least 90% of its new loans to small and medium-sized businesses and, by implication, cutting back dramatically on loans to large corporations. Accordingly, in the spring of 1985, it reviewed its commitments with major clients to determine those with whom it could not be expected to earn an adequate rate of return. Further loan requests from companies such as Teijin, Toray, and Sumitomo Electric were turned down following this review. As one Kyowa executive put it, "Those days when banks are competing for volume of loans are over. Even if the client is a big corporation, the unprofitable loan to the company should be withdrawn and it is quite reasonable to do so."[7]

Although all major banks are not rushing to replicate Kyowa's bold shift in client relationships, some—such as Sanwa, Fuji, and Mitsubishi—have also screened relationships in order to focus on the more profitable ones.[8] When asked if he could ever envision circumstances in which the bank would dispose of some of its stable shareholdings in client companies, a Sanwa Bank executive acknowledged that the question was a live issue

---

7. Yoko Shibata, "Japanese Give the Chop to Former Allies," *Euromoney* (August 1986), p. 92.
8. In a dramatic strategic move aimed at increasing market share and profitability, the Mitsui and Taiyo Kobe banks announced a merger in August 1989. The combination blends Mitsui's large corporate international client list with the retail and middle-market banking strengths of Taiyo Kobe.

at Sanwa. A number of top officers favored such a move if the shares could be sold as a block at a favorable price. At conservative Mitsubishi Bank, a special team studied all aspects of the bank's dealings with major clients preparatory to a decision about which relationships to preserve and which to terminate through a sale of shares. While much of this screening took place as a late response to the 1977 amendment of the antimonopoly law that reduced permitted bank holdings of equity in other companies from 10 to 5% by the end of 1987, it has been kept alive by the new BIS capital requirements.

The buildup of banks' equity ownership would seem to be inconsistent with this heightened selectivity. However, one must take care to separate trends in stable equity ownership from that of bank investment in equity at large. In recent years, most of the increase in bank equity ownership has not been for stable share-owning purposes. Bank executives themselves point out that virtually all of the increases (and then some) in their institutions' equity portfolios have been for short-term investment purposes. A director of research at one bank asserted that more than 10% of the stocks his bank owned were held for such speculative purposes today, whereas none were so held just three years ago. Stock portfolio turnover figures for banks (see Exhibit 8–7) corroborate this story.

A better picture of the trend in stable share ownership by banks is provided by banks' fractional equity ownership in their own industrial group. The data in Exhibit 8–8 reveal that not only do the six largest banks hold less than the maximum amount of equity allowed in their keiretsu companies (5%), but their fractional ownership has actually been trending downward slightly but steadily over the past 10 years.

Moreover, it is likely that the trend will continue. The glut of convertible bond and bond-warrant units Japanese companies issued domestically and internationally creates a significant equity overhang that may be difficult for stable shareholders to absorb. The constant flow of new issues and partial conversions of outstanding issues makes it difficult to assess the size of that overhang. The daily Japanese business newspaper *Nihon Keizai Shimbun* estimates that the equity-linked securities issued by

Exhibit 8-7  Stock Portfolio Annual Turnover Ratio
(% of current value)

| Fiscal Year | Insurance Companies | Banks | Investment Trusts | Corporate Entities | Foreigners | Individuals |
|---|---|---|---|---|---|---|
| 1980 | 2.2 | 5.6 | 91.6 | 9.5 | 70.6 | 52.9 |
| 1981 | 2.0 | 6.9 | 107.4 | 11.1 | 74.8 | 66.7 |
| 1982 | 1.7 | 4.5 | 77.2 | 6.9 | 51.6 | 50.5 |
| 1983 | 1.8 | 5.5 | 96.8 | 8.9 | 64.0 | 60.1 |
| 1984 | 1.4 | 8.8 | 93.5 | 8.2 | 53.8 | 59.8 |
| 1985 | 1.9 | 15.6 | 103.4 | 8.9 | 57.1 | 52.9 |
| 1986 | 2.3 | 39.2 | 188.9 | 21.2 | 103.2 | 106.3 |

Source: Industrial Bank of Japan.

Exhibit 8-8 *Major Bank Equity Holding in its Industrial Group*
(*unit: %*)

|  | 1975 | 1980 | 1985 | 1986 |
|---|---|---|---|---|
| The Fuji Bank, Ltd. | 4.7 | 4.4 | 3.9 | 3.8 |
| The Sumitomo Bank, Ltd. | 4.9 | 3.9 | 3.6 | 3.5 |
| The Mitsubishi Bank, Ltd. | 4.9 | 4.0 | 4.0 | 3.9 |
| The Sanwa Bank, Ltd. | 4.1 | 4.1 | 3.8 | 3.7 |
| The Dai-Ichi Kangyo Bank, Ltd. | 4.3 | 4.3 | 4.0 | 3.8 |
| The Mitsui Bank, Ltd. | 3.3 | 3.5 | 3.7 | 3.6 |
| Average | 4.4 | 4.0 | 3.8 | 3.7 |

*Source:* The Fuji Bank, Ltd.

Japanese companies in the first half of the 1988 fiscal year alone represent a potential share increase of 15.7 billion, which is about 5.4% of total listed shares.[9] The unexpectedly rapid conversion of many of these issues has created problems for some companies as the percentage holdings of their stable shareholders is diluted below target levels. Financial institutions have greeted requests that stable shareholders increase their equity ownership to offset the dilution half-heartedly. Yoh Kurosawa, president of the Industrial Bank of Japan, observed that major city banks and long-term credit banks have so far been among the major purchasers of shares issued on conversion (as well as shares disgorged by smaller banks refocusing their lending activity). He also said that the banks were "getting to the limit of what we are willing to absorb."

Trust Banks and Insurance Companies

Two other logical candidates for picking up the slack in stable share ownership are insurance companies and trust banks. They are large (total assets of the twenty-three life insurance companies amounted to ¥74 trillion and those of the eight domestic trust banks totaled ¥144 trillion as of the end of the 1987 fiscal year) and grew rapidly at rates of 15–20% a year throughout most of the 1980s. Insurance companies have a statutory ceiling of 30% on the amount of their total assets that can be devoted to equity; but unlike banks, they are still permitted to own up to 10% of another company's stock. In any event, insurance companies are presently nowhere near their statutory limit. Their relatively long investment time horizons also naturally dispose these institutions to the role of stable long-term investors.

But like commercial banks, Japanese financial deregulation has changed their product mix, thrusting these institutions into competition with one another in such a way that portfolio performance will begin to count for as much or even more than traditional relationships. As reciprocal trading arrangements be-

---

9. Too Many Issues of Convertible Bonds and Warrant Bonds Have Created Disorder in Corporate Finance," *Nihon Keizai Shimbun*, October 22, 1988, p. 12.

come less significant in increasingly price-competitive markets, the need to cement commitments with reciprocal shareholdings will diminish. So too will the stability of shares held by these other financial institutions.

Take the case of the insurance industry. For life insurance companies, financial deregulation in Japan has meant greater degrees of price competition than ever before. Prior to the 1980s, conventional term and whole life insurance policies were virtually the only types of life insurance products sold by life insurers. Both the pricing and paying of dividends on standard policies are tightly controlled by the MOF. Allowable policy dividends, in particular, are fixed for each insurer strictly on the basis of the institution's income yield on its investment portfolio, calculated as the ratio of dividends and interest received to the book value of the entire portfolio. Capital gains, realized or unrealized, are not counted in this calculation, a regulatory feature creating a bias favoring high-income loans and securities over low-yielding stocks. Even today, insurers compete primarily through intensive door-to-door selling efforts by neighborhood salespeople (predominately by nearly 360,000 housewives trying to augment household income) rather than by yield on the cash value of policies, service, or product design.

Things began to change in October 1981 when the variable life insurance policy was introduced. With this policy the premiums paid and the death benefit remain constant, but the cash value fluctuates according to the actual performance of an investment fund—segregated from the company's general investment fund—underlying the policy. In a sense, it is a kind of investment trust run by the insurance company. The universal life insurance policy, a more recent product introduction in Japan, allows irregular premium payments and combines life insurance with a savings feature (the cash value of the policy) that also provides market interest rates.

New products like these have given rise to a degree of price competition not previously experienced among Japanese insurers. As one might predict, this change had weakened incentives to remain passive and stable shareholders with a long-term, buy-and-hold approach to equity investing. Beginning in 1984, insurance companies could invest up to 3% of their assets in so-called *tokkin* funds. These funds are actually trust accounts opened with trust banks, but managed directly by the supplier of the funds.[10] They developed in their modern form with the 1980 revision of Japan's corporate tax code, which allowed companies to segregate the management of financial assets from other "operating" assets for tax purposes. Specifically, stocks purchased through a *tokkin* account would be given a tax basis equal to their actual purchase price plus fees and commissions. Previously, newly purchased shares were commingled with shares already owned in the same company and assigned a basis equal to the *average* purchase price of the shares. This new practice benefited corporations that wished to trade in equities of companies in which they had acquired a "stable" shareholding position long ago. In most cases, the stable shares were acquired at very low cost and had appreciated tremendously in value. By using *tokkin* funds, corporate treasurers could separate stable shareholdings from new shares purchased for speculative purposes and avoid a large tax bite on the sale of the new shares.

A particular advantage of *tokkin* funds for insurance companies is that capital gains earned on equity investments can be dividended from the fund to the insurance company; hence they can be counted in income-yield calculations used to determine the payment of dividends on policies. This ability has increased the appetite of insurance companies for investing in equities, a fact reflected in the halting of a nearly 30-year decline in the fraction of insurance industry assets held in equities (between 1955 and 1984, equity investments as a fraction of insurance companies' total assets fell steadily from 30% to 15%).

Given the short-term capital appreciation objectives of *tokkin* funds, however, such increases in equity ownership cannot be interpreted as a deepening of the traditional stable shareholding

---

10. Actually, the term *tokkin* refers to both true *tokkin* funds and *kingai* funds, corporate funds actually managed by the trust bank holding the account but in a commingled manner with separate accounting for individual clients. In practice, true *tokkin* funds are managed by brokers assigned to the account as financial advisers. Purchases and sales are made at the discretion of these brokers, who thus become the de facto custodians of the accounts.

relationship. Quite the opposite, in fact. A senior fund manager for one of Japan's largest life insurers hypothesized that were data on *tokkin* funds made available, we would discover that turnover in these funds exceeded turnover in most American institutional portfolios by a wide margin. He noted further that under cover of the anonymity provided by *tokkin* funds, he would cheerfully sell stock held in such an account into a tender offer if a premium were offered over market value—even if the offer were not supported by the target's management and even if his company had a stable shareholding relationship with the client. Other insurance company fund managers were less direct in their assertions, but indicated that they would be likely to use the shares in whatever capacity would best help to "improve the management" of a target company.

Presently, the MOF is considering changes in Article 86 of the Insurance Business Law so that realized capital gains can be counted in the yield calculations. (The law now restricts policy dividends to be paid out of the current-income yield of an insurance company's general investment fund.) Such a move will almost surely mean a shift of money out of *tokkin* funds and high-coupon foreign bonds and into equities to be held in the general fund, but the short-term capital appreciation objective of new investments in equities is unlikely to be affected by such a development. Indeed, without the percentage-of-total assets restrictions currently imposed on money invested in *tokkin* funds, the fraction of insurance assets seeking short-term gains on equity is likely to increase, if anything.

Competition for corporate pension fund management has also fueled the rising performance orientation of both insurance companies and trust banks in the management of equity investments. Historically, corporate pension funds were of almost insignificant size and fund managers, who were restricted to trust banks and insurance companies only, were selected on the basis of relational contracting. According to practice at Toshiba, for example, pension funds were allocated to institutional managers on the basis of their share of loan volume to Toshiba, the extent of their equity ownership, and the volume of equipment purchases made from Toshiba. Until relatively recently, fund performance was not a factor since there was virtually no difference in performance among the trust banks and insurance companies. Typically, the yields they provided on pension funds varied between 8.5% and 9.5%, with very tight clustering within this narrow range. As recently as 1985, the weighted average return on all Japanese pension funds was 8.94%, with less than 1% separating the best fund manager from the worst.[11]

Today, however, pension fund management has become a big, rapidly growing business vital to the long-term prosperity of the trust banks, which have also had to find new sources of growth and profitability to replace their plateauing loan demand. At the end of the 1988 fiscal year, corporate pension fund assets under management amounted to ¥26.3 trillion ($210 billion) and were growing at an annual rate in excess of 15%. Forecasters expect them to reach ¥100 trillion by the end of the century.

Today's corporate pension fund owners have also become more demanding. In response to indistinguishable performance in the industry, the lack of full disclosure about true fund performance, and high management and custodial fees (ranging as high as 2.1%), the Federation of Employee Pension Funds filed a formal complaint with the Ministry of Health and Welfare that sought more competition among managers. Subsequently, nine foreign banks were allowed to enter the trust banking business in Japan and, perhaps more significantly, four major banks (Fuji, Mitsui, Sanwa, and Bank of Tokyo) were permitted to set up investment advisory firms. This move was widely interpreted as preliminary to an eventual authorization of their managing pension fund money. In a similar vein, the Foundation of Welfare Pension Funds in 1986 announced new performance measurement guidelines. These have resulted in quarterly performance evaluation by a variety of measures, some of which include capital gains as well as current income yield on book assets.

Even before these changes, however, corporations were indicating their search for better fund performance by steadily shifting assets away from trust banks to insurance companies. Between 1980 and 1988, trust banks' share of pension assets fell

---

11. "Trust Is Not Enough," *The Economist*, June 25, 1988, p. 76.

from 70% to 62%. Insurers achieved these gains by charging lower management fees (insurers structure their fees as annual premiums that are not fixed as a percentage of total asset value) and by essentially guaranteeing that funds under their management will perform as well as or better than those managed by trust banks.[12]

The upshot of this sort of activism by pension fund owners has been an aggressive pursuit of short-term capital gains by fund managers; the proportion of pension fund assets invested in equities doubled from 12.7% in 1981 to 25.8% in 1988 (equity investment by pension funds is limited to a maximum of 30% of total assets). The average return on pension funds rose to 12.7% in 1988, with a 7% spread separating the best from the worst performance. When Toshiba allocates money among the eight insurance companies and five trust banks that manage its pension assets today, recent fund performance is the key consideration. Relationships now count primarily as tie breakers.

In short, regardless of the product or service in question and however fund management is executed with respect to equities, the demand for performance in terms of total return on investment is being made ever more clear by Japan's major financial institutions. Yutaka Hashimoto, general manager of the Investment Department of Nippon Life, the largest Japanese insurer and second-largest insurance company in the world behind Prudential (and the owner of 3.2% of all listed shares on Japanese stock exchanges), has publicly stated that in the current environment of financial deregulation Nippon Life now sees itself as much as a modern fund manager as a life insurer and therefore has necessarily become "more conscious about asset performance."[13] Elsewhere, in a public relations document, the company states the case plainly as follows:

---

12. Unlike trust banks that are required to segregate pension fund assets and manage them separately, insurance companies can commingle pension assets with their general investment funds. This commingling allows insurance companies to avoid reporting separate fund performance figures and ultimately to provide whatever return on pension assets was thought necessary to meet owner expectations, even if it means subsidizing them at the expense of insurance policy holders.
13. "Nippon Life and Shearson Set an Example to Be Followed," *Euroweek*, a Euromoney publication, June 5, 1987, p. 17.

In the past, Nippon Life, like most institutional investors, took a passive position on its shareholders' rights. However, recent changes in the financial community, which have put more and more emphasis on corporate earnings and competitiveness, have induced changes in the company's stance on equity holdings. Although the company has no direct interest in exercising its rights as a shareholder in management decisions, *it is beginning to assert its position as an investor where it affects the return on investment* [emphasis added].[14]

Many executives in the Japanese insurance industry view these statements as shots across the bows of the major banks. The banks have been asking insurance companies to absorb much of the banks' own issues of new shares, which are allegedly purchased at inflated offering prices that then decline in secondary market trading following the issue. There is some concern among Japanese insurance companies that they may soon be imposed on by industrial companies to take up additional large blocks of stock released by banks and other stable shareholders seeking to redeploy assets to higher-valued uses. But independent of the principal audience for which these statements were intended, their public exposure reflects the beginning of a profoundly important change in the role of insurance companies as shareholders—a change shared with major commercial and trust banks and, in all cases, induced by the evolving nature of the markets in which they compete.

The shifting patterns of Japanese corporate finance, and the competitive and regulatory pressures on Japanese financial institutions to increase their return on assets, are collectively resulting in a gradual unbundling of claims held against industrial corporations. Rather than being key shareholders, lead lenders, and primary vendors of financial services in long-term relationships with clients, Japanese banks are now being reduced to the

---

14. Brian Robins, "Nippon Life Insurance Company: An Ambitious Global Investor," *Tokyo: A World Financial Center*, a Euromoney publication, 1987, p. 275.

position of minority shareholders that must compete fiercely for a client's business on a transaction-by-transaction basis.

Two important effects on corporate governance result. On one hand, Japanese financial institutions, banks especially, are becoming more demanding about the performance they expect on their equity investments. On the other hand, these same institutional shareholders are losing their ability to monitor client companies closely and intervene as needed to correct problems, both heretofore critical safeguards in the Japanese corporate governance system. Together, these effects are destabilizing Japanese financial institutions as corporate stakeholders. This is a necessary condition for change in the Japanese market for corporate control. Should this instability be combined with chronic dissipations of shareholder value by industrial corporations, conditions will then be ripe for the growth of a new type of deal in the Japanese market for corporate control—unsolicited, financially motivated takeover bids.

# 9
# THE HIDDEN COSTS OF SUCCESS

The stage is being set in Japan for overt conflicts among corporate stakeholders and the emergence of struggles for corporate control. Managers in sunset industries are pushing to restructure corporate strategies, particularly in the direction of greater product market diversification. Upholding implicit promises of lifetime employment and maintaining the growth of their enterprises are prominent motives. This restructuring is being undertaken with less bank oversight than ever before and in the face of ever-mounting demands from these important shareholders for better financial returns.

As these trends continue, the bone of contention among Japanese corporate stakeholders will be the use of the excess cash building up on corporate balance sheets. Excess cash tends to be a lightning rod for conflict among corporate stakeholders the world over. Cash is a highly visible asset; its value is easily measured and the amounts available can be quickly ascertained. More important, cash is the most liquid and fungible of all assets. Hence it is the easiest to deploy in the interests of particular stakeholders. Not surprisingly, therefore, decisions about how to allocate cash bring into sharp relief disagreements among stakeholders about the future direction of the firm. In the West, chronic failure to deploy cash in the best interests of shareholders has led to an active and sometimes openly hostile market for corporate control. Through the functioning of this market, corporate ownership is concentrated, management replaced, and cash returned to suppliers of capital.

Shareholder welfare is enhanced when cash is deployed in

those activities promising at least as much value in terms of discounted future cash flows as the amount expended in the present. Other stakeholders might prefer to see cash deployed differently. Employees would presumably prefer richer compensation and greater job security. Upstream suppliers might want to see production capacity expanded. Downstream customers might be expected to favor investments that lead to better quality, lower costs, and more reliable delivery whether or not shareholder value is increased.

Needless to say, such diverse interests need not be mutually exclusive. Many investments will simultaneously expand capacity, provide jobs, and lower production costs, as well as create value for shareholders. Such uses of cash will naturally entail little or no conflict among stakeholders. When internally generated capital is scarce relative to available uses, conflicts on the use of cash are more likely to be resolved in favor of shareholders and/or other suppliers of capital to the firm. The scarcity of internal funds will drive managers to source funds externally, thereby exposing their decisions and plans to the scrutiny of the suppliers of capital. Generally, new capital will be forthcoming only if investors are confident that their interests will be protected and their welfare advanced.

Even if managers elect not to seek external capital, thus avoiding capital market tests of the perceived efficacy of planned investments, product market tests may apply. Rivalry among competitors in the company's product markets will exert a disciplinary force driving managers to seek sustainable competitive advantage, which is the very foundation of value creation for shareholders. The company's internal control systems and incentive compensation schemes tied to equity interests may further constrain the scope of managerial discretion in the use of cash when capital is scarce.

Stakeholder conflict about the use of cash tends to be greatest when internally generated cash is abundant relative to investment requirements. Under these conditions, managers enjoy greater latitude in its deployment. A surplus of cash relative to value-creating investments allows managers to minimize capital market oversight. The imperatives of product market competition can be satisfied without precluding the ability to pursue other stakeholder priorities. Internal monitoring and control may also be less strictly executed when cash is liberally available. Management's incentive alignment with equity may be too weak to overcome desires to act in its own interests or that of other stakeholders demanding a greater share of the firm's economic rents. The result often is the investment of excess cash at rates of return below the cost of capital.[1] If such investment becomes chronic, conflicts among shareholders, managers and/or other corporate stakeholders will eventually emerge. These will be costly to the extent that corporate resources must be devoted to dispute resolution, previously valuable commercial relationships are ruptured, or corporate performance suffers in the course of the dispute.

## MODERN USES OF CASH

The upshot of a decade of adjustment following the first oil shock, is the emergence in Japan of a manufacturing sector that has substantial cash flow relative to its needs and much reduced monitoring of its entrenched managers. But for the possibility of voluntary forbearance on the part of these managers, it seems all but inevitable that cash will begin to be deployed in ways that have little bearing on the achievement of product market competitiveness or parity growth in the value of stakeholder claims. Under present circumstances, cash can be more easily devoted to the pursuit of individual stakeholder goals. Recent evidence suggests that not only *can* excess cash be appropriated by stakeholders other than the true residual claimants (equity), but it actually *is* being so appropriated. The clearest manifestations of such uses of cash can be seen in the unrelated diversification plans being pursued by many major Japanese corporations today and even in the management of cash itself.

---

1. For a further discussion of such agency costs see Michael C. Jensen, "Agency Costs of Free Cash Flow, Corporate Finance, and Takeovers," *American Economic Association Papers and Proceedings* (May 1986), pp. 323–329.

The Treasury Function as Profit Center

As noted in Chapter 8, Japanese corporate financial managers are using their new freedom in global capital markets to experiment and innovate as never before. This might be nothing more than what one would expect. Lowering the cost of capital is at least desirable if not actually necessary to survival in a world where one's competitors are also assiduously procuring low-cost funds. But coming as it does during a cash glut and a period of competitive dominance enjoyed by many Japanese corporations, the exercise of this new-found financial freedom is unlikely to be checked by the rigors normally imposed by the competition for funds in capital markets or the competition for profits in product markets. The result has been the uncoupling of financial policies and financial execution decisions from overall corporate strategy. For a number of prominent Japanese corporations today, the purpose of corporate finance has gone beyond merely enabling operating managers to carry out their plans. Making money through the treasury function has become an end in itself.

This phenomenon is at once sufficiently new yet sufficiently widespread in Japan that it has been dubbed with the journalistic appelation, "*zaiteku*" (perhaps best interpreted in its common usage as "financial technology" or "financial engineering"). The scope of the term is quite wide, referring to virtually any profit-seeking financial activity: stock market speculation, arbitrage, foreign exchange speculation, or the lending of funds at some positive spread. *Zaiteku* transactions can be as simple as borrowing funds in the commercial paper market and depositing them at higher interest rates, or as complicated as the execution of a long chain of transactions that begins with nonyen Euromarket financings and concludes with the purchase of yenbond futures in Tokyo. As an example of a simple transaction, Toshiba claimed an ability in 1988 to issue commercial paper at a 4.0% cost to it while depositing those same funds at a 4.5% rate. Hitachi makes a similar claim with respect to funds borrowed directly from banks. For an example of complexity, Sumitomo Corporation uses at least four offshore subsidiaries in London, Luxembourg, the Cayman Islands, and Panama to execute hundreds of millions of dollars of Eurobond transactions accompanied by currency and interest rate swaps, which are then invested in yen bonds or other Euro-instruments denominated in several different currencies.

One of the most common *zaiteku* maneuvers entails the issuance of low-coupon convertible bonds or bond-warrant units, often denominated in foreign currencies but swapped into yen. The proceeds are then invested in *tokkin* funds that facilitate tax-favored speculation in stocks. An important advantage of trading through *tokkin* funds is anonymity. When its shares are being bought and sold by another, a company can determine only that a *tokkin* investor is doing the trading; it is unable to identify the specific investor. Although accurate data about *tokkin* funds are difficult to obtain, *Euromoney* reported in a special survey that as of the first quarter of 1987, about ¥30 trillion had been invested in such accounts, which were expanding at the rate of ¥1 trillion a month. About 35% was said to be invested in equities.[2]

What is motivating Japanese industrial corporations to become so proactive in their management of excess cash? Historically, they had relegated finance to a backseat enabling function and "stuck to their knitting" as far as operations were concerned. Why, for that matter, is there so much financial slack today on Japanese corporate balance sheets?

One argument may be that corporations in Japan have access to unique financial arbitrage opportunities or information that make them distinctly better managers of cash than their shareholders. *Zaiteku* might be viewed as simply another perfectly valid means of creating value for the firm's many stakeholders.

This is a tenuous explanation at best. Corporate treasurers may face unique investment opportunities and/or have better information than individual shareholders in Japan, but the same can hardly be said for the banks, insurance companies, and other corporate stakeholders making up the bulk of the typical large corporation's ownership. In fact, if anything, treasurers of

2. "Zaiteku Sends Stocks and Tokkin Soaring," *Euromoney: Special Survey*, April 1987, pp. 130–131.

manufacturing corporations and their brokers/advisers may be *less* well situated to assess the risks of their financial positions and discern whether or not a *zaiteku* transaction is creating value for the corporation in the true sense of the word.

Consider those who claim to be earning positive spreads on funds borrowed in the commercial paper market or from banks. These spreads are achieved only by mismatching the maturities of the paired assets and liabilities. The borrowing is done on a relatively short-term basis, while the deposits are committed for a longer period such as a year or more. The company taking such a position generally counts on rolling over its short-term debt on a favorable basis and inevitably takes an interest rate risk in the process. Those who relend low-cost capital at a positive spread are also taking on credit risk, something banks are skilled at evaluating but most manufacturers are not. In both instances, the positive spreads being earned may be barely adequate, and quite possibly inadequate, compensation for the risks involved.

There also seems to be widespread misunderstanding among many corporate treasurers about the gains to be had from *zaiteku* operations involving the issuance of low-coupon convertible bonds and bond-warrant units. Nearly all financial managers in my field sample considered such securities to represent very low-cost funds because of the 3%, 2%, and even 1.5% coupons attached to them. Some treasurers even claimed to have obtained a *negative* all-in cost of financing with such securities when issuing in a foreign currency and swapping into yen! However, these conclusions involve a numerical sleight-of-hand: the value of the option to convert, or the value of the warrant component of a unit, is left out of the analysis. The funds are "cheap" only if these options are mispriced in the company's favor when the security is sold. This reality was either missed or brushed aside by many of the financial managers who were interviewed. They generally replied that any equity issued on conversion of the bonds or exercise of the warrants was still quite cheap in view of the very slight dividend yields paid on the stock (generally substantially less than 1% of the market value of the stock). Perhaps because of the more passive role stable shareholders have played in recent years, there was limited appreciation at best for the generally high implicit costs associated with new equity in the form of investors' expected returns from capital gains.[3]

A prominent, albeit extreme, example of miscalculated financial risk taking is that of Tateho Chemical Industries. A regional supplier of electrofused magnesium for steelmaking, Tateho went public in 1978 with sales of ¥3.4 billion, capital of ¥4.7 billion, and no bank debt. With new access to public capital markets, Tateho began raising funds in the Swiss franc and Eurodollar markets starting in 1983; it also borrowed heavily from local financial institutions. Virtually all of these newly raised funds were devoted to *zaiteku* operations, resulting in a substantial ¥800 million nonoperating profit in fiscal 1984, 80% of reported total pretax profits for that year. The following year, it began investing in the Japanese government bond futures market, which was opened in October 1985, borrowing still more to increase its capital committed to *zaiteku*. By the end of fiscal 1987, Tateho had built its annual securities trading gains to ¥2.2 billion and was confident enough to publish *forecasted* securities gains for fiscal 1988 of ¥23.0 billion!

Unfortunately, the government bond market failed to perform as anticipated. Both the cash and futures markets for government bonds collapsed during May–July 1987 (the benchmark 5.1% Japanese government bond Number 89, due in 1996, lost about 15% of its value during this 90-day period). In mid-May, Tateho owned ¥20 billion of futures contracts to purchase government bonds for which only 3% margin had to be committed. Perhaps because of his success in riding out a short bear market for government bonds in 1986, Takaki Kobayashi, a managing

---

3. Corporate financial managers may still have been right about the cost of their company's equity, but for the wrong reason. When queried about whether or not the Tokyo Stock Exchange was properly valuing their company's stock, many responded that their stock was overvalued. Were that true and if a correction in price was expected soon, then issuing equity-linked securities may indeed have been a way of raising "cheap" capital from the point of view of the pre-existing shareholders. However, to the extent these securities flow back into the hands of existing shareholders before a correction occurs, even this rationale for why equity-linked securities were a source of cheap capital fails to make sense.

director and chief treasurer for Tateho, plunged more deeply into the futures market in early June, building Tateho's position to possibly as much as ¥200 billion at one point during the slide. The bear market failed to turn around, however. By August, Tateho had incurred losses in the futures market estimated at ¥28 billion, an amount exceeding the book value of its net total assets. By September, it sought and received the support of its main bank, Taiyo Kobe, and seven other lenders, who agreed to postpone repayment of ¥20 billion of debt owed to them so that Tateho could cover payments in the futures market.

Although uncharacteristic of the Japanese financial community, it was perhaps predictable that such a dramatic incident would be followed by a round of finger pointing. Japanese banks have roundly criticized the securities industry, which they claim encourages unsound speculation by pushing convertible or bond-warrant underwritings tied to *zaiteku* investments and failing to make margin calls according to regulation. For its part, Taiyo Kobe Bank was charged with laxness in the monitoring of its client; apparently, it was not until August that the bank learned the true depth of Tateho's losses.

Both bankers and brokers question the understanding of the bond market held by Kobayashi, the chief engineer of Tateho's *zaiteku* operations.[4] Naturally, the rest of Tateho's top management has also been severely criticized for exerting inadequate control over Kobayashi and allowing such an exposure to develop in the first place. At a September 1987 news conference, Tateho's chairman, Tadashi Kawabe, and its president, Shigeru Senzaki, were unable to distinguish between the cash and futures markets for government bonds. They lamely explained, "Because they were called government bonds, we thought they were safe instruments."[5] While some managers in Japan view the Tateho *zaiteku* incident as an isolated case not likely to be repeated, many see it as but the tip of an iceberg. In any event,

---

4. Kathryn Graven, "Japanese Executive, Bosses and Broker Dispute Responsibility for Huge Losses," *The Wall Street Journal*, September 28, 1987, p. 28.
5. Yoko Shibata, "The MD Might Have Gone Mad," *Euromoney* (October 1987), pp. 67–73.

as one banker put it, "The case is a very good illustration of the problems embraced by the main bank amid the financial liberalization under which its client business corporations are shunning bank loans and are free to raise funds from the world's capital markets."[6]

If sheer ignorance and folly were what ultimately ensnared Tateho, it was the prospects of offsetting declining operating performance with easy *zaiteku* gains that lured it into the trap. As Japanese steel output declined with the rise of the yen in 1985 and 1986, so did Tateho's profits. In its fiscal year ending in March 1987, operating profits fell by 64%. Yet Tateho's total pretax profit actually rose by 45%, having been buoyed by its ¥2.2-billion securities trading gain for that year. Tateho was not alone in its heavy reliance on *zaiteku* profits to shore up the bottom line. As shown in Exhibit 9-1, net nonoperating earnings (a proxy for *zaiteku* profits) were a large fraction of total pretax earnings for many of Japan's largest and best-known companies. In fact, were it not for such earnings, 47 of Japan's 250 largest corporations would have shown no profit at all in 1987. Thus *zaiteku* has helped many Japanese companies mask eroding earnings from operations, but often at the expense of assuming risks that they are poorly equipped to handle.

Unrelated Diversification

Compared to their American counterparts, Japanese industrial corporations have consistently maintained a higher proportion (about 10% more) of their total assets as cash and marketable securities.[7] Historically, and even for some firms today, three primary considerations may explain the difference. First, cash and deposits were kept relatively high during the rapid-growth period in part because of the high degree of bank borrowing and the common use of compensating balances in conjunction with such loans. Sufficiently large amounts of cash

---

6. Ibid., p. 69.
7. W. Carl Kester, "Capital Ownership Structure: A Comparison of United States and Japanese Manufacturing Corporations," *Financial Management* (Spring 1986), pp. 5–16.

Exhibit 9-1 *Net Nonoperating Income of Major Japanese Corporations, 1987*

| Company | Amount (¥ billion) | Percentage of Pretax Income |
|---|---|---|
| Toyota Motor | 149,644 | 37.6 |
| Nissan Motor | 127,004 | 107.1 |
| Mitsubishi Corp. | 46,329 | 58.3 |
| Matsushita Electric | 40,536 | 79.8 |
| Sharp | 30,917 | 81.7 |
| Sumitomo Corp. | 21,646 | 47.0 |
| Nippon Oil | 21,044 | 106.7 |
| Sony | 19,823 | 150.2 |
| Victor Company of Japan | 17,118 | 132.4 |
| Nissho Iwai | 15,021 | 50.5 |
| Aginomoto | 12,503 | 40.8 |
| Hanwa | 11,446 | 65.0 |
| Murata Mfg. | 10,279 | 50.3 |
| Fujisawa Pharmaceutical | 10,079 | 53.4 |
| Mitsui O.S.K. Lines | 9,253 | 295.9 |
| Settsu | 8,715 | 66.3 |
| Marubeni | 7,916 | 25.6 |
| Kyocera | 7,408 | 21.6 |
| Toyo Engineering | 6,880 | 271.4 |
| Nissin Food Products | 6,289 | 33.7 |

*Source:* NEEDS: Nikkei Financials (magnetic tape). Nihon Keizai Shimbun, Inc. Databank Bureau Information Service Department. Tokyo, 1987.

were tied up in compensating balances (up to 70% of the nominal amount of the loan in some cases) to elevate effective borrowing costs to levels that exceeded the 15% interest rate ceiling established in the Interest Rate Control Law for loans of more than ¥1 million. The practice was sufficiently widespread and frequent that it elicited periodic reprimands from the Ministry of Finance.[8]

A second motive for maintaining relatively large cash bal-

8. Stephen Bronte, *Japanese Finances, Markets, and Institutions* (London: Euromoney Publications, 1982), p. 17.

ances and less debt than might otherwise be optimal was a preference shared by managers worldwide for using internally generated or privately procured funds to support capital investments
whenever possible. Owing to the asymmetry of information that
commonly exists between a corporation and its public capital
markets, issuing risky securities such as equity in order to raise
new funds is often greeted skeptically by potential investors. Is
the issuing corporation raising new funds because it possesses
great new investment opportunities, or is it merely timing the
market—issuing stock today while its price is relatively high
rather than later when it may be lower? To the extent that investors cannot be sure and the company is unable or unwilling to
communicate credibly the superiority of its investment opportunities, investors confronted with this sort of moral hazard will
hedge their bets. They will buy the new securities at a price that
reflects the *average* worth of new projects undertaken by the
company rather than the project's true value. From the company's point of view, this may mean selling the securities at an
unfairly low price. If the price is too low, the company may even
prefer to cancel the project rather than "give away" too much of
its value.

One way to avoid this outcome is to maintain financial slack
on one's balance sheet and/or preserve access to creditors who
can accurately assess the value of the investment opportunities
facing the company. For many large Japanese companies, close
bank relationships were the solution to such a problem. Most of
the companies in my field sample, for instance, did not feel that
they were especially capital constrained during the high-growth
period, primarily because of the commitment their main banks
displayed.

Not all Japanese industrial corporations have identically close
relationships with banks, however. For those that do not, maintaining higher degrees of financial slack on the balance sheet
may be important. One would expect this to be all the more imperative before financial liberalization made possible the issuance of a wide array of securities in highly liquid capital markets. The empirical evidence supports this hypothesis. During
the 1977–1982 period, investment by Japanese companies with

close bank affiliations was unaffected by fluctuations in financial liquidity. For a sample of "independent" companies without close bank ties, however, investment was strongly influenced by their levels of liquidity.[9] Thus, for the latter type of Japanese manufacturer, maintaining some financial slack in the form of excess cash may be a rational adaptation to the information asymmetries and moral hazard dilemmas that inevitably plague large, impersonal capital markets.

Finally, maintaining substantial cash balances may have been a means of making credible a company's commitment to fulfilling implicit contracts with some of its major stakeholders. The promises of lifetime employment and future retirement benefits are good examples. When queried about why so much cash and marketable securities were being held, managers in the field sample most frequently cited labor considerations. As one manager put it, "If we began paying out the cash as dividends, the employees would probably become angry and frightened. 'You are spending our future,' they would say. 'Why are you draining the company of funds rather than keeping it inside and securing our welfare?' I am sure their concerns would ultimately prevent us from giving the cash to shareholders."

These concerns are not unfounded. The promise of lifetime employment is an implicit contract with employees, not a written guarantee that could or would be enforced by Japanese courts or regulators. The company must be alive and solvent in the long run if this promise is to be kept. Promised retirement benefits are of a more explicitly contractual nature, having been formally agreed to through collective bargaining. But until very recently, such benefits were not paid as an annuity from a pension fund. Rather, retiring employees would usually receive a lump-sum settlement on separation from the firm, the amount paid depending on the seniority of the employee and salary history with the company. Companies usually set up accounting reserves related to this liability, but are not required to earmark funds spe-

---

9. Takeo Hoshi, Anil Kashyap, and David Scharfstein, "Corporate Structure, Liquidity, and Investment: Evidence from Japanese Industrial Groups," *Quarterly Journal of Economics*, forthcoming.

cifically for it.[10] Thus, for all practical purposes, retirement benefits in Japan have been unfunded. It is only natural, therefore, that labor should look to the company's liquidity to gauge its ability to maintain employment through adversity and to make good on future retirement settlements.

The deployment of excess cash by some Japanese companies in the post–1985 period can be construed as an attempt to dip into this nest egg for purposes of making good on implicit promises of lifetime employment to labor and management. As shown in Chapter 7, Japanese companies trapped in sunset industries maintained higher levels of employment in their existing businesses in the 1980s than could be justified on the basis of either their near- or long-term outlook. At the same time, they are spending or planning to spend their cash to enter new businesses in order to maintain job continuity for current workers and managers. This reduces current profitability and likely represents a transfer of value from shareholders to employees.

Take the case of Nippon Steel. Only time will tell how successful Nippon Steel's diversification will be, but there are good reasons to view at least some of its new ventures—the most unrelated businesses such as biotechnology and communications systems—with skepticism. For many companies, unrelated diversification strategies have proved to be of dubious value. Alfred Chandler has studied the evolution of modern industrial enterprises in Germany, the United Kingdom, and the United States and finds that the most successful large enterprises were those that developed and nurtured what he calls "organizational capabilities": unique managerial skills and organizational hierarchies to govern technically sophisticated production facilities and distribution networks. The application of these organizational capabilities to an ever-larger market in a company's existing line of business or in new markets for closely related products (e.g., branded food products) allowed them to achieve very large-scale and eventual market dominance. By contrast, com-

---

10. The maximum permissible size of the reserve is equivalent to 40% of the liability that would be incurred if all employees voluntarily separated at the rate of the balance sheet.

panies that pursued unrelated diversification into businesses in which they had no such applicable organizational capabilities foundered or even failed.[11]

Michael Porter's conclusions in a study of diversification strategies of 33 major U.S. corporations pursued between 1950 and 1986 are consistent with Chandler's.[12] In Porter's sample, the most successful strategies were pursued by companies like Procter & Gamble and IBM. Such companies diversified primarily into closely related fields, and even they did poorly when they dabbled in unrelated areas. The worst performers—CBS, RCA, Gulf + Western, and Westinghouse—pursued aggressive diversification strategies into unrelated businesses. For these companies, Porter concludes that "corporate [unrelated diversification] strategies . . . dissipated instead of created shareholder value." For many of them, pressure to perform in the 1980s has meant dozens of divestitures that have effectively undone the strategies followed in the prior decades. Indeed, the American M&A boom of the 1980s is widely viewed as a "supply-driven" wave. The market for corporate control forced underperforming corporate giants to regurgitate poorly fitting businesses, which were ultimately sold to companies with the organizational capabilities needed to manage them effectively.

Even Japan does not lack such examples of severe underperformance due to unrelated diversification. Under its domineering former president, Shinzo Ohya, the Teijin Corporation undertook a far-reaching, American-style diversification strategy starting in 1965. The oldest and once largest textile company in Japan, Teijin entered such new businesses as cosmetics, automobile sales, oil exploration in Nigeria and Iran, large-scale farming in Brazil, and restaurants in England. Deeply entrenched at the center of this far-flung corporate empire was Ohya himself. He became virtually the only person in this functionally organized, highly centralized company that understood its complexity and could administer it. The tenuousness of his

---

11. Alfred Chandler, *Scale and Scope* (Cambridge, MA: Harvard University Press, 1990).
12. Michael Porter, "From Competitive Advantage to Corporate Strategy," *Harvard Business Review* (May–June 1987), pp. 43–59.

grasp was revealed, however, when sharply rising oil prices dras-
tically reduced the profitability of Teijin's core business, synthetic fibers. In the absence of this business's contribution to
consolidated profits, the weak performances of Teijin's many
other smaller businesses became evident. Dramatic restructuring began in 1978, but not until Ohya's death in 1980 did with-
drawal from businesses other than fibers, textiles, and chemicals
begin. Company insiders estimated that Ohya's diversification
strategy cost the company at least ¥30 billion in after-tax profits
(between 35% and 40% of equity's market value in the late
1970s), not to mention the expenditure of immense amounts of
management's time and energy trying to turn the company
around.

However well intentioned their plans, a number of other
large, cash-rich companies in Japan appear to be running a similar risk of diversifying beyond the reach of their existing organizational capabilities. Of the ten companies in my field sample
with threatened or slowly growing core businesses (primarily
steel and metal products, chemicals, textiles, fibers, and
branded consumer products), three were entering or renewing
emphasis on engineering and construction activities, three were
developing advanced materials of various sorts, one-half were
entering some segment of the information processing and/or
telecommunications systems markets. And *all* were seeking
commercial applications of in-house biotechnology research.

For some, the new fields represent natural extensions of their
existing businesses. The commercial application of biotechnol-
ogical research, for example, may be quite appropriate for a
chemical or food products company. But computer electronics,
software engineering, real estate development, and chains of
health clubs appear much less so. Naturally, rationalizations for
entering these largely unrelated businesses are readily available,
but they tend to beg credulity. One manager in the field sample
claimed that sometimes there was no clear rationale for entering
a new business other than that a provocative opportunity presented itself. "Often, we buy an interesting new venture first and
then think up a strategic reason later," he frankly admitted.

Perhaps new organizational capabilities will eventually be de-

veloped to handle these unrelated businesses. The tendency of
Japanese companies to manage many of the new businesses
through joint ventures with partners that have managerial as
well as technical competence in the fields is evidence that diversifying parents frequently recognize their organizational limitations and act sensibly in light of that fact. Moreover, it must be
noted that the new businesses typically account for less than
10% of the parents' total revenues and costs.

However, most hope to see these businesses account for one-
third or more of total revenues by some point in the mid-1990s.
Given the scope of the diversification efforts being undertaken,
it is by no means obvious that successful organizational and
managerial adaptation will take place within the planned time
frame. Some undoubtedly will succeed. But the past unrelated
diversification experiences of industrial enterprises worldwide
make it difficult to be sanguine about the prognosis.

## A Disciplinary Void

Tremendous success in product markets around the
world, the retention of much of their cash flow, and fewer good
investment opportunities in core businesses have produced considerable financial slack for Japanese corporations. Coupled
with freer access to global capital markets, this has led to a distancing of Japanese industrial corporations from their owner/
lender banks, a widening of managerial discretion with respect
to the allocation of resources, and a drive to escape dependence
on a single industry.

The evidence presented here suggests that freedom from
product and capital market discipline is prompting Japanese
managers to deploy cash in ways more likely to benefit themselves and other employees of the firm by preserving jobs than
to benefit other stakeholders, suppliers of capital in particular.
The risky, probably uneconomic use of excess cash to speculate
in financial markets and plunge into strategies of unrelated diversification are two major deployments in this vein.

In this regard, the remarkable success of Japanese companies
in the postwar period has revealed a hidden and potentially de-
bilitating cost. The managerial discretion afforded by excess

cash has given rise to the expression of latent self-interests that were successfully contained during Japan's high-growth period. Today, some Japanese stakeholders appear to be gaining at the expense of others without any immediate prospects of recontracting. With their diminished control over the supply of capital, and being largely owned by their industrial clients, the ability of lending-share-owning financial institutions to undertake corrective action is greatly reduced. It is the voiding of this vital safeguard in the Japanese corporate governance system that will lead to a different Japanese market for corporate control—one that will be more active and more frequently punctuated with bids by investors hostile to incumbent management. Recent struggles for corporate control in Japan signal the advent of this new market.

# 10
# CONTESTS FOR CONTROL
# IN JAPAN

The costs associated with management's discretionary control of excess cash are difficult to hide indefinitely. It is unlikely that many institutional investors or financial analysts in Japan have been fooled by the use of *zaiteku* earnings to mask declining operating earnings or have been oblivious to the risks being taken. Nor are the lessons of wasteful investment in unrelated businesses by some Western companies likely to have been lost on them. One analyst from Nomura Research Institute, for example, flatly stated that he thought Nippon Steel was "wasting money investing in new, diversified businesses." If Nippon is committed to that strategy, the Nomura analyst would prefer to see them purchase established companies rather than attempt to build new units in-house utilizing existing manpower. Even then, he believes "Nippon Steel's management, which has been used to managing a business [steel] with a 30- to 40-year time horizon, will be inferior in running short life-cycle, high-tech businesses."

Lending banks and other financial institutions, the traditional watchdogs of manufacturing enterprises find that their ability to exercise control over the uses of cash are severely impaired in this period of abundant liquidity. Large manufacturers now borrow less money, consult lenders less frequently, and deflect attempts to insert bank officers into their own top management.

Other means of asserting one's voice as a shareholder have always been and continue to be quite ineffective. For example, waging a successful proxy fight to change managerial policies about the deployment of corporate cash (or any other action, for

237

that matter) would seem all but impossible in Japan. From the start, Japanese regulations governing the proxy device have been rather weak.[1] Moreover, in contrast to the trend in the United States, Japan has had a history of gradually relaxing proxy regulations in favor of incumbent management. Among other steps, Misao Tatsuta has pointed out that amendments over time have abolished advance review of proxy materials by the Ministry of Finance even when a contest for control is at stake, and have deleted provisions that the designated proxy agent should follow the voting instructions of the shareholder solicited![2]

In major Anglo-American economies (the United States, the United Kingdom, Canada, and Australia), a chronic transfer of value from shareholders to other corporate stakeholders at the hands of incumbent management, coupled with the high costs—or even the impossibility—of disciplining management through existing corporate governance mechanisms, has given rise to an active market for corporate control. It is, moreover, one often punctuated by successful *unfriendly* takeovers of even large corporations. In such a market, the equity interests can be given a renewed pre-eminence by taking ownership out of the hands of a widely diffused shareholder population and concentrating it in the hands of a smaller shareholder group that can more effectively monitor and govern the company's actions in its own self interest. Usually this entails changes in the board of directors, management, or both, and some recontracting with other key stakeholders such as labor, suppliers, or major customers.

---

1. Blank proxies, for example, were quite common in Japan and generally recognized as valid in support of management's position. Vagueness in the regulations requiring disclosure of potential conflicts of interests affecting a candidate for director have allowed corporations to state routinely that there is no conflict. Shareholders have no right to make proposals and have them included in management proxy statements. Instead, they must own at least 3% of the stock and convene a shareholders' meeting at their own expense. Although penalties for the violation of proxy regulations do exist, no sanctions have ever been imposed. In any event, the majority view among legal scholars in Japan appears to be that violation of proxy rules would *not* affect the validity of an action taken at the shareholders' meeting because the regulations extend only to the *solicitation* of proxies and not to corporate action itself. A concise but thorough discussion of these and other points of Japanese proxy regulation is in Misao Tatsuta, *Japanese Securities Regulation*, edited by Louis Loss, Makoto Yazawa, and Barbara Ann Banoff (Tokyo and Boston: University of Tokyo Press and Little, Brown, 1983).
2. Misao Tatsuta, "Proxy Regulation, Tender Offers, and Insider Trading," in *Japanese Securities Regulation*, edited by Loss, Yazawa, and Banoff, p. 162.

Can such an Anglo-American market for corporate control take root and flourish in Japan? Clearly it has not to date, and many knowledgeable observers doubt it ever will. Some point to technical, legal, and regulatory barriers that might inhibit such an evolution. Most appeal to various extralegal barriers to mergers and acquisitions. These include membership in industrial groups, extensive cross-shareholdings (especially with banks), the potentially high costs of recontracting with other stakeholders, and a sheer cultural bias against such activity.

The effectiveness of these barriers is examined here in the light of two of Japan's most celebrated large-scale takeover attempts: at the Fujiya Co., Ltd. and the Minebea Company, Ltd. The Minebea attempt involved hostile foreign raiders, whereas the Fujiya struggle was incited by a new breed of indigenous Japanese corporate predators. Ultimately, both attempts failed to win control of the companies targeted. But the surprising inroads made in each case demonstrate the extent to which the Japanese market for corporate control has changed and foreshadow the more frequent use of Anglo-American tactics in future battles for control of Japanese companies. While it is premature to forecast a convergence of the Japanese market with the West's, these examples make it evident that a newly active market for corporate control in Japan will fill the void left by receding capital market discipline.


## THE CASE OF FUJIYA CO., LTD.

Fujiya Co., Ltd. is one of the "Big Five" confectionery manufacturers and distributors in Japan.[3] In 1986, each of its two divisional operations, wholesale and retail, accounted for roughly half of Fujiya's ¥124.3 billion in sales and ¥950 million in net income. The wholesale division produced branded Japanese candies, chocolates, cookies, Western-style cakes, and

---

3. Facts concerning the Fujiya case have been drawn from public sources. Many of them were generously provided by Associate Professor Sadahiko Suzuki of Keio Business School. These and other details of Fujiya's greenmailing are contained in Timothy Luehrman, "Fujiya Co., Ltd.," 288-027. Boston: Harvard Business School, 1988. The analysis of these facts and any errors in their presentation are my responsibility.

soft drinks for sale to independent Japanese wholesalers and retailers. Most products were sold under its own brand names, although a few were produced under license (or imported) and distributed under foreign brand names owned by Rowntree Mackintosh, plc., Baskin-Robbins Ice Cream Company, Hershey Foods Corporation, and Frito-Lay.

The retail division managed a chain of 948 retail candy shops, tearooms, and restaurants. Franchisees operated 792 of the outlets, and Fujiya operated the rest. Many of the franchises Fujiya owned and operated were located on prime Tokyo real estate that it also owned. Although these land holdings were carried on its balance sheet at a book value of ¥1.3 billion (representing only 2% of Fujiya's total assets), their market value was undoubtedly vastly higher; many of the sites had been acquired decades ago before the tremendous boom in the Tokyo real estate market. Despite a declining trend in sales and profits per franchise, Fujiya continued to expand its chain operations throughout the decade ending in 1986. During the 1983–1986 period, Fujiya spent 100% of its total cash flow from operating and nonoperating sources (approximately ¥4.6 billion per year) on capital expenditures.

The Japanese confectionery industry is one of the largest in the world, second only to that of the United States. It grew slowly at an average annual rate below 5% in the first half of the 1980s. Industry profitability was also low, showing no growth since the mid-1970s and only a 4% return on total assets in 1986. Significantly, much of this return was provided by nonoperating earnings on substantial cash holdings invested in financial securities; earnings from confectionery operations were actually declining in the early 1980s. Nevertheless, encouraged by rising demand for Western-style chocolates, many foreign producers such as Hershey Foods, Nestlé, and Cadbury Schweppes announced plans to enter the Japanese market. The Japanese government imposed a 20% tariff on imported chocolate in 1986, but most industry observers expected it to be lowered or even eliminated by the end of 1987.

Fujiya was founded in 1910 by Rin-emon Fujii. The Fujii family continued to dominate company management throughout the following decades. Prior to 1982, the Fujii family was thought to control, directly and indirectly, about 20% of the company's stock, which was listed on the First Section of the Tokyo Stock Exchange. Major financial institutions owned about one-third of the company's stock; other corporations owned 6%, and individuals owned the remainder. Two sons of the founder, Goro Fujii and Kazuro Fujii, were the company's chairman and president, respectively. Two grandsons were also directors and were expected to succeed the elder family members.

A significant change in Fujiya's ownership structure occurred in 1982, when Ginzo Korekawa, an experienced private investor, started accumulating Fujiya's shares on the open market. A dramatic series of events ultimately threatened the Fujii family's control of the company, sent Fujiya's stock soaring, and resulted in a ¥76.75 billion ($474 million) repurchase of shares by a related company, the largest such repurchase in Japanese business history. A brief summary of the major events follows.

By March 1983, Korekawa had purchased and registered 15.457 million (12%) of Fujiya's 126.344 million outstanding shares under the name of his private securities and precious metals trading company, Tokiwa K.K. An additional 6.42 million shares (5%) were also registered to Sanyo Securities, a brokerage firm that handled much of Korekawa's trading business, and 380,000 more shares were registered to Korekawa and his wife directly. It was rumored throughout Tokyo that Korekawa actually controlled directly and indirectly closer to 30% of Fujiya's stock through various proxy investors.

During this period of Korekawa's accumulation, Fujiya's stock price rose steadily from ¥295 per share on March 31, 1982, to ¥590 by the end of March 1983. The stock continued to move upward throughout 1983 and 1984, at which time Korekawa offered to sell the shares he controlled to a shareholder of Fujiya's choosing.[4] The offer to sell was reportedly at ¥500 per share.

---

4. Listed Japanese corporations are forbidden to repurchase their own shares. Consequently, an affiliate or other friendly corporation is designated to undertake the purchase with the greenmailed company eventually providing indirect financing.

Management hesitated and Korekawa withdrew his offer. He sold the shares to Video Seller in an off-market transfer at a price estimated to be between ¥500 and ¥600 per share. Ostensibly a company engaged in the selling and leasing of video-tapes and recording equipment, Video Seller was in fact recognized as the leader of a coalition of investors deliberately targeting companies in which they could accumulate large shareholding positions and prompt repurchase of their shares by a related company at a profit to the group. In 1984, Video Seller was building a position in both Fujiya and Morinaga, another major Japanese confectionery company.

It was also at the end of 1984 that Fujiya and other confectioners were targeted by another group: "The Man With 21 Faces," a gang of extortionists. The gang sent letters to all the major confectioners about its intent to lace candies on retailers' shelves with poison just before Valentine's Day unless each threatened company paid ¥100 million. Payment was not forthcoming and poisoned candies were discovered in Tokyo and Nagoya on February 12, 1985 (fortunately, the poisoned candies had labels warning of the contamination). Sales and profits of the confectioners were hurt as products were hastily pulled off retailers' shelves. Similar threats followed in December 1985, this time resulting in ¥500,000 payments by Fujiya and Meiji Seika. Other confectioners again refused to submit to the extortion.

Meanwhile, by June 28, 1985, Video Seller was thought to control in excess of 50 million Fujiya shares (39.6%), which by then had risen to ¥1,620 per share in value despite the threats of the extortionists. Two months later, Video Seller approached Fujiya's management with an offer to sell its shares. Confident that it still had a majority of shares in stable hands and believing Video Seller to be bearing substantial interest expenses on debt used to purchase the stock, management declined the offer. Nevertheless, it approached its banks and other sympathetic shareholders to encourage them to hold more stock in order to ensure a majority was held in stable hands.

In October 1985, the price of Fujiya's stock fell precipitously from ¥2,160 to ¥1,540 on news of the death of Video Seller's president, but later recovered when leadership was assumed by Yoshio Kurihara, a former stockbroker. Further gains in price were made in December, when Daisuke Kawai registered a block of 5.4 million Fujiya shares (4.3%). Kawai was unrelated to the Video Seller group, but he had been involved in an earlier attempt to take over Yomiuri Land, a real estate company. Analysts in Tokyo believed that some seemingly "stable" shareholders were actually the source of Kawai's newly purchased stock and that he could be expected to cooperate with Video Seller in an effort to force a repurchase of shares by a Fujiya affiliate.

In 1986, rumors began to circulate that Video Seller had engaged agents in New York to find a U.S. buyer for its Fujiya shares. Furthermore, a number were said to be seriously interested. Trading in Fujiya's stock became furious, with the price eventually reaching ¥3,790 by the end of April 1986. However, the volatility of its price prompted the Tokyo Stock Exchange to impose limits on its daily movements, increase margin requirements on the stock, and limit the number of shares that could be purchased on margin.

By September, six participants in the Video Seller group registered their collective holdings of 14,489 million shares, and the president of Video Seller announced that the group actually controlled more than 60 million shares (47.5%). He also confirmed that Video Seller intended to continue to seek a majority, but that it was still willing to sell to Fujiya and that buyers were being sought elsewhere. By late November, trading in Fujiya stock was suspended indefinitely after finally trading at ¥2,810 (earlier that month, Kawai committed suicide, allegedly because of involvement with gangsters in connection with Fujiya stock trading).

The drama ended on December 7, 1986, when it was announced that Fuji Merchant, a producer of alcoholic beverages and a Fujiya affiliate, agreed to buy all of Video Seller's position for just under ¥1,250 per share. Funding for the ¥76.75 billion purchase was arranged through banks and insurance companies. Goro Fujii acknowledged that the decision to arrange the purchase was made after learning that a U.S. food products company had expressed interest in buying Video Seller's position.[5]

From a Western perspective, there may be little remarkable about the Fujiya case. It is a classic story of what can happen to a listed company with high cash flow, substantial liquidity, considerable real estate holdings, unused debt capacity, but a languishing stock price and an investment policy of pouring cash back into poorly performing businesses. In the United States, a battle for control of such a corporation would seem inevitable, and one way or another, a substantial amount of cash would be disgorged from the corporation to shareholders.

If there is anything eyebrow-raising about the case, it is that it occurred in Japan, the land of entrenched management, and that control was very nearly lost but for the fact that the company *did* make a timely dispersal of cash to several of its major shareholders. What does this say about barriers to takeover activity in Japan? Is the Fujiya situation such an extreme case as to be safely dismissed from consideration, or does it represent the cutting edge of domestic acquisition activity in Japan?

## FINANCIAL GAIN VERSUS SOCIAL LEGITIMACY

Social and cultural norms are frequently mentioned as constituting at least as formidable a barrier to merger and acquisition activity in Japan as do legal and regulatory restrictions and equity ownership structure.[6] At the root of this barrier is the Japanese concept of *ie* (family; see Chapter 2) and the perception of companies as modern forms of *ie*. Selling a company, Japanese managers frequently say, is like selling a family. The very language used to express the concept of one organization

---

5. "Affiliate Buys Fujiya Stock, Ending Hostile Takeover Attempt," *The Asian Wall Street Journal*, December 8, 1986, p. 24.
6. See, for example, Walter L. Ames and Michael K. Young, "Foreign Acquisitions in Japan: Hurdling the Ultimate Barrier," *The Journal of the American Chamber of Commerce in Japan* (January 1986), pp. 10–29; and Kelly Charles Crabb, "The Reality of Extralegal Barriers to Mergers and Acquisitions in Japan," *The International Lawyer* (Winter 1987), pp. 97–128.

taking over another, *nottori* (hijacking) and *baishu* (bribery), connotes unsavory behavior. The idea smacks of "fleshpeddling" and is simply not to be done except under extreme circumstances. Even then, continuing feelings of loyalty to the separate premerger "families" and a complex network of principal-agent relationships shadowed by implicit contracts are said to frustrate the successful blending of companies. Even if an acquisition target is allowed to maintain its own identity and to be managed in a highly decentralized manner, anything less than a takeover warmly welcomed by all the target's stakeholders (employees especially) is thought likely to demoralize the target company's work force.

The opprobrious image of M&A in Japan has been reinforced in the postwar period by *yakuza* (organized crime syndicates such as "The Man With 21 Faces") that specialize in the use of shareholder positions to extort money from corporations. One means by which these gangs operate is to acquire shares in a target company and then threaten to disrupt shareholder meetings with public disclosures of scandalous management behavior unless they are paid off. In other cases, *yakuza* money has been alleged to support efforts by *shite* (stock-cornering) groups. These groups attempt to drive up the price of thinly traded stocks through the purchase of a large number of shares on margin. Then they threaten to use special large-shareholder rights (e.g., to inspect the company's books or call a special shareholders' meeting) to hamper management's control unless the shares are repurchased by one of the target's affiliates at a substantial premium.

Although most common in the late 1960s, such illegal activities continued in the 1980s. Sony's 1984 annual meeting, for example, was stretched to more than 13 hours because of the actions of *sokaiya* (thugs specializing in the disruption of shareholders' meetings as a means of extortion). Three leaders of prominent *shite* groups are either dead (Kazuo Kengaku, former president of Cosmo Research, killed by *yakuza* that later admitted their guilt), missing (Yasutsugu Ikeda, former president of the bankrupt Cosmopolitan *shite* group), or being prosecuted on illegal weapons charges (Kazuma Kimoto, former president of the Nihon Tochi *shite* group and reported to have a prior criminal record).

The illegal activities of such groups will never achieve social legitimacy in Japan. To the extent the public confuses them with genuine contests for corporate control, it will be that much harder for the Japanese business community to accept such future contests as legitimate shareholder responses to breakdowns in the traditional Japanese corporate governance system. But if these breakdowns become sufficiently severe, and if the financial returns forgone by shareholders and appropriated by other stakeholders such as labor and management become sufficiently large, economic self-interest will override cultural taboos and the derogatory connotations associated with unfriendly acquisitions.

This already appears to be happening. Recently, the rewards to legal (albeit, in the eyes of many Japanese, distasteful) greenmailing and risk arbitrage activities have been substantial indeed. The private status of *shite* groups and their secretive nature make impossible any precise calculations of gains from these activities, but some estimates are possible. Toyota Motor purchased shares of one of its group companies, Toyota Automatic Loom Works, from Nihon Gendai Kigyo (a dummy corporation of Nihon Tochi) at an estimated profit to the *shite* group of at least ¥10 billion. Video Seller claims to have earned about ¥1.5 billion in its first risk arbitrage position in Nihon Lace, which was involved in a struggle for control with Sanyo Kosan. Later, it made approximately ¥3 billion in a similar play for Fujita Sightseeing and is conservatively estimated to have earned about ¥15 billion in its greenmailing of Fujiya. The size of the positions taken in each of these cases is not known. But because stock of target companies is usually purchased on thin margin, it is likely that the equity committed to these deals was small. The probable returns were commensurately high and risky.

The greenmailing of listed Japanese companies is both more widespread and frequent than most people realize. Although most successful greenmailings are not publicly announced, a list of those reported in the business press between 1976 and 1987 is provided in Exhibit 10-1. The increasing incidence of greenmailing starting in 1985 is undoubtedly related to the buoyant

Exhibit 10-1 *Successful Greenmailings in Japan*

| Target | Owner | Date of Repurchase | Estimated Shares Repurchased | | Estimated Value of Repurchase (¥ billion) |
|---|---|---|---|---|---|
| | | | Number (million) | % | |
| Mitsui Mining | Mr. Toguri | 1976 | — | — | — |
| Daido Sanso | Nihon Tochi | 1977 | — | — | — |
| Ohji Paper | Hong Kong-based companies | May 1978 | 29.0 | — | 10.0 |
| Okamoto | Sasagawa group | May 1978 | 24.0 | — | — |
| Takara Brewery | Juzenkai | 1979 | — | — | — |
| Chiyoda Engineering | — | 1979 | — | — | — |
| Diesel Machinery | — | January 1980 | — | — | — |
| Yuasa Battery | Nihon Tochi | October 1980 | 9.3 | — | 3.4 |
| Tachikawa | — | February 1981 | — | — | — |
| Copia | Daishowa | September 1981 | 6 | 23.6 | — |
| Shochiku | Mr. Kono | October 1981 | 6 | — | — |
| Tsukamato Shoji | — | November 1981 | 0.7 | — | — |
| Yamada Machinery | Kurosawa Gakki | December 1981 | 1.3 | 10.8 | — |
| Tokyo Nissan | Shuwa | April 1981 | 7.8 | 22.9 | 3.5 |
| Sumitomo Mining | Mr. Korekawa | May 1982 | 5.5 | — | — |
| Tokyo Juki | — | July 1982 | 8.8 | 13.0 | — |
| Takasago Netsugaku | Namirei | October 1982 | 3.6 | — | — |
| Kobe Electric Railway | Sasagawa group | November 1983 | 4.0 | — | — |
| Kobe Silk | — | July 1984 | 10.0 | — | — |
| Meito Sangyo | — | 1985 | — | — | — |
| Nippon Lace | — | 1985 | — | — | — |
| Mitsui Toatsu | Nihon Tochi | January 1985 | — | — | — |

Exhibit 10-1  Successful Greenmailings in Japan (continued)

| Target | Owner | Date of Repurchase | Estimated Shares Repurchased | | Estimated Value of Repurchase (¥ billion) |
|---|---|---|---|---|---|
| | | | Number (million) | % | |
| Takasago Kohryo | Aibi Cosmetics | January 1985 | — | — | — |
| Tosco | — | March 1985 | — | — | — |
| Shin-Nippon Zohki | Asahi Kakaku | June 1985 | 0.67 | 4.7 | — |
| Miroku Firearms Manufacturing | Shoeido | October 1985 | 1.01 | 8.3 | — |
| Matsuzakaya | — | October 1985 | — | — | — |
| INAX | Marumo | April 1986 | 20.0 | 19.0 | — |
| Nankai Electric Railway | Ryusho Tekko | May 1986 | 33.0 | — | 31.4 |
| Kitano Construction | Jyutaku Ryutsu Center | August 1986 | 3.5 | 10.7 | — |
| Fujiya | Video Seller | December 1986 | 61.4 | 47.5 | 76.8 |
| Calpis Foods | Harada Real Estate | 1987 | — | — | — |
| Tobishima Construction | Cohlin Industry | March 1987 | 17.55 | 9.2 | 22.8 |
| Nihon Matai | Taiyo Koson group | April 1987 | 4.96 | 23.6 | — |
| Morinaga Confectionary | Video Seller | May 1987 | 12.0 | 5.4 | 7.6 |
| Toyota Automatic Loom Works | Nihon Tochi | May 1987 | 17.7 | 7.1 | 35.4 |
| Japan Steel Tower | Kurosawa Gakki group | August 1987 | 1.62 | 9.0 | 11.3 |
| Tsukishima Machinery | Mr. Ohira | September 1987 | 6.94 | 19.8 | 6.9 |
| Ishihara Construction | — | February 1988 | 3.7 | — | — |
| Teikoku Sangyo | Cosmo Research | May 1988 | 5.0 | — | 3.5 |
| Koike Sanso Kogyo | Nippon Trust | May 1988 | 4.3 | 13.8 | 3.7 |

stock market in Tokyo, which made it easier for freelance Japanese risk arbitrageurs to support large positions in stocks purchased on margin. But the phenomenon is by no means a purely stock-market-related play. The Tokyo market crashes of 1987 and 1990, for example, bankrupted a handful of *shite* groups but did not eliminate the activity in general. An indicator of this persistence is the number of open positions roughly half a year after the 1987 crash. A list published by *Ohru Toshi* (*All Investment*) magazine in its July 15, 1988 issue, showed 120 private investors, companies, and groups with experience in greenmailing or associated risk arbitrage holding positions in 156 different listed corporations (a list of the most active and better-known Japanese greenmailers is provided in Exhibit 10-2). Collectively, they accumulated registered positions with a market value of

Exhibit 10-2  *Active Shite Groups*

| Company Name | Business |
| --- | --- |
| Aichi | Finance |
| Akebono Kikaku | Real estate |
| Akomu | Finance |
| Asahi Kikaku | Real estate/management consulting |
| Auto Life | Electronics wholesaling |
| Azabu Jidosha | Commerce/real estate |
| Chishima Tochi | Real estate |
| Cosmopolitan | Real estate |
| Daiichi Fudosan | Real estate |
| Daio | Apparel wholesaling |
| Jemco | Finance |
| Kanon | Yarn wholesaling |
| Kita Shoji | Real estate |
| Koshin | Finance |
| K.T.T. | Finance |
| Kurosawa Gakki | Musical instrument retailing |
| Misato Sangyo | Real estate |
| Miyama | Real estate |
| Musashifuji | Finance |
| Nihon Tochi | Real estate |
| Shin Jigyo Kaihatsu Hombu | Finance |
| Shuwa | Real estate |
| Toa Denki | Electronics retailing |
| Zenrin | Publishing |

*Source: Ohru Toshi* (*All Investment* Magazine), July 15, 1988, pp. 50–53.

Exhibit 10-3 *Shite Group Investment by Industry, 1988*

| Industry | Size of Investment (¥ million) | Percentage of Total |
|---|---|---|
| Marine products | 9,321 | 0.6 |
| Foods | 136,676 | 9.2 |
| Textiles | 74,947 | 5.0 |
| Pulp and paper | 17,882 | 1.2 |
| Chemicals | 37,596 | 2.5 |
| Pharmaceuticals | 6,434 | 0.4 |
| Tire and rubber | 8,162 | 0.5 |
| Cement, concrete, and ceramics | 25,606 | 1.7 |
| Metals and metal products | 85,916 | 5.8 |
| Machine tools | 9,705 | 0.7 |
| Industrial machinery and parts | 210,223 | 14.1 |
| Automotive manufacturing | 32,236 | 2.2 |
| Bicycles | 27,864 | 1.9 |
| Electrical machinery | 87,541 | 5.9 |
| Consumer electronics | 32,982 | 2.2 |
| Miscellaneous manufacturing | 52,405 | 3.5 |
| Trading and wholesale commerce | 76,629 | 5.1 |
| Banking and insurance | 113,143 | 7.6 |
| Real estate | 21,936 | 1.5 |
| Department stores and chains | 48,343 | 3.3 |
| Construction and engineering | 266,468 | 17.9 |
| Transportation and warehousing | 49,784 | 3.3 |
| Hotels and theme parks | 48,594 | 3.3 |
| Communications | 8,836 | 0.6 |
| Total | 1,489,229 | 100.0 |

Source: *Ohru Toshi* (*All Investment Magazine*), July 15, 1988, p. 344.

¥ 1.5 trillion (the average registered position was 5.7% of the target companies' stock). Fifty-eight percent of the targets were listed on the First Section of the Tokyo Stock Exchange. Among them were some well-known companies, including *keiretsu* members, such as Konica, Teijin (Sanwa group), Sapporo Breweries (Fuyo group), Mitsubishi Rayon (Mitsubishi group), and Mitsubishi Steel (Mitsubishi group). A profile of the industry classifications of the target companies is shown in Exhibit 10-3.

The Real Estate Connection

    Profit is obviously the motivating force behind these mavericks of the Japanese business community, but what is the source of their funding, and how do they select their targets? Not surprisingly, direct answers to questions like these are not provided by these highly secretive, private organizations. However, indirect evidence from Japanese securities industry professionals who monitor their activities points to real estate and excess cash as common denominators among greenmailers, freelance risk arbitrageurs, suppliers of finance, and the target companies.

The booming real estate market in Japan pushed up the value of corporate real estate prices by nearly 100% between 1984 and 1987. Prices have continued to rise since then, giving Japan the highest property values in the world. The clear winners in this price appreciation were the large real estate development companies and anyone else owning substantial amounts of real estate in and around Tokyo prior to the 1980s. In 1987, *Forbes* magazine traced the bulk of the fortunes owned by 14 of the 22 Japanese billionaires it identified (undoubtedly there are more) to real estate profits.[7] Adding to the pools of private capital created by these profits is the debt supported by appreciated property. It provides good collateral for loans—a highly important consideration given the inflexible, asset-based lending practices of most Japanese banks.

While much of the liquidity created by real estate gains has been reinvested in property inside and outside Japan, some of it is apparently also being devoted to the greenmailing and risk arbitrage operations of the *shite* groups. In fact, almost half of the *shite* groups listed in Exhibit 10-2 are real estate companies. Seven others are finance companies with considerable real estate-based lending practices. Professionals in the securities companies believed that some large, publicly held real estate development companies in Japan were also using *shite* groups as fronts for greenmailing and risk arbitrage operations that might otherwise be carried out by them were it not for adverse reputation effects. Similarly, they believed that even some major commercial banks were indirectly providing capital to *shite* groups through small, wholly owned finance companies. Not surprisingly, in view of the risks involved, such loans bear very high interest rates. They are viewed as an effort by the banks to make

---

7. Andrew Tanzer, "Land of the Rising Billionaires," *Forbes*, July 27, 1987, pp. 66–80.

up for lost corporate loan business and, most recently, from a decline in real estate lending following a 1987 MOF requirement that all property financing be reported to it.

Although the veil of secrecy similarly obscures the reasons for targeting specific companies for greenmailing, what evidence there is points to the presence of valuable real estate and financial slack on the balance sheets of targeted companies. In explicit statements about their greenmailing activities, Kurosawa Gakki group, Nippon Trust (a Tokyo real estate broker), Ryusho Tekko (a mid-sized Osaka trading company), Cohlin Industry (later Koshin), and Kenji Corporation have all identified the misuse of valuable real estate holdings or mismanaged "hidden assets" (which generally implies real estate holdings) as reasons for their respective attacks on Nippon Tekko Kogyo (Japan Steel Tower, the nation's largest builder of steel-pipe towers and bridges); Koike Sanso Kogyo (a producer of gas-powered machine tools); Nankai Electric Railway; Janome Sewing Machine; and Mitsui Wharf (a port-harbor transport company belonging to the Mitsui group owning waterfront property in the Tokyo area). On average, the greenmailed companies did have more land (5.7%), more cash (18.8%), and less debt (26.8%) as a percentage of total assets prior to being targeted than that of all companies listed on the First Section of the Tokyo Stock Exchange. Consistent with this real estate focus is the very high concentration of current targets in construction and engineering (see Exhibit 10-3). Many of the targeted firms in this business acquired considerable real estate holdings in the 1980s as they put their own equity into large-scale, develop-and-sell projects to replace subsiding public works projects.

The Vulnerability of Closely Held Companies

Interestingly, past and present targets are not companies that are obviously vulnerable because of a large float of shares outside the control of stable shareholders. As often as not, targets are group companies with more than 50% of their shares in the hands of friendly financial institutions and other corporations, a classic Japanese ownership structure. Possibly the targets are more vulnerable than they appear. With access to insider information regarding the willingness of apparently stable shareholders to sell, *shite* groups may be taking positions with a real threat of obtaining control and an initial information advantage over the target's management.

More likely, however, the *shite* groups are actually turning the close, stable ownership of targets to their advantage. The number of stable shareholders holding a majority of the outstanding stock is typically no more than a few score companies. Hence, one well-financed *shite* group, or several acting in concert, can buy up sufficient outstanding stock to reduce the total number of outstanding shareholders to a level below the minimum required for listing on the Tokyo Stock Exchange (for a typical Japanese company, this level would be about 2,500 separate shareholders). Issuing new shares to existing stable shareholders is no defense in this case, and finding a sufficient number of reliable new shareholders on short notice can be problematic. When caught in this position, Japanese companies have generally capitulated rather than face delisting or hastily expanding the circle of stable shareholders.

The methods of *shite* groups, although technically legal, are outwardly despised by Japan's business establishment. Nevertheless, they are effective. Through the concentration of available shares in their hands, they manage to accomplish what has not been forthcoming from the management-controlled boards of most Japanese companies: the disgorging of excess cash to (some) shareholders and reductions in unnecessary financial slack. In and of itself, this activity is unlikely to provide any widespread social acceptance of greenmailers in Japan: certainly, leaders of *shite* groups are implausible candidates to head the Keidanren.

But, however begrudged they may be, wealth and success have a way of creating their own legitimacy. Evidently, the returns to this activity are currently attractive enough relative to the risks involved to attract more capital and, significantly (if the allegations of some finance executives in Tokyo are accepted), the tacit cooperation and even financial support of some major financial institutions. By demonstrating the value that shareholders can appropriate for themselves through unilateral action outside the traditional coalition of corporate stakeholders, hostile *shite* groups are functioning as catalysts fostering the development of a more Anglo-American market for corporate control in Japan. They may never be invited into the mainstream Japanese business fraternity. But their success in a period marked by rising levels of excess cash, widening managerial discretion, and declining levels of monitoring and control by financial institutions is gradually seducing that fraternity into methods of obtaining returns on equity investments previously considered anathema.

## HOSTILE BIDS BY FOREIGNERS

The 1980s also saw several foreign investors become unfriendly bidders for Japanese companies. Although unsuccessful in gaining actual control over a Japanese company, they appear to have reaped financial rewards nonetheless. Consider the targeting of the Minebea Company, Ltd. by foreign bidders in 1985. Minebea was a diversified Japanese company with 1984 sales of ¥131 billion. It had grown extensively through acquisition under the leadership of its flamboyant and outspoken chairman, Takami Takahashi, who controlled 6% of Minebea's stock through a foundation. By 1985, it was selling products that ranged from kimonos to computer keyboards, although the bulk of sales was made up of ball bearings (33%) and various electronic devices (43%).

Minebea was steadily profitable with return on sales averaging about 3.1%, but return on book equity was low at 5%. Market returns on equity averaged less than 2% per year between 1980 and 1984. Although roughly half of its ¥200-billion capital base consisted of various forms of debt, this was offset somewhat by ¥61.5 billion in cash and marketable securities, which constituted 27% of total assets (long-term investments other than plant and equipment and intangibles constituted another 27% of total assets).

In August 1985, Minebea attempted a hostile takeover of Sankyo Seiki Manufacturing Company, a producer of robots and musical boxes. Sankyo Seiki vowed to fight the takeover. Terence Ramsden, a former British stockbroker and specialist in Japanese securities trading in the Euromarkets, then moved quickly to acquire 10 million Minebea shares (4.6%) on the open market through his investment firm, Glen International Financial Service Company.[8] Earlier, without Minebea's knowledge, he had quietly accumulated large blocks of equity warrants and convertible bonds that Minebea issued in the Euromarkets between 1982 and 1985. It was estimated that the stock, warrants, and convertible bonds collectively amounted to a $125 million investment and gave Glen International control of 30% of Minebea's common stock on a fully diluted basis (exercise of the warrants would require an additional investment of $150 million). On acquiring this stake, Ramsden is said to have offered Minebea the chance to repurchase it at a price per fully diluted share of ¥1,150, nearly double the value of Minebea's stock on the Tokyo Stock Exchange. Minebea rejected the offer, which was reportedly then presented to Sankyo Seiki. This proposal was also turned down.

At this juncture, Glen International sold an option to purchase its stake in Minebea to Trafalgar Holdings Ltd., a small investment bank started by Charles W. Knapp, former CEO of Financial Corporation of America, a California savings and loan bank. Glen International and Trafalgar Holdings then formed a partnership, Trafalgar-Glen, to pursue the Minebea situation further. News of the sale and partnership drove Minebea's stock price from ¥600 to ¥845 in less than two weeks.

Minebea responded by announcing on September 11 that its board had approved the issuance of ¥16 billion of subordinated debentures convertible into 20 million shares of common stock (5.6% of fully diluted shares outstanding). The debentures were to be placed with stable shareholders such as Takahashi, the Long-Term Credit Bank of Japan, and other banks with which Minebea did business. Although a decision to issue the bonds

---

8. Glen International's investors were anonymous, but were reported to include a number of influential Japanese investors as well as wealthy Swiss, Arabs, and Germans.

would actually be made at a later date and the dilutive impact would be minimal, the mere announcement of the issue caused Minebea's stock to fall about 10% in price.

Finally, on October 25, Trafalgar-Glen communicated to Minebea's directors a formal offer to purchase all Minebea's outstanding shares. The offer for each fully diluted share was a unit consisting of $.70 cash, a 20-year 3¼% yen-denominated convertible bond valued at ¥550 (approximately $2.56), and a 30-year zero-coupon bond with an estimated current value of ¥200 ($.93) and a par value of ¥2,000 ($9.30) at maturity.[9] The total package was valued at nearly ¥900 per fully diluted common share of Minebea, or approximately $1.4 billion. Special incentives were also offered to any Minebea executives who cooperated with the bidding partnership. A November 4 deadline was placed on the offer. If accepted, the Trafalgar-Glen partnership would buy all the shares and then merge with Minebea in Japan.[10]

Minebea's reaction to the tender offer was swift and sharp. Iwao Ishizuka, Minebea's executive vice president, declared the offer was an insult to Minebea's Japanese shareholders. Takahashi vowed that Minebea would use all necessary measures to thwart the takeover attempt. This vow was followed in a matter of days with the announcement that Minebea would merge with an affiliate, Kanemori Company (a clothing sales business), in which it already held a 48% equity interest. The merger would be structured as a stock-for-stock swap entailing the issuance of 30 million new Minebea common shares. The move was expected to increase equity ownership in Minebea by stable shareholders to 53%.

Four months later, Trafalgar-Glen filed suit in a Japanese court to try to stop the planned Minebea-Kanemori merger. It also filed a notice with the Bank of Japan that it intended to

9. Values reported were estimated by Trafalgar-Glen. The convertible carried an exercise price of ¥1,125 per share and would be convertible into shares of the new (postacquisition) Minebea. The zero-coupon bond was to be secured by U.S. Treasury bonds.
10. Strictly speaking, this would not have been possible since the Japanese Commercial Code permits mergers only between Japanese companies; Trafalgar-Glen would have had to set up a Japanese subsidiary to consummate a merger.

acquire more than 10% of Minebea's issued and outstanding shares. The suit was rejected in a preliminary court ruling in March 1986, while a ruling on Trafalgar-Glen's notice with the Bank of Japan was postponed in early April. However, negotiations between Minebea and Trafalgar-Glen aimed at getting the foreign partnership to divest its investment had already begun in March. By mid-April, Minebea was able to announce that the Trafalgar-Glen stake had been purchased by an unnamed Japanese buyer at an undisclosed price.

Although many observers view this case as an example of an ill-conceived and unsuccessful foreign takeover, it is doubtful that actual ownership and managerial control over Minebea was Trafalgar-Glen's objective. It is more likely that the foreign financiers were aiming for a profitable repurchase of their shares—in other words, a typical greenmailing of Minebea. Because the value of the repurchase was undisclosed, Trafalgar-Glen's actual return on the deal is not known. However, one professional risk arbitrageur on Wall Street, claiming knowledge of the parties and the deal, asserts that an attractive return was realized. The assertion seems plausible on the basis of currency movements alone: between August 1985 and April 1986, the yen rose 40% against the dollar and 30% against the pound. Since the yen price per share of Minebea's stock around the time of the repurchase was at or above its trading range at the start of the Trafalgar-Glen partnership, attractive dollar returns were possible so long as the buyout occurred at, or not much below, current market prices for the stock.

Obviously, international bidders cannot routinely count on the beneficial effects of favorable exchange rate movements to render profitable a stake taken in a foreign target. Even if one does have strong expectations about the direction, magnitude, and timing of exchange rate changes, there are certainly cheaper ways to speculate on currency movements. Nevertheless, even if serendipity determined any financial success Trafalgar-Glen enjoyed, the Minebea case illustrates the emerging vulnerability of some Japanese companies as they alter financing patterns to take advantage of global capital market opportunities. Not only have many Japanese companies turned to offshore markets to raise external funds, but a very substantial proportion (approximately 40% between 1984 and 1986) of securities issued offshore have been convertible bonds and bonds with warrants attached.[11] The new equity potentially created by such securities (most are, in fact, converted because of the closeness of conversion and exercise prices to market prices of the stock at the time of issuance) dilutes the ownership share of stable Japanese shareholders and creates an opportunity for foreign investors to target a Japanese company quietly, beyond the observation and reach of management.

Even though such stakes are unlikely to approach anything close to majority ownership in the target company, considerable leverage may result. The presence of an unfriendly major foreign shareholder may make the Japanese company in question a target for local *shite* groups, who can use the foreign threat to their own advantage. Although there is no evidence of this happening in the case of Minebea, Japanese *shite* groups have been known to exploit the threat of foreign takeover in the past. Recall the threat of sale to foreigners by Video Seller in its successful 1986 greenmailing of Fujiya. In a similar vein, Kitaro Watanabe, who had tried unsuccessfully for a year and a half to get Toyota to repurchase his 20% stake in Koito Manufacturing, sold his stake (valued at ¥145 billion, or about $1.19 billion at prevailing exchange rates) to Boone Co., a merchant bank controlled by T. Boone Pickens, in 1989. Koito is Japan's largest producer of halogen lights and other auto parts and is part of the Toyota group. Toyota itself owns 20% of the company. Despite the ap-

---

11. On the basis of comments made by Japanese financial officers, two factors appear to be driving this preference: the desire to generate reported earnings from financial investment activities (*zaiteku*), and a belief that their companies' stock prices may be overvalued. The issuance of warrant bonds and convertible bonds are attractive for *zaiteku* purposes because of the low coupons attached to these equity-linked forms of debt. These are made all the lower by fixing the exercise price of the warrants or the conversion price of the convertibles within just a few percentage points of the market price of the stock. Despite the valuable option being sold with these securities, most of the Japanese executives interviewed viewed this low-coupon debt as low-cost capital that would allow them to earn a positive spread easily on the funds so raised. Interestingly, many of the same executives would also say that they thought their companies' stock prices were probably too high. To the extent this is true, selling equity-linked debt at current market prices would indeed be a way to raise cheap capital.

parent security of Koito as part of the Toyota group, the emergence of Boone Co. as a major shareholder triggered concern and action on the part of Koito's management to a degree not previously displayed during 18 months of Watanabe's unwelcome share ownership.

It is unlikely that this concern is due to a genuine fear of losing majority control to a foreigner. A more plausible explanation may lie in some of the rights afforded to minority shareholders: for example, the right to demand an audit of the company's books if the investor, or group of investors, holds 10% or more of the outstanding shares. Whether or not this represents a real threat depends on what the books show, how an outsider may interpret them, and whether or not access can truly be obtained. Given the complex and generally customized trading agreements that normally exist among manufacturers and suppliers in the same group, an audit might well reveal off-market transfer prices among group members. This might not raise eyebrows in Japanese business circles but could be of great interest to parties abroad who are eager for any evidence of predatory pricing by Japanese exporters. Closer to home, the Recruit influence-peddling affair, which went so far as to bring down the Takeshita cabinet, raises the specter of scandal and loss of face should any evidence of misuse of corporate funds come to light. Hostile foreign shareholders may sometimes be better situated to bring such breaches of good conduct to light than their Japanese counterparts, some of whom may be subject to investigation themselves.

Perhaps none of these was an actual concern in the specific case of Minebea or Koito. Even so, these examples suggest that (1) it is possible for foreign investors to acquire a substantial, albeit minority, position in a Japanese target without the target's foreknowledge or consent, and (2) under some circumstances, foreign investors may be uniquely situated to capitalize on that minority position. Such action would appear to require a combination of local business knowledge (e.g., who owns large blocks of stock or convertible bonds, who are truly stable shareholders and who are not, what are the likely vulnerabilities of the target company), trading skills, and a credible threat to the normal conduct of business. Even if majority control of a Japanese target remains an elusive outcome for hostile foreign bidders, cross-border alliances between Japanese and non-Japanese investors could prove to be profitable vehicles for targeting the affiliates of cash-rich Japanese companies.

## CONTESTED TAKEOVERS IN JAPAN?

The development of the modern Japanese corporation is fundamentally a history of innovation in the face of changing economic circumstances. Prevailing contracts among corporate stakeholders become obsolete to a degree that makes incremental adaptation of those contracts prohibitively costly or even impossible. When this has occurred, the stakeholders with the most to gain from recontracting, be they equity owners, managers, or labor, have swept aside past arrangements even at the expense of creating open rifts within the coalition of stakeholders and violating prevailing cultural norms.

Today, the changed economic circumstances facing modern Japanese corporations are the slower rate of real growth in their main businesses, a newfound abundance of internal cash flow, and ownership of real estate that has soared in value and in many instances can be redeployed easily to other uses. These circumstances have afforded incumbent managers far greater discretion in decision making than ever before. Unwilling to breach implicit contracts with key stakeholders (lifetime employment commitments especially) and unable to execute past strategies of growing themselves out of their plight, they are using this discretion to devote resources to the sustaining of marginal businesses and/or the pursuit of unrelated diversification strategies. In so doing, they are reallocating the economic rents of these enterprises from shareholders to other stakeholders, primarily employees.

Once again, innovation is occurring. This time it is in the form of a more active market for corporate control where the disciplining of management and a more parochial pursuit of shareholder interests are much in evidence. This has led some to point to Japan as the next frontier of M&A dealmaking, thus lending credence to Joe Perella's forceful assertion that Japan's market for corporate control is inexorably bound for convergence with the Anglo-American market and will involve Western bidders and financial advisers.

Until recently, such an outcome might have been dismissed out of hand as highly improbable if not impossible. But evidence that has accumulated since the mid-1980s no longer permits such a quick dismissal of the idea. The official legal and regulatory framework governing takeover bids is not insurmountably biased against unfriendly tender offers (see Chapter 4). Nor, in the current environment, is the unofficial position assumed by the bureaucrats with responsibility for administrating those laws and regulations. As companies have distanced themselves from their financial institutional owners, and as those same financial institutions have come under pressure to produce better returns on their assets, shareholdings by financial institutions and other corporations have become less stable than generally realized. Finally, while public opinion still weighs against the idea of unfriendly takeovers, the increasingly visible success of unfriendly *shite* groups has begun to attract the attention and even involvement of more mainstream players in the Japanese business community. Tolerance of unfriendly agitation by shareholders against selected companies is developing, even if widespread acceptance is not. As long as publicly held Japanese companies remain engorged with cash or other easily redeployable assets, and as long as the returns from the use of this corporate wealth flow primarily to stakeholders other than equity investors, this agitation will persist.

Profound change in the Japanese market for corporate control has been made inevitable by the stresses that abundant cash and waning bank authority over corporate clients have placed on the traditional Japanese corporate governance system. Whether or not that change will lead to an Anglo-American type of market (as some predict) hinges on how the Japanese corporate governance system adapts to these stresses. Convergence with the West is not impossible, but it is by no means inevitable. Indeed, it is just as likely—if not more so—that Japan will emerge from the 1990s with a market for corporate control that is unique in its structure and conduct, and only partially integrated with similar markets in the rest of the world.

# 11
## GLOBAL PLAYERS, WESTERN TACTICS, JAPANESE OUTCOMES: THE NEW JAPANESE MARKET FOR CORPORATE CONTROL

TOKYO, 1997

Ryuichi Kawakami sat in grim silence watching the coffee in his cup ripple as the latest tremor shook his office building. This one seemed stronger than usual. The sloshing coffee had soaked some papers on his desk. But it was unlikely to do any serious damage to the building itself—the modern Tokyo high-rise had been built to absorb more serious quakes than this.

In any event, Kawakami's mind was on other matters. For months now, he had been preoccupied with an unexpected and unwelcomed struggle for control of his company, Meiwa Manufacturing, a broadly diversified corporation whose main business was producing stamped metal products for two of Japan's major auto assemblers. His antagonist was one of the increasingly common and vexing alliances of Japanese *shite* groups and Western risk arbitrageurs. His "allies"—if they could still be called that after that morning's meeting—were his bankers, customers, and major suppliers.

Meiwa Manufacturing had been targeted by Takeo Kaneko, a well-known Osaka real estate developer with a penchant for greenmailing cash-laden and land-rich companies. He had been attracted to Meiwa by its comparatively low (by Japanese standards) price-earnings multiple of 20, its ownership of marketable securities and Tokyo real estate that together accounted for 40% of its market value, and some overseas assets unrelated to Meiwa's main manufacturing business. A year earlier, Kaneko had quietly amassed a 15% stake in the company, launched a

263

negative publicity campaign critical of Kawakami's chairmanship, and asked to be made a director of the company.

At first, Kawakami treated Kaneko's position as an annoying but foolish gamble. Kawakami and his family controlled 18% of Meiwa's stock. Four large banks; two major auto companies (for which Meiwa was a major supplier of stamped metal parts); and about a dozen other long-time customers, suppliers, and subcontractors collectively owned another 45% of the company's stock. Meiwa seemed invulnerable to takeovers.

Even so, coping with Kaneko's dogged pursuit of Meiwa proved to be a time-consuming embarrassment. What finally spurred Kawakami to seek a final resolution of the situation was Kaneko's recent announcement that he had sold two-thirds of his position to offshore investors: a well-known American financier with eyes on a U.S. leasing business Meiwa owned and an Australian multinational interested in Meiwa's chain of British pubs. The latter had quietly maneuvered in the Euromarkets to accumulate a large block of Meiwa's equity warrants. This block gave it control over an additional 5% of Meiwa's stock on a fully diluted basis. The three were pooling their investments in Meiwa in a new joint venture named Global Investors, Ltd. They also announced that they had secured substantial additional sources of credit and were going to pursue their intent to increase their ownership of Meiwa and obtain representation on Meiwa's board of directors.

A global alliance with deep pockets now controlled 20% of Meiwa's stock. Other *shite* groups and risk arbitrageurs almost surely controlled another 10% to 15%. These *ronnin* of the capital markets could be expected to cast their shares into the hands of whomever offered the highest price. Furthermore, the concentration of shares in their hands would threaten Meiwa with delisting on the Tokyo Stock Exchange. Things had gotten a little too close for comfort. What was needed was a decisive move by Meiwa to convince the hostile investors once and for all that acquiring majority control would be impossible.

Kawakami knew that such a demonstration of support would be tricky to arrange. Meiwa Manufacturing had not been paying much in dividends, and its stock price was depressed—a reflection, perhaps, of the profitability foregone while Kawakami attempted to transform Meiwa into a globally diversified company less dependent on a handful of Japanese customers. Moreover, some of his bold, independent moves in the last decade had not endeared him to Meiwa's stable shareholders. The company's relationship with its banks had become rather "dry" in the 1980s when he repaid Meiwa's loans ahead of schedule with funds raised from a series of Eurobond offerings. Exacerbating the strained relationships with the banks had been Kawakami's requirement that, beginning in 1992, all senior officers and directors above the age of 65 in Meiwa's subsidiaries retire to make way for younger blood. Since a number of them were former career bank officers, this action had been taken as a direct affront to the status of these institutions and a breach of the implicit understanding that had existed between the banks and Meiwa for decades. The auto companies holding Meiwa stock had also been distanced during a soft market when Kawakami had refused to employ temporarily some of their workers at unskilled wage rates. At that time, Kawakami pleaded difficulties of his own while trying to implement his strategy of global diversification.

Still, these relationships had not withered altogether. Kawakami believed that the roots intertwining Meiwa with all these companies went back too far to suppose they would come apart now. Meiwa was still an important supplier to the two auto companies as well as a shareholder and purchaser of their vehicles. Indeed, Meiwa's engineering staff was virtually an extension of theirs. It also continued to own bank stock, maintained deposits in its traditional banks, relied on their cash management services, and executed virtually all foreign exchange transactions with them. New promises could be made, he figured, and old grievances would have to be pushed aside during this time of crisis.

It was under this belief that Kawakami had met that morning with Meiwa's traditional underwriters. The purpose of the meeting was to discuss possibilities for issuing new shares or convertible bonds to reliable investors in order to dilute the ownership of Global Investors, Ltd. and signal the solidarity of Meiwa's stable shareholders.

What Kawakami learned came as a shock. First, he discovered that Meiwa's position was far more precarious than he had imagined. The underwriters had looked carefully into the trading activity of Meiwa's stock and had reached the conclusion that *at least* 40% had found its way into the hands of the Kaneko alliance and other *shite* groups, significantly more than the 30–35% he had thought. Obviously, this meant that some stock had been bled from stable shareholders. It also meant the outsiders had reached a point of sufficient strength, and the stable shareholders had displayed sufficient weakness, that a successful takeover bid was a realistic threat. At the very least, delisting now seemed an imminent possibility.

Second, the full extent of the stable shareholders' frustrations with Kawakami was revealed. Evidently they had lost patience with his wayward management, which had gradually stripped them of adequate returns on investment as well as of the clout to do something about it. The current attack on Meiwa played into their hands. They were wiling to put up a defense, but at a stiff price. Meiwa must create two new executive offices, "Chief Secretary of the President's Office" and "Deputy Secretary of Financial Operations," to be filled by nominees of Meiwa's main bank. Both new officers would have board membership and would assume immediate day-to-day responsibility for company operations and finance. Other bank nominees for directors of subsidiary companies would be named later. Finally, within the year, Meiwa's chief financial officer would be expected to retire, and Kawakami himself would be expected to give up his present responsibilities to assume the post of honorary chairman of the board. If these arrangements were not acceptable to Kawakami, Meiwa's main bank regretfully said it could not guarantee that other stable shareholders would take up the new equity or even remain firm in the face of an attractive tender offer by one or more of the outside investors.

Kawakami felt checkmated. He could scarcely expect to defy both the banks and the hostile investors at the same time. A new set of stable shareholders would be impossible to develop on short notice, for it took years to build the underlying basis of trust that such relationships required. Restructuring the company on his own also seemed problematic. Japanese laws forbidding the repurchase of stock would leave cash from asset sales sitting on his balance sheet for some time to come. A management buyout would necessarily entail the severing of reciprocal shareholding arrangements. This might jeopardize important long-term business relationships and further depress profitability. Fearing job losses, the company union would probably also oppose such a move.

Kawakami expected that his desperate situation with stable shareholders would eventually be leaked to Kaneko, along with word that Meiwa's main bank would not mind being put in the position of arranging a "friendly" rescue. The course of events to follow was all too easy to imagine. Global Investors would launch a takeover bid at a small premium over the market price. An industrial client of the bank would then respond by launching a somewhat superior counteroffer, pledging to manage the company prudently and preserve jobs. The main bank would declare its support for the second bid, as would the company union, both citing the importance of job preservation and the instability that would be engendered by unfriendly foreign owners. Having served its function, Global Investors would then withdraw its offer and tender its shares to the main bank's proxy bidder instead. Meiwa would lose its independence, and Kawakami his job.

Thinking through his other alternatives, Kawakami reasoned that defecting from the stable shareholders and cutting a separate deal with Kaneko would likely yield a Pyrrhic victory. Already dissatisfied with Meiwa's conduct, they could only be further distanced by such a move. Acting unilaterally at this juncture would probably trigger their dumping Meiwa's stock and cancelling contracts with the firm, effectively gutting the profitability of its core business. In fact, paradoxically, the last thing Kaneko would probably want was to cut such a deal with Kawakami if it meant leaving the company and management intact and assuming a long-term ownership position. His greatest gain at the least risk would likely come from the sale of his stock to the stable shareholders at a reasonable margin above his average cost.

Kawakami knew that in the final analysis he had little practical alternative but to acquiesce to the main bank's demands and step aside gracefully. All his efforts to escape the constraints imposed on Meiwa by its close involvements with a few major banks and customers had come to naught. The freedom to do as he wished for the past 15 years had been an illusion—an indulgence eventually terminated by changes in the Japanese market for corporate control, which in 1997 featured Anglo-American bidding tactics and even Western bidders. One thing remained constant, however. The destiny of Japanese industrial targets remained in the hands of their large, institutional shareholders.

## An Orchestrated Takeover Market

This composite sketch of a future Japanese takeover battle portrays a Japanese market for corporate control considerably different from that of the past. The specifics of actual struggles for control will, of course, vary from one situation to the next. In general, however, they will tend to display the same broad characteristics depicted in this sketch. That is, they will feature global players and Western tactics, but will have distinctly *Japanese* outcomes.

Future Japanese M&A activity will differ from the past in the important catalytic role that hostile foreign and domestic bidders play. It will differ from current Anglo-American activity in that these bidders will begin and end their roles in the drama only as catalytic agents of change, rarely ever becoming victors in open, competitive bidding for the target company. Though appearing nominally independent, the bidders will in fact be used by major stable shareholders as their cat's-paws in the disciplining of target-company management. In short, the threat of takeover will gradually substitute for direct stakeholder intervention as the latter safeguard weakens in the face of corporate restructuring and financial liberalization.

There may be numerous indirect and tortuous avenues by which resolution of contests for control will be reached in Japan, but the final outcomes will be carefully and deliberately orchestrated by, and to the advantage of, pre-existing stable corporate stakeholders. In this major respect, the future Japanese market for corporate control will not mirror completely the Anglo-American market. It may display some of the trappings of this market, but it will retain a distinctly Japanese character.

## CORPORATE GOVERNANCE: THE DECISIVE
## DETERMINANT OF JAPANESE M&A ACTIVITY

Neither "500 years of tradition" nor an intrinsic economic superiority of the Anglo-American market for corporate control can adequately explain the past quiescence of the Japanese market, its current state of flux, and its likely future status. To explain all three, one has to understand how Japanese companies coordinate the actions of various corporate stakeholders and resolve conflicts of stakeholders' interests—a problem shared by economic institutions worldwide and throughout time. The Japanese system of corporate governance has been remarkably effective at this coordination and control. As shown in Part I of this book, this past success has contributed significantly to the attenuation of Japanese M&A activity.

This attenuation has occurred because until now two of the major driving forces for acquiring and merging with other firms have been substantially mitigated. One force was the need to extend hierarchical control over a market exchange relationship to relieve trading hazards (vertical integration). By successfully containing self-interested opportunism, the Japanese corporate governance system made it easier for Japanese companies to build and maintain stable, long-term exchange relations with suppliers, distributors, customers, subcontractors, and so on. Such relationships often prove to be superior to the imposition of direct hierarchical control over an exchange partner because of the bureaucratic disabilities and loss of high-powered market incentives that such control frequently entails. Hence the need to integrate vertically in order to secure upstream sources of supply or downstream markets was lessened by the classic corporate governance system.

The second takeover motive blunted by the Japanese corporate governance system was the need to exercise voting control in order to effect change in corporate strategies and policies detrimental to the welfare of the company's owners (discipline). Again, the sheer mitigation of self-interested opportunism on the part of various stakeholders, management included, reduced the need to use takeovers as a disciplinary mechanism. Abuses stemming from hidden action or the use of hidden information for private gain were simply fewer, less severe, and less costly to correct by means other than battles for majority control.

Given a choice between acquiring and managing another company outright versus embracing it with a set of long-term implicit contracts reinforced by reciprocal minority shareholding arrangements, Japanese companies have opted for the latter nearly every time. Combining with another company has happened only when the survival of an important business relationship has been called into question by the possibility of financial distress or a significant competitive threat.

The same kind of behavior has characterized Japanese activity abroad. If Japanese companies have been able to achieve their strategic aims through marketing and manufacturing agreements, joint ventures, or alliances of some sort other than majority ownership, they have generally elected to do so. If and when they have become active bidders for control, two conditions have typically prevailed: (1) the target company has had some kind of an existing relationship with the Japanese bidder, and (2) that relationship was threatened with disruption in some material way.

In this regard, Japanese manufacturers have acted abroad much as they have at home. An important difference, however, has been that the more common threat to the Japanese company's relationship to the target was the threat of takeover by some other American or foreign competitor. That is, their bidding activity abroad has been more *defensive* of an established relationship than an offensive or proactive deployment of cash to take advantage of what they view as undervalued dollar assets. Even today, Japanese companies may delight in studying sell lists brought to them by investment bankers, but unless an acquisition opportunity is a very small deal or a party with which they already do important business, most of their analysis will be mere window-shopping.

In summary, the comparative absence to date of an active market for corporate control in Japan has not been simply the result of a locking up of shares, self-serving entrenchment of management, or government prohibition. Neither has it been the product of Japanese social taboos about mergers and acquisitions nor individual bonds of loyalty to one particular group. Japan has not had a deep and active market for corporate control primarily because it has not needed it, not because it did not want it or could not tolerate it. It has not needed such a market because of the efficiency with which the traditional Japanese corporate governance system has dealt with the trading hazards of the marketplace and the agency problems of large organizations. Corporate governance, in short, has been and will remain the decisive determinant of Japanese M&A activity.

This governance thesis assigns secondary roles to cultural norms and social attitudes as determinants of Japanese takeover activity. There are, indeed, some cultural impediments to mergers and acquisitions in Japan. The company-as-family simile first promoted by Meiji industrialists has clearly taken root and flourished. This view of the firm undoubtedly predisposes Japanese business people against the buying and selling of companies.

But while such cultural biases are part of the M&A story in Japan, they are only part, and not the greater part at that. Little in the evolution of the modern Japanese industrial enterprise suggests that adherence to traditional cultural norms would long stand in the way of reform if private economic gain were an expected result. On the contrary, in Japan as elsewhere, the history of corporate evolution is replete with far-reaching change undertaken in relatively short intervals of time and sometimes characterized by sharp, overt conflict among corporate stakeholders motivated by economic self-interest. Culture may have created a predilection for experimenting with one type of organizational innovation versus another in response to a new opportunity or trading hazard. It also may have shaped the tactics of change. Japanese industrialists have tended to package innovations in such a way as to lend social legitimacy to their actions.

However, it was fundamentally the lure of private gain and the clash of self-interests that brought about evolution in Japanese corporate governance. That an active market for corporate control has not so far evolved as part of that system speaks less to the power of Japanese society's aversion to such activity and more to the lack of strong economic incentives motivating corporate takeovers.


## STRESSES FOSTERING CHANGE

Because the roots of Japanese merger and acquisition activity are more economic than cultural, change in that activity need not wait for a shift in the cultural climate. Rather, it can be expected to occur as economic incentives alter, potentially rapidly if the alteration is sufficiently far-reaching.

The evidence presented in Part II of this book suggests that incentives are beginning to change, in large measure because of emerging weaknesses in the traditional Japanese corporate governance system. Ironically, part of the cause of that weakness is the very fruit of competitive success: an abundance of cash. The combined effects of decelerating real economic growth and considerable success in product markets around the world have been the buildup of tremendous free cash flow. With this have come profound changes in the financing patterns of large corporations. Net new investment by Japanese corporations has been growing less quickly and is increasingly being funded internally. External financing is increasingly being raised from securities markets, not banks. This has meant a shift in the balance of power among corporate stakeholders away from financial intermediaries, the traditional primary suppliers of capital, and into the hands of industrial managers. It is now commonplace to observe Japanese companies repaying their loans completely and even refusing to accept former bank officers as nominees for director.

With financial emancipation has come the deployment of cash in ways that are of dubious value. Much corporate free cash flow in Japan is being used in *zaiteku* operations—essentially speculation on the stock market and other types of financial risk taking. In effect, Japanese treasury operations have begun to be used as profit centers. There is little evidence, however, to suggest that the finance departments of industrial corporations are able to earn returns from these operations any greater than are required to compensate for the risk taken. In fact, many managers seem to be unaware of the nature and extent of the risks involved. Despite some impressive earnings from *zaiteku* operations, there have also been some colossal losses.

Another debatable use of cash has been the pursuit of unrelated diversification strategies. Life sciences, electronic communications, advanced materials, engineering and construction, and services dominate the list of businesses that mature manufacturers in Japan are trying to enter. Every Japanese industrial company I researched in connection with this book was investing heavily to break into one or more of these five areas. The rationale for doing so was to escape the limitations and intensifying rivalry of mature core businesses and, in particular, to keep personnel continuously employed, thereby honoring implicit promises of lifetime employment.

However well-intentioned these efforts may be, there is little reason to be sanguine about their prospects for success. Many of the new businesses being pursued have only the loosest of connections with the investing firm's organizational capabilities. To the extent that these capabilities are exceeded, underperformance will result and capital will have been wasted, at least from the point of view of capital suppliers. Should unrelated diversification plans progress unabated, it is plausible that Japanese industrial corporations will appear as poorly strategically configured in the 1990s as American companies were in the 1980s following their diversification efforts of earlier decades.

Concomitant with the exercise of wider discretion by corporate managers has been an increase in the performance demands of banks and other financial institutions regarding their relationships with client companies. For the large banks, this trend is partly a result of increased capital requirements as they extend their activity abroad. Better returns on investment is one means of meeting these requirements. For nearly all financial institutions, it is also a result of the disintermediation of corpo-

rate borrowing and increased competition in previously protected businesses. Large corporate clients now borrow less and
shop more for financial services.

These trends have begun to reverse the blending of claims that
has characterized the link between companies and institutional
suppliers of capital. As investors, banks are increasingly being
relegated to the role of straight equity holders and vendors of
financial services. The close monitoring that once accompanied
heavy borrowing has begun to atrophy. So too has the banks'
ability to intervene quickly if necessary. Owing to the price-
oriented shopping of clients for other financial services, it has
also become more difficult to extract excess returns from other
pieces of business that might make up for inadequate returns on
equity. Not surprisingly, therefore, banks have begun to act more
like conventional institutional equity investors. Clients with
whom their trust relationship has evolved into a price-oriented
one are being culled from portfolios if returns are inadequate.
Stability of share ownership is no longer a foregone conclusion,
even in the event of hostile attack.

What all this has meant to Japan is the weakening of its classic corporate governance system. With this weakening will come
a higher incidence of unilaterally self-interested actions by corporate stakeholders and the eruption once again of overt conflicts of interest among stakeholder groups. One symptom of this
is the rash of successful greenmailings that has developed in recent years. The lure, in most cases, has been target companies'
cash and so-called hidden assets: vastly appreciated land and
securities, good collateral for bank debt presently eschewed by
large Japanese companies. So long as these features persist on
Japanese corporate balance sheets, this rash will spread and
endure.

Spearheading this movement are figures like Takeo Kaneko of
Meiwa—wealthy entrepreneurs with experience in real estate
and finance. Because they are likely to be considered mavericks
of the Japanese business establishment, their activities have
been dismissed as peripheral and inconsequential. But their importance as catalysts of change in the Japanese market for corporate control has been underestimated. Their activities dem-

onstrate that even in Japan, the use of Anglo-American-style tactics with respect to the ownership of equity in publicly listed firms is now both *possible* and *profitable* as a result of the weakening of the traditional Japanese corporate governance system.


## CHANGE WITHOUT CONVERGENCE

The genie is now out of the bottle as far as Japanese shareholder activism and contests for corporate control are concerned. Perhaps it can be recaptured, but not without a major economic shock.

A prolonged deflation of Japanese real estate prices is one contingency that might have a curtailing effect. Such a drop would almost certainly create a lengthy bear market on the Tokyo Stock Exchange, for equity prices there have risen with the run-up of corporate real estate values. These simultaneous erosions of wealth would slow, if not actually halt and reverse, some of the trends that are now propelling the Japanese market for corporate control down a new path. Industrial corporations that have been raising funds externally through equity-linked securities and using them in *zaiteku* operations would find themselves back on the doorsteps of their main banks, subject once again to bank monitoring and control. The banks, in turn, would likely become more circumspect in their lending as deflating real estate prices eroded the value of loan collateral. For their part, the *shite* groups that have proliferated in Japan's bull markets for real estate and equity would be seriously set back if not substantially wiped out by the prolonged pressure. For a while, at least, we would see a reassertion of the classic Japanese corporate governance system and continued quiescence of the Japanese market for corporate control.

Extreme change in the opposite direction—the complete Westernization of the Japanese market for corporate control— would require a similarly dramatic shock. If a deep and prolonged liquidity crisis ever engulfed Japanese companies, corporations and banks alike might be forced to disgorge their reciprocally held shares, even at the risk of jeopardizing long-term trading relationships. The unraveling of such a vital element of the Japanese corporate governance system might well create the conditions necessary for the emergence of an Anglo-American market for corporate control in Japan once the crisis passed.

In the final analysis, however, it is unlikely that major Japanese corporations will go all the way down the line as far as assuming an Anglo-American approach to mergers and acquisitions is concerned. There is too much transacting efficiency and value inherent in the classic Japanese corporate governance system to suppose that it will degenerate completely. It successfully reasserted itself despite the shocks of World War II and the strenuous reform efforts of the occupation government. Thanks to the exchange efficiencies it still fosters, it will almost certainly also adapt to and survive today's pressures for change.

The new condition to which Japanese corporate governance must now adapt is the pronounced lessening of product and capital market discipline, the latter in particular. The decline of corporate lending in Japan has placed banks on tenuous footing as far as effective monitoring and selective intervention is concerned. Here lies a role for an active Japanese market for corporate control. Change that can no longer be effected through suasion by major suppliers of capital might better be accomplished through actual or threatened change in ownership and replacement of top management.

This begs the question, however, as to who the new potential owners are likely to be. Recall the prevalence of implicit, relational contracting among Japanese companies, the high degree of human-asset specificity that often accompanies those contracts, and the common use of reciprocal equity ownership to reinforce long-term trading relationships. In light of these practices, an unsolicited transfer of ownership to someone outside the industrial group or other network of relationships in which the target company is enmeshed would sever a long-term trading relationship. This is likely to happen only in extreme cases. Poorly performing companies without tight network affiliations and companies that have severely abused trust relationships are the only probable candidates for such abandonment to outside bidders.

In general, the value-maximizing outcome for the stable shareholders of an errant company will be one patterned after that depicted in the Meiwa Manufacturing case. That outcome is one that results in a change in the target company's use of cash, but otherwise leaves intact its trading relationships with the rest of the group. Absent an ability for core shareholding companies to dictate the reforms needed, the accumulation of stock by a potential hostile bidder can be used to threaten exile from the group with the concomitant loss of employment status and stature by incumbent management. Private acquiescence with the demands of aggrieved share-owning stakeholders will be the price of a defense orchestrated by the main bank. But this defense, it must be pointed out, will not necessarily result in continued independence of the target company. Depending on the depth of its problems and the degree of trust others continue to hold in its management, defense may result in a forced combination with another group member designated by the major stable shareholders, much the way arranged mergers have been used to resolve problems of financial distress within the context of the classic Japanese corporate governance system.

In short, hostile bidders may be used to put target companies into play in Japan as in markets for corporate control elsewhere. But once in play, the outcome will likely be determined administratively by the main bank and other core companies in the shareholding group rather than by a true, open contest for control. Thus Japan's future "market" for corporate control is likely to display a controlled, symbiotic relationship between traditional stable shareholders and maverick corporate raiders, foreign as well as domestic. It will be more of a system in which a comparatively small number of important institutional shareholders exercise discipline over managers who fail to perform according to expectations than a true market with relatively free entry, competitively set prices, and control passing to the bidder with the best offer, regardless of group affiliations.

The adaptation of the classic Japanese corporate governance system to modern stresses will prevent a full integration of the Japanese market for corporate control with Western markets any time soon. This in turn means that the business of buying and selling companies with the Japanese will remain fundamentally different. Companies that would normally appear to be attractive targets in other parts of the globe might not be so in Japan. To ascertain a target's availability and value, one has to go beyond the balance sheet and income statement to know something about the nature, history, and current status of the target company's relationship with its stable shareholders.

Even if the target comes under attack by hostile bidders, interested foreign companies should not anticipate success as a white knight—not, that is, unless they have been hand-picked by the target's pre-existing stable shareholders. Within the Japanese corporate governance system, it is *these* players that matter more than incumbent management, and their predisposition toward foreign ownership will almost surely hinge on whether or not the hopeful foreign bidder has a history of successful commercial interaction with the target's various other stakeholders.

So too, large-scale Japanese takeovers abroad will continue to be shaped by the Japanese propensity for managing implicit contractual relationships rather than controlling corporations outright. The key to determining where and when Japanese companies will buy next will not be found in offering prices, breakup values, or even strategic fit per se. Rather, it will be in the desire to preserve an existing valuable foreign business relationship and thus avoid the recontracting that might follow a change in foreign ownership.

Certainly it was the case that the surge of Japanese foreign takeovers in the 1980s came amidst a strengthening yen, a buoyant Tokyo stock market, and a tremendous buildup of excess cash by Japanese companies. These financial developments undoubtedly enhanced the bidding power of Japanese corporations. But this enhancement played more of a supporting than a leading role in the stimulation of large majority acquisitions by Japanese companies. The primary stimulation in the United States was the wave of other foreign and U.S. domestic junk-bond-financed takeovers that threatened to disrupt important Japanese strategic alliances with even very large American corporations. Had the Japanese bidders of the 1980s not been so cash rich and had the yen not been so strong, the pricing of many of their foreign acquisitions would probably have had slimmer premiums. But the final outcome of displacing threatened contractual relations with outright control would likely have been the same.

The wealth of Japan, its seemingly relentless economic expansion, and its fascination with things Western will undoubtedly give it a high profile as a buyer in many markets around the world. But we would be mistaken to anticipate the same sort of Japanese acquisitiveness in the market for corporate control as, say, in the markets for real estate or collectibles. The many offshore minority-equity stakes acquired by Japanese companies in the late 1980s may one day prove to be the basis of an even larger wave of Japanese foreign takeovers. But this development is not inevitable. As long as the underlying contractual and managerial relationships sought by the Japanese remain unthreatened, so too will the independent ownership of foreign corporations.

# Bibliography

Abegglen, James C. *The Strategy of Japanese Business.* Cambridge, MA: Ballinger, 1984.

Abegglen, James C., and George Stalk, Jr. *Kaisha: The Japanese Corporation.* New York: Basic Books, 1985.

"Affiliate Buys Fujiya Stock, Ending Hostile Takeover Attempt." *The Asian Wall Street Journal,* December 8, 1986, p. 24.

Ames, Walter L., and David N. Roberts. "Foreign Acquisitions in Japan: Hurdling the Ultimate Barrier." *The Journal of the American Chamber of Commerce in Japan* (January 1986), pp. 10–29.

Aoki, Masahiko, ed. *The Economic Analysis of the Japanese Firm.* Amsterdam: North Holland, 1984.

Aron, Paul. "Japanese Price Earnings Multiples: The Tradition Continues." New York: Daiwa Securities of America, Inc., August 31, 1989.

Ballon, Robert J., and Iwao Tomita. *The Financial Behavior of Japanese Corporations.* Tokyo: Kodansha International, 1988.

Ballon, Robert J., Iwao Tomita, and Hajime Usami. *Financial Reporting in Japan.* Tokyo: Kodansha International, 1976.

Beer, Michael, and Stephen Marsland. "Nippon Steel Corporation," 482–057. Boston: Harvard Business School, 1981.

Berle, Adolph A., and G. C. Means. *The Modern Corporation and Private Property.* New York: MacMillan, 1932.

Boyer, Peter J. "Sony and CBS Records: What A Romance!" *The New York Times Magazine,* September 18, 1988.

Bronte, Stephen. *Japanese Finances, Markets, and Institutions.* London: Euromoney Publications, 1982.

Browne, Lynn E., and Eric S. Rosengren, eds. *The Merger Boom.* Boston: Federal Reserve Bank of Boston. Conference Series No. 31, 1987.

Caves, Richard E., and Masu Uekusa. *Industrial Organizations in Japan.* Washington, DC: The Brookings Institution, 1976.

281

Chandler, Alfred D., Jr. *Scale and Scope: The Dynamics of Industrial Capitalism.* Cambridge, MA: Harvard University Press, 1990.

Coase, Ronald H. "The Nature of the Firm." *Economica N.S.* 4 (1937), pp. 386–405.

Crabb, Kelly C. "The Reality of Extralegal Barriers to Mergers and Acquisitions in Japan." *The International Lawyer* (Winter 1987), pp. 97–128.

Cramb, Gordon. "Official Calls for End to Tokyo Taboo on Hostile Takeovers." *Financial Times,* November 21, 1988, p. 3.

Dodwell Marketing Consultants. *Industrial Groupings in Japan 1988/89.* 8th ed. Tokyo: Dodwell Marketing Consultants, 1988.

Dore, Ronald. *Flexible Rigidities: Industrial Policy and Structural Adjustment in the Japanese Economy 1970–80.* Stanford, CA: Stanford University Press, 1986.

———. *Taking Japan Seriously: A Confucian Perspective on Leading Economic Issues.* Stanford, CA: Stanford University Press, 1987.

Fallows, James. "Containing Japan." *The Atlantic Monthly,* May 1989, pp. 40–54.

Fox, Alan. *Beyond Contract: Work Power, and Trust Relations.* London: Faber & Faber, 1974.

French, Kenneth R., and James M. Poterba. "Are Japanese Stock Prices Too High?" Cambridge, MA: National Bureau of Economic Research working paper, February 1990.

Fruin, W. Mark. *Kikkoman: Company, Clan and Community.* Cambridge, MA: Harvard University Press, 1983.

Gerlach, Michael. "Business Alliances and the Strategy of the Japanese Firm." *California Management Review* (Fall 1987), pp. 126–142.

Graven, Kathryn. "Japanese Executive, Bosses and Broker Dispute Responsibility for Huge Losses." *The Wall Street Journal,* September 28, 1987, p. 28.

Hanley, Thomas H., John D. Leonard, Diane B. Glossman, Ron Napier, and Steven I. Davis. "The Japanese Banks: Emerging Into Global Markets." New York: Salomon Brothers, September 1989.

Hirschmeier, Johannes, and Tsunehiko Yui. *The Development of Japanese Business: 1600–1980.* London: George Allen & Unwin, 1981.

Hoshi Takeo, Anil Kashyap, and David Scharfstein. "Bank Monitoring and Investment: Evidence from the Changing Structure of Japanese Corporate Banking Relationships." In R. Glenn Hubbard, ed., *Asymmetric Information, Corporate Finance, and Investment.* Chicago: University of Chicago Press, forthcoming.

———. "Corporate Structure, Liquidity, and Investment: Evidence from Japanese Industrial Groups." *Quarterly Journal of Economics,* forthcoming.

Ishizumi, Kanji. *Acquiring Japanese Companies*. Tokyo: The Japan Times, Ltd., 1988.

"Is Japan Adjusting Enough?" *World Financial Markets*. New York: Morgan Guaranty Trust Company of New York, March 18, 1988, pp. 1–17.

Japan Securities Research Institute. *Securities Market in Japan 1988*. Tokyo: Shoken Kaikan, 1988.

Jensen, Michael C. "Agency Costs of Free Cash Flow, Corporate Finance, and Takeovers." *American Economic Association Papers and Proceedings* (May 1986), pp. 323–329.

————. "Takeovers: Their Causes and Consequences." *Journal of Economic Perspectives*, vol. 2, no. 1 (Winter 1988), pp. 21–48.

Jensen, Michael C., and William Meckling. "Theory of the Firm: Managerial Behavior, Agency Costs, and Capital Structure." *Journal of Financial Economics* 3 (October 1976), pp. 305–360.

Johnson, Chalmers. *MITI and the Japanese Miracle*. Stanford, CA: Stanford University Press, 1982, pp. 246–248.

Kester, W. Carl. "Capital Ownership Structure: A Comparison of United States and Japanese Manufacturing Corporations." *Financial Management* (Spring 1986), pp. 5–16.

Lincoln, Edward J. *Japan: Facing Economic Maturity*. Washington, DC: The Brookings Institution, 1988.

Loss, Louis, Makoto Yazawa, and Barbara Ann Banoff, eds. *Japanese Securities Regulation*. Tokyo and Boston: University of Tokyo Press and Little, Brown, 1983.

Luehrman, Timothy A. "Merck-Banyu," 288-127. Boston: Harvard Business School, 1987, rev. 1988.

————. "Fujiya Co., Ltd.," 288-027. Boston: Harvard Business School, 1988, rev. 1989.

Metz, Tim. *Japan's New Directions in U.S. Mergers and Acquisitions*. New York: Japan Society, 1989.

Mitsui & Co., Inc. *The 100 Year History of Mitsui & Co., Inc. 1876–1976*. Tokyo: Mitsui & Co., Inc., 1977.

The Nikko Research Center, Ltd. *The New Tide of the Japanese Securities Market*. Tokyo: The Nikko Research Center, Ltd., 1988.

"Nippon Life and Shearson Set an Example to Be Followed." *Euroweek*, June 5, 1987, p. 17.

Nishimura, Toshiro. "M&A Law in Japan: Rules of the Unplayed Game." *Mergers and Acquisitions*, vol. 17, no. 4 (Winter 1983), pp. 20–24.

Pettway, Richard H., and Takeshi Yamada. "Mergers in Japan and Their Impacts upon Stockholders' Wealth." *Financial Management* (Winter 1986), pp. 43–52.

Porter, Michael. "From Competitive Advantage to Corporate Strategy." *Harvard Business Review* (May–June, 1987), pp. 43–59.

Rappaport, Carla. "Japanese Tyre Maker Aims to Become World's Largest." *Financial Times*, May 14, 1988, p. 1.

Roberts, John G. *Mitsui: Three Centuries of Japanese Business*. New York: John Weatherhill, Inc., 1973.

Robins, Brian. *Tokyo: A World Financial Center*. London: Euromoney Publications, 1987.

Shibata, Yoko. "Japanese Give the Chop to Former Allies." *Euromoney* (August 1986), p. 92.

———. "The MD Might Have Gone Mad." *Euromoney* (October 1987), pp. 67–73.

Shleifer, Andrei, and Lawrence H. Summers. "Breach of Trust in Hostile Takeovers." In A. J. Auerbach, ed., *Corporate Takeovers: Causes and Consequences*. Chicago: University of Chicago Press, 1988.

Shleifer, Andrei, and Robert W. Vishny. "Managerial Entrenchment: The Case of Manager-Specific Investments." *Journal of Financial Economics*, vol. 25, no. 1 (November 1989), pp. 123–139.

Smith, Lee. "Merck Has an Ache in Japan," *Fortune*, March 18, 1985, pp. 42–45.

Suzuki, Sadahiko, and Richard Wright. "Financial Structure and Bankruptcy Risk in Japanese Companies." *Journal of International Business Studies* (Spring 1985), pp. 97–110.

Tanzer, Andrew. "Land of the Rising Billionaires." *Forbes*, July 27, 1987, pp. 66–80.

"Too Many Issues of Convertible Bonds and Warrant Bonds Have Created Disorder in Corporate Finance." *Nihon Keizai Shimbun*, October 22, 1988, p. 12.

"Trust Is Not Enough." *The Economist*, June 25, 1988, p. 76.

United States General Accounting Office. "Foreign Investment: Growing Japanese Presence in the U.S. Auto Industry." Washington, DC: GAO/NSIAD-88-111, March 1988.

Viner, Aron. *Inside Japan's Financial Markets*. London and Tokyo: The Economist Publications Ltd. and The Japan Times Ltd., 1987, pp. 23–26.

Williamson, Oliver E. *The Economic Institution of Capitalism: Firms, Markets, Relational Contracting*. New York: Free Press, 1985.

———. "Corporate Finance and Corporate Governance." *The Journal of Finance*, vol. 43, no. 3 (July 1988), pp. 567–591.

Yamamura, Kozo, ed. *Japanese Investment in the United States: Should We Be Concerned?* Seattle, WA: Society for Japanese Studies, 1989.

Yoshino, Michael Y., and Thomas B. Lifson. *The Invisible Link: Japan's Sogo Shosha and the Organization of Trade*. Cambridge, MA: MIT Press, 1986.

"Zaiteku Sends Stocks and Tokkin Soaring." *Euromoney: Special Survey*, April, 1987, pp. 130–131.

# GLOSSARY

| | |
|---|---|
| **Anmoka no ryokai** | Unspoken understandings. |
| **Baishu** | Bribery; synonymous with corporate acquisition. |
| **Banto** | Trusted retainer. |
| **Bunsho-ka** | Corporate archive section (legal department). |
| **Daimyo** | Japanese feudal lord. |
| **Dozoku** | A clan consisting of several *ie*. |
| **Endaka** | High yen; generally used to refer to the yen's rise subsequent to the September 1985 Plaza Accord. |
| **Honnin** | Experienced factory workers. |
| **Ie** | A stem family or descent group. |
| **Ikebana** | Classical Japanese flower arrangement. |
| **Keidanren** | The Federation of Economic Organization, the leading Japanese business association representing private-sector business interests. |
| **Keiretsu** | Postwar federations of interrelated companies around a major bank or industrial corporation. (*See* zaibatsu.) |
| **Kingai fund** | Tax-advantaged trust fund managed by trust banks, but in a commingled manner, with separate accounting for individual clients. Used by corporations to achieve capital gains through securities investments. (*See tokkin* fund.) |

285

**Meiji Restoration**  Restoration of imperial power under Emperor Meiji (1868–1912).

**Miso**  Fermented soybean paste.

**Nemawashi**  "Wrapping"; used to describe the preliminary process of consultation and consensus building in Japanese dealmaking.

**Nottori**  Hijacking; synonymous with corporate takeover.

**Oyakata**  Labor recruiters.

**Propa**  Short for "propagandist," retailers for pharmaceutical companies who call on doctors to sell drugs.

**Ronnin**  Masterless samurai, often acting as mercenaries in feudal Japan.

**Samurai**  Member of the feudal warrior class, usually bearing lifelong allegiance to a particular lord.

**Sangyo-damashii**  "Spirit of industry" slogan.

**Shite group**  Private investors collaborating in the accumulation of a listed company's stock for purposes of gaining control or, more commonly, to induce a repurchase of their shares at a large profit. *Shite* is derived from the term used to describe the protagonist in Noh dramas.

**Shogun**  The supreme military authority in the feudal Japanese government.

**Shoyu**  Soy sauce; a seasoning made from fermented soybeans.

**Sohyo**  National Labor Confederation.

**Sokaiya**  Shareholders' meeting men; generally racketeers who specialize in attending shareholders' meetings to intimidate participants and disrupt normal proceedings.

**Toji**  Factory foremen.

**Tokkin fund**        Special tax-advantaged trust accounts handled by trust banks, often actually managed by brokers, and redeemable in cash. Used by corporations to achieve capital gains through securities investments. (*See kingai fund.*)

**Tonya**              Licensed wholesale merchants.

**Yakuza**             Japanese gangsters and racketeers.

**Zaibatsu**           Prewar industrial groupings of related firms around a holding company. (*See* keiretsu.)

**Zaiteku**            "Financial engineering"; slang for financial speculation with corporate funds.

# APPENDIX

The conclusions reached in this book about Japanese M&A activity are founded primarily on field data—that is, direct observation of actual companies involved one way or another in the market for corporate control or in the process of managing change among stakeholder relations. Two factors influenced the choice of data: (1) a general dearth of reliable quantitative data concerning large Japanese takeovers (compared to U.S. experience, there have been significantly fewer of them, and less is disclosed about those that do occur), and (2) my belief that Japanese activity in the market for corporate control ought to be studied at the individual corporate level to grasp the subtleties of corporate governance that drive the activity.

Ultimately, my field research involved interviews with scores of executives from dozens of different organizations. Among them were senior bureaucrats at the Ministry of International Trade and Industry (MITI) and the Ministry of Finance (MOF), representatives of the Keidanren (Federation of Economic Organizations), and numerous foreign bankers, lawyers, and consultants who specialize in Japanese corporate finance. They provided general background and orientation information, assistance in the interpretation of some of my observations, and corroboration of statements made by my primary sources.

The core of my field sample, however, consisted of 16 industrial corporations, one of which was an American pharmaceutical company, Merck, and 15 Japanese financial institutions. They are identified here.

## Japanese Industrial Corporations

| Company | Primary Businesses | Group Affiliation |
|---|---|---|
| Asahi Chemical Industry Co., Ltd. | Synthetic fibers | Asahi Chemical (Sumitomo) |
| Bridgestone Corp. | Tires and rubbers | — |
| Canon, Inc. | Cameras | Fuyo |
| Dainippon Ink and Chemicals, Inc. | Inks and resins | — |
| Hitachi, Ltd. | Electrical machinery; consumer electronics | Hitachi |
| Kikkoman Corp. | Soy sauce | — |
| Minebea Company, Ltd. | Miniature bearings | — |
| Mitsubishi Chemical Industries, Ltd. | Basic chemicals | Mitsubishi |
| Mitsubishi Corp. | Trading (especially oil and heavy industrial products) | Mitsubishi |
| Nippon Mining Co., Ltd. | Nonferrous metal mining and fabrications; petroleum refining | Kyodo Oil |
| Nippon Steel Corp. | Steel | Nippon Steel |
| Sony Corp. | Consumer electronics | — |
| Teijin, Ltd. | Polyester | Sanwa |
| Toray Industries, Inc. | Synthetic fibers | Mitsui |
| Toshiba Corp. | Electrical machinery | Toshiba-IHI |

## Japanese Financial Institutions

| Institution | Type | Group Affiliation |
|---|---|---|
| The Bank of Tokyo, Ltd. | Foreign exchange bank | — |
| The Dai-Ichi Kangyo Bank, Ltd. | City bank | DKB |
| The Dai-Ichi Mutual Life Insurance Company | Mutual life insurer | — |
| Daiwa Securities Co., Ltd. | Security broker | (Sumitomo) |
| The Fuji Bank, Ltd. | City bank | Fuyo |
| The Industrial Bank of Japan, Ltd. | Long-term credit bank | IBJ |
| The Long-Term Credit Bank of Japan, Ltd. | Long-term credit bank | — |
| The Mitsubishi Bank, Ltd. | City bank | Mitsubishi |
| The Mitsui Trust & Banking Co., Ltd. | Trust bank | Mitsui |
| The Nikko Securities Co., Ltd. | Security broker | (Mitsubishi) (Tokai) |
| Nippon Mutual Life Insurance Co. | Mutual life insurer | Sanwa |
| The Nomura Securities Co., Ltd. | Security broker | — |
| The Sanwa Bank, Ltd. | City bank | Sanwa |
| The Sumitomo Trust & Banking Co., Ltd. | Trust bank | Sumitomo |
| Yamaichi Securities Co., Ltd. | Security broker | — |

( ) = Indirect or loose affiliation

# INDEX